RUNNING

WHILE BLACK

RUNNING

WHILE BLACK

Finding Freedom in a Sport

That Wasn't Built for Us

ALISON MARIELLA DÉSIR

Portfolio | Penguin

PORTFOLIO / PENGUIN
An imprint of Penguin Random House LLC
penguinrandomhouse.com

Most Portfolio books are available at a discount when purchased in quantity for sales promotions
or corporate use. Special editions, which include personalized covers, excerpts, and corporate
imprints, can be created when purchased in large quantities. For more information, please call
(212) 572-2232 or e-mail specialmarkets@penguinrandomhouse.com. Your local bookstore
can also assist with discounted bulk purchases using the Penguin Random House corporate
Business-to-Business program. For assistance in locating a participating retailer,
e-mail B2B@penguinrandomhouse.com.

Grateful acknowledgment is made for permission to reprint an excerpt from
"Ahmaud Arbery and the White Man's Justice" by Mitchell S. Jackson.
Copyright © 2021 by Mitchell S. Jackson. Used by permission of The Wylie Agency LLC.

Image credits: page 45 photo courtesy of Dwight-Englewood School;
photos on pages 62 and 247 by Alison M. Désir; page 91 photo courtesy of Terria Clay
Photography; page 90 photo by Amir Figueroa; page 109 photo by John Le Tran;
page 111 photo courtesy of Jacob Pritchard; photos on pages 131, 132, and 133 © Rachel
Link; page 139 photo courtesy of Ted Corbitt Archives; page 232 image copyright © 2018 by
Strava, Inc., used with permission; map on page 233 from the National Archives and Records
Administration, image courtesy of the Map Collection, Sheridan Libraries & Museums, Johns
Hopkins University; page 100 illustration by Emanu, www.emanu.se, used by permission.

Library of Congress Cataloging-in-Publication Data

Names: Désir, Alison Mariella, author.
Title: Running while Black : finding freedom in a sport that
wasn't built for us / Alison Mariella Désir.
Description: New York : Portfolio / Penguin, [2022] | Includes bibliographical references.
Identifiers: LCCN 2022026898 (print) | LCCN 2022026899 (ebook) |
ISBN 9780593418628 (hardcover) | ISBN 9780593418635 (ebook)
Subjects: LCSH: Running—United States—History. | African Americans—
Social conditions. | Runners (Sports)—United States. | Running—
Psychological aspects—United States. | Racism in sports—United States.
Classification: LCC GV1061 .D47 2022 (print) |
LCC GV1061 (ebook) | DDC 796.420973—dc23/eng/20220627
LC record available at https://lccn.loc.gov/2022026898
LC ebook record available at https://lccn.loc.gov/2022026899

Printed in the United States of America
1st Printing

BOOK DESIGN BY ALISSA ROSE THEODOR

To my parents, who taught me where I came from,
and to Kouri Henri and Amir, who inspire me
to advocate for a better future

And what sport/pastime is more emblematic of America's promise of liberty than jogging, the prospect of moving free through these usurped lands? Running is both a literal and symbolic expression of America's supposed ideals. And for that very reason, it's a kind of fool's gold for Black folks. A pursuit with the power to lure us into believing we just might own the same rights as white folks to pass through space unfettered, unbothered, unchastened—alive; that we too deserve the happy boost of a runner's high to fuel our pursuits.

~MITCHELL S. JACKSON

Author's Note

This is a work of nonfiction. In some instances, I've changed the names of people to protect their privacy.

Also, part of the story I share in these pages is how running helped my depression. Exercise is a powerful tool for managing mental health, but it is not a substitute for counseling and medication. If you are suffering from depression or another form of mental illness, please work with your doctor to find the best treatment for you.

Contents

Part 2

Part 3

Timeline:
Freedom of Movement

U.S. RUNNING HISTORY	BLACK PEOPLE'S REALITY
	16th to 19th centuries Large numbers of African people are forcibly kidnapped and sold into slavery in U.S. colonies and islands in the Caribbean.
	1791–1804 The enslaved people of Haiti rise up against their French colonizers, launching what's believed to be the largest slave revolt in history and establishing the first Black republic.
	1838 Separate rail cars are instituted on the Eastern Railroad between Boston and Salem, the first known origins of segregation.
	1865 The Thirteenth Amendment passes, ending slavery; Southern states begin to pass Black Codes.
	1865 The white nationalist group the Ku Klux Klan (KKK) is founded; it wages a campaign of violence against Black people.
1887 Boston Athletic Association (BAA) is established.	**1882–1968** 4,743 lynchings occur in the U.S.
1896 The first modern Olympic Games and the first running of the marathon are held.	**1896** In *Plessy v. Ferguson*, the U.S. Supreme Court (all white men) rules that racial segregation laws do not violate the Constitution, a doctrine that came to be known as "separate but equal."
1897 The BAA holds first Boston Marathon.	**1896–1964** De jure and de facto segregation divide cities and towns across the U.S. in all manner of public space—railroads, streetcars, theaters, parks, schools, restaurants, pools, restrooms, drinking fountains, etc.—dictating where Black Americans can eat, drink, sit, and walk.
1909 Charles Burden, a Black man, wins the first marathon held in the South.	**1909** An interracial group establishes the National Association for the Advancement of Colored People (NAACP) and lobbies for anti-lynching laws.
1909 Howard Hall, a Black man, wins the Pittsburgh Marathon.	**1915–1970** The Great Migration takes place, during which six million African Americans move out of the South to points in the North, West, and Midwest.

U.S. RUNNING HISTORY	BLACK PEOPLE'S REALITY
1914–1926 Earl Johnson becomes the first known Black man to be internationally ranked as a distance runner.	
1919 Aaron Morris becomes the first known Black man to run the Boston Marathon, finishing sixth.	**1920** The KKK reaches four million members. Oregon has the highest membership rate per capita.
	1930s Redlining and other forms of housing discrimination begin, eventually leading to the creation of "inner cities."
	1930s–1960s Most cities and suburbs adopt racial covenants prohibiting Black families from owning or renting in white areas.
1936 The New York Pioneer Club is established by African Americans Joseph J. Yancey, Robert Douglas, and William Culbreath in Harlem, New York, as a running and civil rights group.	**1932–1942** Most Southern states bar Black people from using state parks.
1942 The New York Pioneer Club changes its constitution to allow members no matter their race or creed, becoming one of the first large-scale interracial clubs in any sport, amateur or professional. The New York Athletic Club prohibits Black people from joining.	
1946 The U.S.'s top Black track athletes plan a boycott of the Amateur Athletic Union (AAU) championships in San Antonio due to Jim Crow conditions.	**1949–1974** City and state governments conduct urban renewal projects, a practice that disproportionately harms Black communities. As James Baldwin said, "Urban removal . . . means negro renewal."
1952 Ted Corbitt becomes the first Black man to represent the U.S. in the marathon at the Olympics.	**1950s** Civil rights lawyers file multiple lawsuits in an attempt to desegregate state parks. South Carolina shuts down its park system rather than comply.
	1950s–1970s White people leave cities and move to the suburbs to avoid integration, a process known as "white flight."
	1950s–1980s Move-in violence is used to terrorize Black families and prevent them from moving to white areas.

U.S. RUNNING HISTORY	BLACK PEOPLE'S REALITY
1954–1972 Ted Corbitt runs the Boston Marathon in under three hours, nineteen times, tying Clarence DeMar's streak from 1922 to 1940.	**May 1954** The Supreme Court rules school segregation is unconstitutional in *Brown v. Board of Education*.
	1954–1960s White Americans violently resist integration, notably school integration. Southern white people form the White Citizens' Council to delay school integration.
1955 The New York Pioneer Club wins the Boston Marathon's team competition. They win again in 1957.	**August 1955** Fourteen-year-old Emmett Till is beaten, shot, and dumped into the Tallahatchie River by two white men.
	December 1955 Rosa Parks is arrested for refusing to give up her seat on a bus.
	January 1957 Sixty Black ministers and leaders establish the Southern Christian Leadership Conference to promote civil rights. Martin Luther King Jr. becomes first president.
February 1958 The Road Runners Club of America (RRCA) is founded to promote distance running.	**1957** Lucía María Désir, Alison's mother, immigrates to the United States from Colombia.
April 1958 New York Road Runners (NYRR) is founded as the New York chapter of the newly formed RRCA.	**1959** Wilfrid Désir, Alison's father, immigrates to the United States from Haiti.
	1960 Six-year-old Ruby Bridges is accompanied to school by four federal marshals for the year to ensure her safety against mobs of white adults hurling racial slurs at her each morning.
	1960 Students hold sit-ins across the South to protest segregated lunch counters.
1961 At the Houston Relays, all Black track and field athletes boycott the event due to Jim Crow seating in the stadium. The following year, event organizers integrate the stadium.	**May 1961** Thirteen men and women (seven Black, six white) ride a bus from Washington, DC, to New Orleans to protest segregation. The Freedom Riders are attacked and beaten during their journey.
1962 The RRCA hosts over six hundred races around the country, compared to the previous handful of races nationwide.	

U.S. RUNNING HISTORY	BLACK PEOPLE'S REALITY
January 1963 The RRCA expands to include thirteen districts nationwide.	**Spring 1963** Civil Rights leaders launch Project C, also known as the Birmingham Campaign, a large-scale, direct-action effort aimed at undoing the city's segregation system.
February 1963 Coach Bill Bowerman creates jogging programs for people in Eugene, Oregon, in what is one of the nation's whitest states due to exclusion laws prohibiting Black people from living there.	
	June 1963 Medgar Evers, field secretary in Mississippi for the NAACP, is assassinated by white supremacist Byron De La Beckwith, whose trial twice ends in a hung jury before he is sentenced to life in prison.
	August 1963 Martin Luther King Jr. leads the March on Washington.
	September 1963 16th Street Baptist Church is bombed, killing four Black girls who were attending Sunday school.
1964 The Atlanta Track Club is established; it will become the second largest running organization in the United States.	**July 1964** The Civil Rights Act of 1964 is signed into law, ending legal segregation and prohibiting discrimination based on race, color, religion, sex, or national origin.
1964 RRCA begins offering "Run for Your Life" fun-run events.	
August 1964 Jogging begins to make national news: *Chicago Tribune* publishes a story on jogging, "Jog Way to Physical Fitness in Middle Age."	**1964** Riots erupt in Harlem, Philadelphia, Chicago, and other cities due to racial discrimination.
1965–1970 Mainstream media helps popularize jogging for health with articles such as "Top Track Coach Thinks Jogging Ideal as Exercise for Older Men," (*Washington Post*, 1965); and "Jogging for Heart and Health—It's Catching On," (*U.S. News & World Report*, 1967).	**February 1965** Malcolm X is assassinated.
	March 1965 Alabama state troopers use whips, sticks, and tear gas to beat back six hundred peaceful demonstrators participating in the Selma to Montgomery march, an event that became known as Bloody Sunday.
	August 1965 The Voting Rights Act is signed into law.
1966 Bob Anderson, a high school senior in Kansas, starts a newsletter called *Distance Running News*.	**June 1966** Stokely Carmichael, a leader of the Student Nonviolent Coordinating Committee (SNCC), rallies protesters using the term "Black power." Television cameras catch the moment, and the slogan enters the mainstream, fueling civil rights and the push for self-determinism.

U.S. RUNNING HISTORY	BLACK PEOPLE'S REALITY
April 1967 Kathrine Switzer runs the Boston Marathon when women are not permitted to participate.	
1967 Blue Ribbon Sports, a precursor to Nike, opens on 3107 Pico Boulevard in Santa Monica, California.	**June 1967** The Supreme Court hands down a unanimous ruling on *Loving v. Virginia*, outlawing laws banning interracial marriage.
1967 Bowerman publishes the book *Jogging*.	
1967 An estimated five million Americans are running recreationally.	
1968 Kenneth H. Cooper publishes *Aerobics*, in which running is listed as the preferred exercise.	**February 1968** *The Kerner Commission* is released; it finds that white racism, not Black anger, was responsible for the riots that swept across the country during the Civil Rights Movement.
	April 1968 Martin Luther King Jr. is assassinated.
	April 1968 The Fair Housing Act (Civil Rights Act) is signed into law. White communities turn to the practices of planning and zoning to perpetuate segregation.
1969 Ted Corbitt sets an American record for running one hundred miles on the track. His time is 13:33:06 at age fifty.	**October 1968** At the Olympic Games, sprinters Tommie Smith and John Carlos each raise a gloved fist in support of human rights and civil rights. Wyomia Tyus wears near-black shorts as a form of protest against discriminatory treatment of Black people.
1970 *Distance Running News* is renamed *Runner's World*.	
1970 The inaugural Seattle Marathon is held.	
July 1970 Atlanta's Peachtree Road Race launches.	**1971** President Nixon declares a "war on drugs," leading to disproportionately higher rates of arrests and incarceration of Black people.
September 1970 The New York City Marathon launches.	
1971 The book *Aerobics* hits two million in sales.	**1971** U.S. Olympic coach James E. Counsilman perpetuates a stereotype about Black athletes as better suited to power sports: "I'm not saying the Black man is inferior or superior. I'm just saying he is better adapted for speed and power."

U.S. RUNNING HISTORY	BLACK PEOPLE'S REALITY
1972 NYRR launches the Mini 10K for women. The Portland Marathon begins in Oregon. And the Boston Marathon allows women to run.	**1972** New York congresswoman Shirley Chisholm is the first Black person to campaign for the Democratic presidential nomination. She loses the nomination.
	June 1972 Title IX is enacted into law, prohibiting federally funded educational institutions from discriminating against students or employees based on sex.
September 1972 Frank Shorter wins the Olympic marathon, a turning point in shifting running from a fringe sport to a mass-participation sport of largely white Americans.	
1973 The Cherry Blossom Ten-Mile Run in Washington, DC, is created. The Falmouth Road Race begins.	
1976 The New York City Marathon expands to all five boroughs.	**1976** Black History Month is celebrated nationwide for the first time.
1977 Jim Fixx publishes *The Complete Book of Running*.	
September 1977 The Chicago Marathon is founded.	**1978** The Supreme Court rules in *Regents University of California v. Bakke*, allowing affirmative action to be used as a legal strategy to manage discrimination.
1979 South Fulton Running Partners is founded in Atlanta; it is one of the first African American running groups.	
1980 Twenty-five million people in the U.S. are running, up from five million a decade earlier. The number of marathons in the U.S. increases to 305 marathons, up from 73 a decade earlier.	**1980** The wealth gap widens; the median white household wealth is $100,000; for Black families, it is $25,000.
1980 The New York City Marathon's participation swells to more than 13,000 runners, up from 127 in its first running in 1970. Participation at the Boston Marathon rises from around 1,000 runners to 5,400.	**1982** A national campaign against environmental racism is launched when Reverend Benjamin Chavis and his congregation block a toxic waste dump in North Carolina.
August 1984 Joan Benoit Samuelson wins the first women's Olympic marathon.	**April 1989** A white woman is raped in Central Park and left for dead. Five Black and Latino teenagers are falsely convicted.
1990s Women's participation in road races rises to 25 percent of finishers.	**March 1991** Rodney King is beaten by LAPD officers. Riots follow in 1992 after the officers are acquitted.

U.S. RUNNING HISTORY	BLACK PEOPLE'S REALITY
	September 1994 Nicholas Heyward Jr., age thirteen, is shot and killed by police.
March 1995 Oprah Winfrey appears on the cover of *Runner's World* after completing the Marine Corps Marathon in October 1994.	**1995–2000** Forty different major media outlets use the term "super-predator" to demonize Black youth at least 280 times.
2004 The National Black Marathoners Association is founded.	**1996** California's 1994 "three strikes" law leads to the imprisonment of Black people at thirteen times the rate of white Americans, with no data supporting a higher violent crime rate among Black people.
2006 Samia Akbar runs the fastest marathon by an American-born Black woman, 2:34:14, a record that still stands as of this writing.	**2007** The wealth gap between white and Black families quadruples between 1984 and 2007.
	2008 Barack Obama is elected as the first Black president of the United States.
2009 Black Girls Run is founded.	**January 2009** Oscar Grant is killed by a Bay Area Rapid Transit police officer.
2009 Meb Keflezighi wins the New York City Marathon and is the first American to do so in twenty-seven years. Some publications say that as an African immigrant, he's not "really" an American.	
2010 Women surpass men as the majority of runners in the U.S.	
2011 Nearly 14 million people run a road race in the U.S.; 54 percent are women.	
2012 Alison Mariella Désir runs her first marathon.	**February 2012** Trayvon Martin is shot and killed by a neighborhood watchman.
2013 Black Men Run is founded.	**2013** The #BlackLivesMatter movement is founded in response to the acquittal of Trayvon Martin's murderer.
2013 ESPN article furthers the "anybody can do it" myth citing the rise of women's running, failing to see the exclusion of Black women.	
2013 Harlem Run is founded.	**2014** Eric Garner, Michael Brown, and Tamir Rice are killed by police.
2015 Seventeen million people finish a race in the U.S.; 57 percent are women.	**2015** Freddie Gray and Sandra Bland are killed by police.
	2016 The wealth gap between Black and white Americans is as wide as it was in 1960s.

U.S. RUNNING HISTORY	BLACK PEOPLE'S REALITY
2017 Run 4 All Women is founded.	**2017** White nationalists hold a "Unite the Right" rally in Charlottesville, Virginia; it leads to multiple deaths and injuries.
2017 Black people are 7 percent of runners, up from 1.6 percent in 2011.	
February 2020 Out of a record 500-plus women running in the women's Olympic marathon trials in Atlanta, only four are Black; only one is African American.	**2020** On average, Black women in the U.S. are paid 36 percent less than white men and 20 percent less than white women. That amounts to one dollar for white men, seventy-three cents for white women, and fifty-eight cents for Black women.
	2020 Over the past decade, twenty-five states implement voting restrictions that disproportionately affect Black Americans.
	2020 Ahmaud Arbery is shot by a vigilante. Breonna Taylor, Tony McDade, and George Floyd are killed by police.
October 2020 The Running Industry Diversity Coalition is founded.	**2020–2021** Black Americans are three times more likely to be killed by police than white Americans.
	January 6, 2021 Thousands of white nationalists try to take over the U.S. Capitol and attempt to halt the certification of the presidential election.
March 2021 RRCA inducts Marilyn Bevans into its hall of fame. In her speech, she notes her confusion in being inducted so many years after racing and competing.	**2021** Whitelash erupts around educating children about America's past. A push to remove critical figures from history emerges.
	December 2021 White supremacists march through the Lincoln Memorial to "reclaim America."
February 2022 One hundred and thirty-five years after its formation, the BAA names the first woman of color to its board.	**February 2022** A federal jury finds three men guilty of hate crimes in connection with the killing of Ahmaud Arbery.
	March 2022 After a century of trying, lynching is made a federal hate crime for the first time; the bill is named in honor of Emmett Till.
	March 2022 Stop WOKE Act passes in Florida state legislature; it prohibits trainings that cause someone to feel guilty or ashamed about the past collective actions of their race or sex, limiting DEI training.

RUNNING

WHILE BLACK

Introduction

It's 6:00 p.m. and I'm getting ready for a run. I add electrolytes into my water and shuffle through my drawer. I toss clothes around, searching for an appropriate outfit. It's unseasonably warm, so it might be nice to rock a sports bra and shorts, but I shake my head. I want to be seen as a runner, but I don't want to call extra attention to myself. I settle on a bright, long-sleeved shirt with reflective bands, a shirt that screams "I'm running! Don't shoot!"

As I dress, I debate my route. I could head toward the trail. But then I'd pass the house with the American flag and start wondering if it's safe, and then I'd be annoyed that white nationalists have somehow claimed the flag, as if the rest of us aren't Americans, too. Oh, and that street also has the house with the oversized pickup truck. Dammit. I tell myself to stop generalizing, but decide it's not worth the risk or the stress. I'll go right, down the street that parallels the lake and once I hit the halfway mileage point, I'll loop back, an easy out and back. Yes, good, that's it. The route has a pretty view of the mountains and the (white) woman picking up her mail the other day waved at me. I run downstairs, kiss the baby on the forehead, tell my partner I'll be back in an hour, and go.

The first miles of a run are always terrible for me. I plod down Lake View Drive feeling heavy, my body working out the kinks. By this point, I've started my tracking app and shared my location with my partner. A safety ritual. But is it really? The likelihood that a tracking app would protect me from a white vigilante trying to kill me is tenuous at best. *Don't go there*, I tell myself. *Enjoy the run, stick with the routine. The routine works, the routine keeps you safe; ensures Kouri will grow up with his mama.* I convince myself this is true because I have to.

On my right, the peaks appear in the distance, the highest covered in snow. My mind wanders to the conversation my partner and I have been having about summiting the mountain someday, inspired by a team of all-Black climbers attempting to summit Mount Everest. I drift out of the running lane; a car honks and I jump back and wave. The man inside screams a response I can't hear, and judging by the "Trump won!" flag on the back of his pickup, it likely wasn't something nice.

I live in a small town outside a major city, with a population of 35,000; 85 percent of the people are white, and only 2 percent are Black. I spend too much time negotiating my safety while running. The other day, I ran down the sidewalk, and a white man with a scruffy beard in a blue baseball cap and work boots was coming in the opposite direction. My app was on, telling my partner where I was, which gave me some relief. But my mind kept saying, *Cross, Alison, cross,* so I did. I bolted to the other side of the road, worried the whole time that a sudden move might provoke him. The man didn't even adjust his gaze. It's hard to know whether I'm invisible or hypervisible in these moments. I can't know, so I play it safe. Better to assume bad intentions. This way I increase the chance that my name won't be added to the list, the ever-growing catalog of Black people harassed or killed for daring to exist, for taking up space in a white world. I act as though changing my behavior will somehow prevent me from an unprovoked, racist attack. It seems both silly and essential. It's all I have.

When I go for a run, I'm not just going for a run. I am stepping outside as a Black body in a white world. I am Alison Mariella—mother, runner, activist, wife—and I am also a Black woman forced to carry the stereotypes that whiteness has assigned to Black people. I would prefer to just be me, but my country has not given me this choice. I learned from a very early age that I am never just myself in white spaces; I must be aware of how whiteness sees me.

My freedom of movement, our freedom of movement, is very much influenced by our collective memories of the cultural trauma inflicted on us by a white supremacist nation. We carry these memories—those from centuries ago and those from last week—with us. They create a hypervigilance, a hum of what can happen when we are doing ordinary things like running. It is a hum that increases in volume when I read that a Black person was killed by a white person, which puts me on high alert for days afterward. Sometimes the worry is too great and I skip a run altogether. Safer inside. Other times, the hum is low, and moving through white space is routine, even mundane. But the hum is never shut off. There is no mute button.

Except, sometimes, when I run.

There are moments on a run when I hear only my breath and footfall. When life's problems get shaken out and resolved over a five-miler. In those moments, the world around me ceases to be any particular type of space. It becomes air and trees, or buildings and traffic, or nothing at all. I am just a body moving through space, propelled by my own muscles and emotions, my own drive and power. My legs at times seem to be the legs of someone else, someone in better shape than I am, faster than I am. And yet, with each stride, I know it's me. I am this runner. I am this powerful. These moments are when I feel most free. But at some point, the world returns. A dog barks. A car speeds by. And I am jolted back to reality and the possibility of some type of harm.

I often think of sociologist Elijah Anderson's seminal paper, "The White Space," in which he talks about the overwhelmingly white landscape of the United States as a place Black people can be disrespected (or worse) and reminded that they "don't belong." He describes the "criminal stereotype," which means "virtually every public encounter results in a degree of scrutiny that a 'normal' white person would certainly not need to endure." The scrutiny, the arrests, the violence Black people encounter in the white space exists for us at all times.

Running is no different. When I started running, I was the only Black person in a crowd of white people. The space was infused with white culture, i.e., a belief that whiteness is the norm and should be. Running also brought its unique brand of whiteness, with its hierarchy of who belongs at the top—white, thin, fast people. The sport's whiteness sent a message about who a runner was, and it wasn't a Black woman. And yet I kept hearing how running was democratic and a sport "for everybody" kept getting repeated: *The world's most democratic sport! All you need are shoes! Just show up!* It was both annoying and funny, because it was clear that this message came from white runners in a white sport inside a white country, and they had no idea what it was like to be a Black body in such a climate.

Running hadn't made space for us, so I set out to change that. I started a running club in Harlem. At first, my goal was simply to have other Black people to run with. But as I continued to run and evolve personally, I realized that by our very existence as Black runners we were disrupting the white narrative, carving out space for ourselves. It became my goal and purpose, my lifelong mission, to welcome more Black people to running. I want to make the sport more racially inclusive, to make running a space where we all belong.

That's the story I tell in this book. It is the story of a woman seeking a place of belonging and finding she has the power and voice to bring about change, both internally and in the larger world. My story is a running journey, but at its heart, it's a story for anyone who has experienced the harm and powerlessness that comes from not fitting into society's expectations, anyone who has ever existed in the margins. It is a story of finding and creating your place and space.

My journey to finding a sense of belonging began when I started running. Running showed me change was possible. It showed me how transformative movement can be. Simply put, running changes lives. That is where this book begins, with the story of how running saved me.

PART

ONE

1

The Only

The train pulled into the station at Seventy-Second and Central Park West, and I climbed the stairs to the sidewalk. New York surrounded me the way that New York does—tall buildings, humming buses, steam rising from a sidewalk vent. I was struck, not by the beauty, but by the coldness. I don't mean the temperature, though it was February. It was the sterile, detached feel of white space, when what I wanted was to be entering the familiar warmth of Harlem. The bodegas with their playful chaos of music and laughter. The people on the stoops making eye contact with you, nodding to acknowledge your presence. A place where I could be myself, be seen as myself. But there were no marathon training programs in Harlem, so I waited for the cars and buses to clear from Central Park West, crossed the street, and cut into the park.

Time collapsed then as it does for me sometimes in white spaces. As I walked down the footpath, I wasn't consciously thinking about Seneca Village and the Black families whose homes were razed so white people could build a park for themselves. But I felt them there, raising their families, making meals, taking care of one another the way our families do. A Black space until white people took it.

A place is never separate from its history, even if you don't know it. It's in the trees and grass, in the buildings and the air, and in the people. I saw it as the cyclists cranked by—white men—and as the runners jogged down the path—white women—and in the white people carrying little dogs across the grass. There weren't a lot of us here, I noted. Always disconcerting, but my mind that morning was buoyed by the idea of the marathon. So I put my head down, relegating the hum of whiteness to background noise, to white noise.

The blue dot on my phone led me to a wide pavilion at Bethesda Terrace. No one else was there yet, so I wandered down the stairs toward the fountain, meandering through the seven arches of the walkway, before climbing back up to the meeting spot and sitting on a bench. I was about forty-five minutes early, a habit I picked up from my dad, who believed being on time was late. I pulled my jacket around me against the chill and waited. Slowly, people began to arrive, wearing tights and jackets. Everyone was white, and no one was talking to each other, a habit of white people I find odd—a default to being stoic and standoffish. I'm never quite sure: are they not talking to me because I'm Black, or because they're white?

By nine o'clock, the terrace had filled with fifty or so bodies. I scanned the crowd to see if any other Black people had come, a habit of mine. I focused on hair, looking for anything textured: kinky, braided, thick. In this crowd, hats made the ritual difficult, but I went section by section, searching and finding no one. *Shit*, I thought. *Maybe I shouldn't have come. There's a reason I'm the only one—we run track, not distance, not marathons. Do I really want to be The Only in this space?*

I scanned the crowd again and felt relieved to spot two women wearing the same jacket I was. A small sign that I might fit in. They saw me, too. "Oh my God, look at that," one of them said, "we must take a picture," with the overenthusiasm some white women employ when greeting Black women, a forced casualness to hide whatever discomfort might be there. To fit in as a runner, it seemed, you needed to look the part.

We made small talk. I'm careful, as I always am in such spaces, to present what I've learned is the most palatable version of myself to white people: quieter, less forthright. "I'm a little nervous," one of the women said, "I've never done a marathon before." "Me, too," I said, without adding that my nerves also came from being the only Black person. I wondered what they thought of me being there, then, second-guessed if I was being paranoid and silly. But I knew I wasn't, that 85 percent of white people have anti-Black bias, conscious or not. *Maybe I won't come back*, I thought. But I rejected that. The marathon seemed like the only possible solution.

U p until that moment, I'd spent my days on the couch. When I was able, I stole Xanax from my mom, taking a few pills when I woke in the morning, then more when I woke again six hours later. If I was out of Xanax, NyQuil could do the trick. On the weekends—which seems odd now, because I had no job to mark the days—alcohol put me out. A part of me wanted to sleep and not wake up. But what I really wanted was to be better, and sleep seemed like the best solution. If I could shut my eyes through this bad patch and wake up sometime after it passed, my life would be back on track.

In my waking moments, I scrolled through Facebook. My friends seemed to be thriving—getting promotions, living in expensive Midtown apartments, paying for nightly bottle service. One was training for a marathon. I didn't know him that well, but he was Black and training for a marathon, and Black people didn't run marathons. I knew this because the lines had been drawn for me in high school. The white kids ran cross-country; the Black kids ran track. I myself ran the 400 meters and 400-meter hurdles. Distance was for white folks; sprints were for Black people. So it stood out to me that my friend had crossed the color line. A common phrase among Black people is "I don't go there/do that, that's white people's shit"—a defense mechanism. (The once-popular website stuffwhitepeoplelike.com listed running marathons as number twenty-seven.) Sometimes it's easier to pretend something is white people's shit than it is to reckon with the historical and cultural factors that have stolen everyday activities and places and made them off-limits to us.

Yet there was my friend, a Black man training for a marathon, wearing a purple singlet advertising Team in Training, the flagship fundraising program for the Leukemia & Lymphoma Society. It might have worked in my mind if he'd had the body of a distance runner, but my friend was on the chubby side. Plus, he wasn't just Black, he was Black-Black. He had locs and was a Que: an Omega man, a member of Omega Psi Phi, a Black fraternity with a loud, unapologetically proud culture that was not at all "running."

I couldn't keep my eyes off his feed. He posted and I devoured each one. He wrote about the joy and hardship of his daily run, about the case of runner's knee he developed from wearing an old pair of sneakers that sent him to the physical therapist for the first time. He wrote about the pain of the long run and how, after the agony of it all, he somehow felt surprisingly good afterward. He said he felt better than he ever had in his life. He saw himself in ways he never had before.

On the surface, I was watching a man train for a marathon, but really, I was witnessing a transformation. Could the marathon transform me?

I messaged him on Google Chat with all of my questions. *Do you eat while you run? What do you do if you have to poop or pee? How do you run, physically? I mean, how do you run so far for so long?* He replied each time. *Yes, you eat. If you have to go, you go. You're essentially at war with your body, so you have to will yourself to get through it. It's all about using your mind to override the body. It's hard, but it works.* We had hours-long conversations this way.

Six months passed, and I did not move from the couch until New Year's Day came. I'm not much of a resolutions person, but the combination of a new year, coupled with a push from Phil McGraw, got me to really consider registering for a marathon. Dr. Phil wrote in his book *Life Strategies: Doing What Works, Doing What Matters*: "The key is to go from awareness and consciousness to putting what you want on project status. Make it a project. Think about it. If you were just aware that you wanted the garage to be painted, it wouldn't get painted. But, if you make it a project with a deadline, it will get done." *All right*, I thought. *I'll make the marathon a project.*

What compels a person with depression to get off the couch, get dressed, walk a mile from her co-op in New Jersey to the base of the George Washington Bridge, catch a bus to the city to board the A train, then the C train down to Twenty-Third Street, and be among the living? Hope would be the easy answer, but it was more desperation. A therapist had helped me understand that feelings of hopelessness and worthlessness were not how I would feel forever, but he hadn't told me how to change the feeling. Running seemed to offer a path.

The woman at the Team in Training office pointed me to a conference room. I took a seat in the back, not just because I was the only Black person, though that was part of it—you get tired of eyes on you—but also because I was no longer used to being in public or interacting with people. A woman explained the fundraising and the training. I signed on the dotted line and left.

It was January 12, 2012, a date I remember because it was the second anniversary of the earthquake in Haiti, the country of my father's birth. My dad had been diagnosed with Lewy body dementia a number of years earlier and it seemed his mind was back in the period right before he left Haiti, when so much harm was being done by the dictator. He would go on about how hordes of people were trying to kill him. As the dementia got worse, he stopped making sense, though I knew he was talking about the injustice of the world. Signing up to run the Rock 'n' Roll Marathon in San Diego on the anniversary of the earthquake seemed meaningful, and I left the office already feeling different.

Within a week, an email came explaining what to expect and what preseason training sessions were available. I pulled out a notebook, drew a calendar, and began plotting upcoming dates, adding structure to my life.

The thought came: *To do this, you will need to stop self-medicating.* Then it was gone, and I focused on shopping. I'd need the right outfit, so I took a trip back into the city, way downtown to Paragon Sports, and bought a pair of Nike tights and a bright orange, long-sleeved jacket. Shoes were too expensive, so on the day of the first preseason session, I slipped on an old pair of Adidas and went out the door.

The head coach, a lanky white man, welcomed us, and the crowd moved in to hear him. He talked about the sixteen-week training plan we would receive via email and assured us that at the end of the program, we would be able to finish a marathon. I was incredulous. How could this coach, who knew nothing about me, make such a big promise? A part of me wanted to go home, take a Xanax, and prove him wrong. Another part of me, the part that stayed, wanted to be awake again.

The run that day was a 5K out and back along Central Park's East Drive. We lined up and the coach sent us off. He'd told us the run would serve as a baseline for our training, so I set off thinking I needed to run as fast as possible. The runners around me fell into pace groups. I barreled ahead on my own, channeling the running I knew, which was sprinting. In high school, the 400 meters was a game of going as hard as you could for as long as you could, so without knowing how long a 5K was, I pushed ahead.

By the turnaround, the metallic taste of effort was heavy on my tongue. As I passed runners on the way back who were still on their way out, I worried about collapsing in front of everyone. But there was also a comforting, familiar feeling: I was running at a highly uncomfortable pace, and while I wanted to stop, I was convincing myself to keep going. This felt like something. A part of me knew I could keep going and another part of me questioned my ability: *Go, don't go; stop, don't stop.* But one foot was landing in front of the other. My arms were swinging back and forth, nudging my legs to hang on. I don't know if my pace was waning, but I knew I was winning this battle within myself.

I walked back through the park lighter, excited, feeling almost faint from effort and discovery. I replayed the run in my head. I was moving down the road, detached from the world around me, hearing my breathing and my feet. My mind was inward, focused only on movement. At one point, I had felt free. There was a sense of being myself in my body, a singular human being bolting through time and space. The moment was brief but powerful. It had returned me, momentarily, to the person I was seeking.

kept going. Every Wednesday and Saturday, I walked the mile from my apartment to the base of the George Washington Bridge and caught the bus to the city, where I boarded the A train to 125th Street, then the C train to Seventy-Second and Central Park West to run with a group of strangers to try to make myself feel alive again. Since the first session, the group had diversified somewhat. Along with myself, a Black woman growing out a fro, there was an overweight Black man, a Black woman who looked like a model, a brown Brazilian woman with beautiful curly hair, and an Indian woman. As we gathered, most of the white people grouped together, forming the main group, and by default the people of color became the "misfit" group of those of us outside what is considered "the standard": white, thin, fast, experienced—which meant a couple of heavyset white people were over with us. I welcomed the larger presence of people of color, of course, but it didn't change the white culture of the group. It meant we all had to endure whiteness. I don't know what that meant for them; once the workout began and we were separated into pace groups, I was surrounded by white people again. I'd say hi and they'd say hi, but that was it. There was no conversation. The coaches were similar. No one said, "Hey, welcome, how's your running going?" and so it seemed to me that maybe I was not part of the "everybody" noted in the advertising.

I was managing the normal anxieties of starting something new, along with the additional weight of being one of The Only. You know you are going to be perceived as speaking for all Black people. What you do will be categorized, labeled, and judged. Sometimes I wanted to play it up for the white runners and really be "Black" for them—sassy, ill-mannered, quick to anger. Feed their stereotype, stoke their discomfort. But I didn't. Too exhausting. More often than not, I put my head down and ran. Other times, I performed as I did on the first day, presenting the vanilla version of myself that white people would be comfortable with.

None of this was new. But it was eased in part by running. After a few miles, my body seemed to relax into itself. Feeling the pavement beneath me was a sort of grounding. Going farther gave me a sense of accomplishment. I remember being nervous the morning we were scheduled to run a 10K, our longest run yet. It was March, almost spring, and you could feel the weather was turning. I had decided 10K was the distance that made you a long-distance runner, and while I felt fit, our last run had been only four miles. Six seemed far.

We ran up through Central Park, the once-unfamiliar paths now recognizable. Passing that tree on the right meant we had hit mile three. I felt weightless, unstoppable. A woman in my pace group named Caitlyn and I ran a steady, even pace. The coaches had told us that pacing was the key to distance running, so I'd become very conscious of pace. As we ticked off the miles, I was amazed I *still* felt good. I waited for the fatigue to set in during the fifth mile, but it never came. As we were closing in on mile six, I felt like I could run forever. I thought of the platitudes the head coach had made earlier—that at the end of the program we'd be able to run a marathon. *Maybe*, I thought, *he was right*.

One night, early in marathon training, I stood in the kitchen and stared at a bottle of Xanax, trying to figure out how the pills could fit into training. I worked backward. If I took a pill the night before the Saturday morning run, I'd sleep through the alarm, so that wasn't an option. But if I took a pill on Tuesday nights, I could be awake by noon on Wednesday, which would give me enough time to eat, get ready, and get to the park for the evening workout. But then I'd have a pill hangover—I'd feel slow, sluggish, groggy. My dependency was more emotional than chemical. The pills had made me believe I'd be okay. Now, running did. So I stopped taking them.

But my hold on my mental health was tenuous. My father's dementia had progressed and left him with delusions and the inability to control bodily functions. He needed someone nearby all the time, a responsibility that fell to my mom and me. A couple of times a week, she dropped him off at my apartment on her way to teach at a college north of the city. I would feed him, get him to the toilet, change a diaper if needed, help him get on and off the bed. She was usually back by five thirty so I could be in the city by seven. One Wednesday when she wasn't back by six fifteen, I broke down, crying hysterically, believing that if I missed one run, everything would fall apart.

Other times, when I needed to go to my parents' house to help with my dad, I drove the three hours to Delaware sobbing, convinced that something bad was about to happen, a symptom of anxiety I'd later learn was called catastrophic thinking. Although I was often at my parents' house, I didn't miss a run. I looked up the closest Team in Training group and drove forty-five minutes to run with them. If there was an award for consistency, I would have received it.

Without the self-medicating, I began to feel things. The ache in my legs the day after a workout. The pounding in my chest as I ran up a hill. The efficiency of my body when my breathing was even and steady. It seemed to me I was a machine: heart and lungs, legs and head propelling me forward. Week after week, running made my body—and me—feel alive. Afterward, there was a good hangover, one that lit me on fire, made me alert, lighter.

I was so used to muting every feeling that feeling was weird. I called my friend Sean, whom I had met a decade earlier in college. "Is this what normal people feel like?" I asked, telling him that the weight and anxiety in my chest was gone.

Though I hadn't been in touch much over the last few years, I could hear him grinning over the phone. "Yes," he said. "Yes, it is."

I couldn't quite believe it, so I asked my mom on the phone, "What do you feel right now?"

"I feel fine," she said.

"So, are you telling me that nothing is bothering you, like you don't have any anxiety?"

"No, honey, I feel good. But mostly because *you* feel good." I rolled my eyes, but it was comforting that I could laugh at that and not feel annoyed, now that I was feeling better.

Riding the bus into Manhattan, I was surprised to realize that I was there, actually present, looking out over the Hudson. The sun sparkled on the water. Runners and cyclists were on the bridge. You could see all the way down to lower Manhattan. I'd never noticed that before.

At practice, we ran as a group farther and farther up the park, going to the East Side, past the Metropolitan Museum of Art, the statue of Fred Lebow at Engineers' Gate—landmarks I had once barely noticed before—all the way to North Woods. I'd get into the zone and feel like I could do anything. Running, it seemed, worked similarly to antidepressants. The effect was cumulative. The medication needs time to get into your bloodstream, and so does running.

During my first run with the group, I had felt a desperation to feel better. A couple of months in, I felt good during the run and for a little while after. Now, running was in my bloodstream. The aftereffect had somehow become how I felt all the time.

I discovered a different version of myself during those months. Gone was the couch potato who considered finger-scrolling cardio. I got an email from my cousin with a link to therapists in my area, a kind gesture. I emailed back: *Thanks*, I said. *I'm no longer obsessive or homicidal lol. Hope the feeling doesn't return!!!* I started returning to my life. I ran on Saturdays with the group, then caught the train to Harlem to have brunch with Sean and another friend from college, Sasha.

The real proof I'd changed, though, was that I had to miss a Saturday session to help my mom, and I didn't panic. I could do the run on my own, a simple, obvious idea that never would've occurred to me ten weeks earlier. I left for the run, a ten-miler, feeling nervous but oddly aware that I could cover the distance on my own. I was likely bolstered by the fact I had followed the instructions of the coach: I'd gone to bed early, eaten what I planned to eat on race day, and allowed two hours for digestion before setting off.

From my cousin's house in Harlem, I headed south down St. Nick. I was wearing headphones, but I didn't start the music; I wanted to hear Harlem as I ran. St. Nick hugged one side of St. Nicholas Park and as I ran, a group of old men sitting on the benches shouted, "All right now!" and whistled, encouraging me on. Young men shooting dice were so engrossed in their game that they didn't look up when I passed, but I smiled. I loved that about Harlem, the outdoor community. You didn't see people in Midtown tossing dice; Harlem was special this way. Near the end of the park, a group of elderly women held out their hands, gingerly giving me high fives as I passed. The kids with them raced me to the end of the block and clapped, bent over and out of breath, when I continued on. I looked back and waved as they made their way to their grandmothers.

When I got to 110th and Central Park West, the color line, I turned my music on. The scenery began to shift. Instead of Black people, the sidewalks were filled with white folks walking dogs and pushing strollers. No one nodded or said hello. A white runner who passed me going in the opposite direction refused to look my way or acknowledge me with the runner's nod.

I hit Columbus Circle in no time, feeling strong, and cut through the park to Fifth Avenue. I felt good, so I headed east, weaving my way through the Upper East Side along Park Avenue to add mileage. The streets were beautiful and clean; no trash had been left on the ground as it was in Harlem. The disparity between these spaces was always stark to me, a sign of where the city's investments are: which places, which neighborhoods, which people, are resourced. I ran back up to 110th Street and felt Harlem embrace me. I turned off my music and pushed the pace a little back to my cousin's house. My watch read 12.95 miles. I worried the added miles would mess up the rest of my training. Still, I circled the block a few times to get 13.1, a half marathon, feeling embarrassed that people saw me go round and round, but also elated that I'd run that far.

A few weeks later, I met Caitlyn on a corner near my apartment in Fort Lee, and we walked to join the other Team in Training runners at a park on the Hudson for the Escape from Palisades Half Marathon, a "tune-up," the coaches called it, before our marathon. Many of the other runners were chatty with me now; I'd gotten faster, so I'd moved up, so to speak, in the runner hierarchy. We gathered at the start at the base of a hill. I looked around at the white people around me and shook off the feeling of being The Only. The gun fired and I ran, feeling both the joy of the sport that was saving me and the awareness that while I was participating, I didn't really belong.

2

White Space

Running with that group wasn't the first time I'd felt a lack of belonging. I've spent my whole life navigating the discomfort of white spaces. Being a racial interloper is a role I know well. When I read Ijeoma Oluo's book *So You Want to Talk About Race*, I saw myself in her words: "As a Black woman, race has always been a prominent part of my life. I have never been able to escape the fact that I am a Black woman in a white supremacist country."

I became aware that I would be required to navigate white spaces when I was in the first grade. We were living in Teaneck, New Jersey, a suburb five miles outside of New York City. It was a mixed town, with a white majority population and a wide range of ethnicities and immigrants like my parents. Both my mom and dad had moved to the United States when they were young—my dad from Haiti in 1959, my mom from Colombia in 1957. They met on Welfare Island—now Roosevelt Island—in 1964 when my father was doing his medical residency and my mom was working at the hospital as an executive secretary, and started dating soon thereafter. She used to tell me she was drawn to my dad's intelligence and curiosity, and that they'd go for long walks and talk about ideas, history, and the world. It was my father, my mom said, who encouraged her to pursue her Ph.D. in anthropology and become a professor.

My parents moved to Harlem in 1969. Like other Black immigrants and African Americans, they loved the neighborhood's vibrancy. While Harlem's heyday was decades earlier—the renaissance of the 1920s, Malcolm X and Martin Luther King Jr. in the '60s, James Brown and Aretha Franklin stirring up the crowd at the Apollo—the vitality remained. My parents lived in Lenox Terrace, the most sought-after residential building on Lenox Avenue (aka Malcolm X Boulevard) in Harlem, and hung out at the Cotton Club and Smalls Paradise.

But in the 1970s, when they started thinking about having children, New York City's crime rate was rising and the crack epidemic was growing. So my parents began looking for a safer place with good schools and bought a house in Teaneck.

Teaneck was divided the way many towns are, along racial and class lines. There was a wealthy section with million-dollar homes and big lawns, where a lot of white people lived. The northeast was where houses were smaller and the lawns dimmer, and where most of the Black people lived. More fast food and liquor stores lined these streets; what I remember was that the streets had double yellow lines, meaning they were busier and noisier. Years later, I'd learn that when more Black families began moving to Teaneck in the first half of the twentieth century, white people didn't want to live next to people who looked like me, so they moved to another part of town. Real estate agents would show Black people homes only in the northeast, and they would not sell homes to Black families in the white parts of town, forcing segregation on the community.

We lived in a middle-class neighborhood, on a tree-lined street straight out of Pleasantville, surrounded by white families, but also a few families of color. Streets had a single traffic line, or none at all. About a mile from our house was the bus stop my dad used to get into the city for work.

All this meant to me growing up was that I couldn't easily play with the Black kids at my school because they didn't live in my neighborhood. I mostly played with white kids: Lauren, who lived down the block, and Lindsey, who lived up the block. We climbed trees and biked the streets. There was a boy, Josh, who was a friend of my older brother, Christopher. We were like a little troop. When my parents decided we were going to take art lessons, all of us took art lessons. We played soccer together. Over the summer, we were off to camp. One year it was Summer Sonatina, where we were expected to practice piano four hours a day. Another year was Frost Valley, when we were scheduled with outdoor activities from sunup to sundown. I was such a busy kid, my dad nicknamed me Pye Poudre, or Powdered Feet, a Haitian Kreyòl saying that describes someone who is so active that you never see them, just the footprints they leave behind.

I knew I was Black, of course, and that the girls I played with were white. I also knew I was different from the African American kids at my school because their parents were from the United States, and mine were from Haiti and Colombia. I felt most like the African kids and the Trinidadian student, because their parents were from different countries. My friend Lindsey and I had that in common, too, because her mother was from Finland, but she was white, and so nobody asked her where she was "from-from."

These differences were just facts until Mrs. Weaver, my first-grade teacher, couldn't remember my name. I was seven and sitting at my desk at Whittier Elementary. Mrs. Weaver, a white woman, was calling out the name Raisha. Raisha was the other Black girl in my class, and since I was not Raisha, I didn't say anything. But the teacher kept saying the name Raisha and looking at me. When it finally dawned on me what was going on, I said, "I'm Alison." Mrs. Weaver looked at me, then at Raisha. "Oh, I'm sorry, you look so much alike."

But Raisha and I did not look alike. No more than the white girls in our class with the same blond or brown hair. Raisha and I both wore braids, so I thought I could rectify the situation with a new hairstyle. I started wearing my hair in twists with bows. Our teacher still couldn't figure out who was who.

The name mix-up happened with other white teachers, too. None of these teachers made any overt racist comments. None of the other kids teased us or said anything. But I began to understand that the color of my skin was salient. I learned that I wouldn't be seen as myself, an individual, and that Raisha would also not be seen as herself. We were the Black girls.

The implications of this began to emerge when I went to a birthday party at a hair salon. Despite the party's theme—hair makeovers—my mother dropped me off with a meticulously constructed hairstyle—multiple twists all over my head. She was, I think, following the decades-old rule of respectability for Black families: Don't send your kids out into the white world ungroomed. A groomed child is a safer child, less likely to have to deal with the biases and prejudices of white people. I also think my mom knew that no one at the salon would know what to do with Black hair. She thought she could save me by giving the stylists a head start. In her mind, all they had to do was add bows.

The birthday girl, who was white, announced to the assembled group of girls that each of us would have the opportunity to have our dream makeover. All the other girls squealed and ran to look at photos of their future hairstyles. I hung back. I knew the styles in the book were for white hair. I learned that white places were not called white places; they were *the* places. There were Black salons. Black barbers.

Black neighborhoods. But the "regular" salon, barber, and neighborhood were white spaces. If it was Black, it was other.

I sat and watched while the other girls had their hair done. The stylists tried to engage me. "Do you want to do something?" one asked. "We can figure something out," another said. It was strange to me that these white people didn't have a language for race or an awareness of it. No one said the word "Black," as if it should not be spoken. They were pretending that "Black" did not exist and that whiteness had no meaning while treating my difference as something that was strange, even wrong. I shook my head no. I wouldn't have it. I wasn't going to let white women touch my hair.

This was the moment I really understood that to be Black was to be something deemed undesirable. The air in the room had shifted around me when the women spoke. I was simply not white, I deviated from the norm, and I understood that I would be treated differently.

Thankfully, my parents' home was a counterpoint to the white world I was moving through. Our house was filled with warmth and love, and the rhythms of our Afro-Caribbean heritage. The sound of cumbia thumped against the walls when my mom vacuumed. She moved around the living room with one arm raised, shuffling her hips and feet, half-stepping the traditional dance moves. Sometimes, she would grab my hand and try to pull me off the couch to join her, but I pulled away, feigning embarrassment. My dad played Kompa on Saturday mornings while cooking scrambled eggs for Christopher and me. He, too, tried to get me out of my chair, but I refused. Secretly, though, I rehearsed alone in front of the bathroom mirror, trying to emulate their easy sway.

Our home was a place where those on the margins were centered and celebrated. A Huichol yarn painting from the Yucatán Peninsula hung on one wall, opposite a Préfète Duffaut framed print. Upstairs, we had a room we called "the library," a study full of thousands of books—the histories of South America, Africa, Palestine, the Caribbean, along with anthropology textbooks and sociology primers. There were titles like *Medical Apartheid* and *Pathologies of Power*, and a wide range of writers—Black, African, South American, American. Writers like Frantz Fanon, Toni Morrison, bell hooks, James Baldwin, C.L.R. James, Paulo Coelho, and Susan Sontag. These books, my mother used to say, were open to me whenever I was ready.

My dad was an emergency room physician at Harlem Hospital, so most nights, he would get home at midnight after working twelve-hour shifts. My brother and I would wake up, run downstairs, and sit on his lap at the kitchen table and eat dinner with him. In the mornings before he left, I would jump down the stairs into my father's arms. This went on until I was twelve, when my dad finally said, "Okay, we have to stop, you're going to kill me."

My parents, like many immigrant parents, were highly focused on our education, and my dad took every opportunity to expand on our lessons. I'd be at the dinner table doing homework and would ask my dad what a word meant. Rather than telling me, he would have me open the dictionary, read the definition, and use the word in a sentence. If I was studying for a test on the Civil Rights Movement, for example, he'd ask, *Did you know that Rosa Parks was not a tired old Black woman who suddenly refused to give up her seat?* He didn't wait for an answer. He went on to tell the full story, explaining that she had been an activist her whole life, active in the Montgomery chapter of the NAACP, and before the now-famous moment, she'd been kicked off the bus multiple times by the same driver for refusing to give up her seat. She wasn't tired; she was tired of giving in. Despite my protests—"Dad, it's not on the test; can we focus on what's on the test?"—he would go on, telling me she was chosen to be the face of the bus boycott because of her light skin and her humble profession as a seamstress, which fit the idea of respectability. There were textbooks, and then there was my father.

I was in the fourth grade when I had my first set of Black friends at school. There were five of us. Some of us were in the same class, others we met up with at lunch and recess. My white girlfriends were convenient for my parents, though Lauren and I got on each other's nerves, and truth be told, we didn't really like each other very much. The Black girls were the first friends I chose for myself.

The girls all lived in the Black part of town. We played double Dutch and talked about boys. I felt more comfortable around them than my white friends, even though we were different in many ways. They were less inhibited, had more freedom, and were mostly unsupervised. I was quiet, even reserved, compared to their loud playfulness. One girl, Charisse, was confident and had an in-your-face forthrightness; I wished I could get away with half the things she felt comfortable saying. We discovered Charisse's mom was in her twenties and my mom was in her early fifties. We thought this was just wild; my mom could literally be her mom's mom.

The biggest difference was that they got to just hang out while my life was scheduled. We were nine or ten years old, and on Saturdays, I went to music school while Charisse and the girls simply chilled. *Wait,* I wanted to say, *I want to chill, too.* Plus, they got to go to the mall by themselves, or with an older sibling, something I was never allowed to do.

We never talked about race or skin color. We didn't compare notes on whether our teachers knew our names or if the places we went were Black or "regular." We didn't talk about all the whiteness around us, but being together, at least for me, made it a little easier to exist in these spaces.

My family had a ritual on Sunday mornings. My brother and I would wake and join our parents in the living room, where they would be deep in conversation about some world event. I'd take my place on the couch and open a book, but would often end up listening to my parents talk instead of reading. Discussions about world events often led to analysis—a conversation on Cuba, for example, would be followed by a discussion on the benefits of socialism and communism. An article that referred to a group of Black kids as thugs prompted talk of the way Black people are portrayed in the media—as dangerous and criminal, or as the sanitized version white people prefer, like Martin Luther King Jr. He was depicted as a peacemaker, when in reality, he was a radical activist, a moral powerhouse, and such a threat to the white power structure that the FBI followed him until he was assassinated.

These conversations took the narrow lens of the white world I moved through and expanded it, showing me that there were many perspectives. The broadening of my worldview continued when I was eleven or twelve in my mom's anthropology classes. She taught at Mercy College in Dobbs Ferry, New York, and rather than hiring a babysitter or leaving my brother and me home alone to fight, she brought us to her classes. We sat in the front row and did our homework. I finished quickly so I could follow the lesson.

I remember one in particular. My mom displayed a photo of a man in a Speedo and asked, "Where would you wear something like this?" The students piped up, saying, "Oh, the beach." She nodded, then changed the slide to a woman in a burka and posed the same question. The students wondered why anyone would cover up so much. "Well," my mom said, "this is somebody who is also at the beach." She then engaged the class in a conversation about different cultures, emphasizing that one is not better than the other, one is not right and another wrong. Instead, there are different ways of living and being in the world that reflect varying beliefs and cultures across all kinds of people.

At the dinner table, or really at any time or place, my father would turn to my brother and me and say, "Have I told you about the Black Jacobins?" The line was a running joke in our family. There was never an inappropriate time to bring up the story of the Haitian revolution; how his people, our people, took back our country from French colonists. We were required to say no, so we said no, and then my dad would dive into the story of Toussaint L'Ouverture: how he was born into slavery and became a general, and how as a strategist and negotiator he helped lead the early rebellion to reclaim the country.

In his professorial manner, my father emphasized the powerful minds and creative thinking of the revolutionaries. He talked about their knowledge of the situation in France, their belief in universal human rights, and their ability to outsmart their captors. It was only when he got to the defeat of Napoleon that my father became animated, emotional. His voice rose when he told us Commander Dessalines and his forces led a second revolt in 1803 against Napoleon, who tried to reinstitute slavery. The Haitians were victorious, establishing an independent nation and becoming the first Black republic. Dessalines turned the French flag on its side and *ripped out* the white stripe with his sword, my dad said, mimicking the action with his hands. Dessalines then had his goddaughter sew the red and blue pieces together, representing a union between the Black and mulatto citizens. Later, the words "L'union fait la force," or "In Union There Is Strength," would be added to the Haitian flag. The creation of the flag was my dad's favorite part of the story, and so it was mine, too.

I remember being surprised to learn that slaves were smart enough to overthrow their owners, which is embarrassing to admit, but true. When we learned about slavery in school, Black people were called "slaves" and shown in textbooks either in chains, as cargo at the bottoms of ships, or as servants in cotton fields and in white people's houses. But the way my dad talked about slavery was different. The Haitian people were enslaved, they were not slaves. This flipped a switch in my mind. "Slave" was not their identity; it was a label and a life forced upon them. Suddenly, I saw the Black people in our history books walking through their villages in Africa. I saw them going to the market, going to school, playing ball in a wide field near a cluster of homes. I saw doctors and craftspeople, merchants and tradespeople, teachers, mothers, fathers, husbands, wives, and sisters and brothers. They were vibrant, creative, smart, human.

I remember learning from my dad that after Napoleon was defeated by the Haitians, he gave up his ambitions in the Americas and sold his land (really the land of multiple native peoples) to the United States in what would be called the Louisiana Purchase. In class, the Louisiana Purchase was billed as a great land grab, an extraordinary real estate deal that would eventually add five states and parts of nine others to the Union, nearly doubling the size of the nation. We were taught in class that Napoleon sold the land because he needed money to fund wars in France. There was no mention of the Haitian victory that precipitated the sale. I remember thinking: *How is it possible that I know more than a textbook?*

What my parents were teaching me was the truth. They were rooting me with a strong sense of pride in my Blackness in a world that would tell me I was worthless. They were teaching me to question what was presented, and who benefited from the way something—a story, history, a news article—was told or phrased.

I thought my classmates could use similar instruction, and when the opportunity presented itself in fifth grade, I took it. Teaneck's centennial was approaching. Our teacher assigned us a research project that was to be displayed for everyone to see, like a science fair, but for history. I was excited. My mom had done research for her dissertation, and I kept a small notebook and pen in my purse and would occasionally stop to scribble notes, telling anyone who asked that I, too, was researching my dissertation. Now, the research was real.

I felt a thrill walking into the library. My cousin worked there and I sat on her lap, flipping through old newspaper clippings to try to find a topic for my project. I stopped at a story about Teaneck in 1949. The headline shouted something about Teaneck being selected as a model town. This was phenomenal. I imagined none of the other kids would find something so cool. I studied the images in the microfiche. Photo after photo showed the faces of white people: kids in school, adults in a meeting, firefighters in uniform standing in front of their stations. My young mind absorbed this with confusion. Where were all the Black people?

I thought maybe the article would say something, but it only said that the Civil Affairs Division of the U.S. Army had selected Teaneck to represent a model town in the United States. The goal was to showcase democracy to the outside world as part of the federal government's reeducation program in Germany and Japan after World War II. Ah, I understood. If something was good, if it was a "model," it was white.

I knew enough to know that Teaneck in 1949 didn't just happen to be completely white. I wasn't fluent in the language of segregation or the specifics of how government policies and anti-Black propaganda segregated the country. But I knew that Black people were in the U.S. in the 1940s and '50s, and that they were either intentionally excluded in the model town project or they were intentionally excluded from living in the town. Here's what else I understood: the government was intentionally broadcasting an image of whiteness.

I was reminded of how I felt when the teacher couldn't remember my name, when there were no hairstyles for Black girls at the salon. I had been invisible. I connected the dots to the history lessons in school, to the exclusion of a Black victory in Haiti from the material, to the one-dimensional and passive depiction of Black people as slaves. We were being taught the story of our nation through a white lens. Even the parts about the Civil Rights Movement were told as if Black and white people had come to a big, amicable understanding, and racism—poof—just disappeared.

I imagined the majority of my classmates would see the white people in the photos and not think to wonder why everyone was white, so I decided I would prompt the question and lead us into a discussion of race.

I went around town with a disposable camera and took photos of my friends and me, as well as other kids in class—a diverse mix that included a boy from Ghana, a Black girl, a Taiwanese girl, and my good friend Phil, who was Italian American. I went to many of the places the U.S. Army had: the school, the library, the police station, the firehouse. On a three-panel posterboard, I pasted the 1949 photos on one side, under the headline "What Is Wrong with These Pictures?" On the other side, I pasted the pictures of my Black, brown, and white classmates and me.

On the designated day, we put our posterboards up around the classroom and took turns looking at each student's work. My classmates weren't really into my project. I don't remember anyone asking me questions, meaning it wasn't the racial intervention I'd hoped it would be. But it had a lasting impression on me. I understood that the world was not made for me, that it was not "for" me, but that I'd have to exist in it one way or another.

3

Belonging

My parents did what they could to prepare my brother and me for a white world. They never sat us down for a big talk about being Black in the United States. The issue of race was more of an ongoing dialogue in our house, more rooted in an understanding of the history of the white supremacist world we lived in. If my parents were talking about the Haitian Revolution, we were talking about French colonialism and oppressive governments. There were conversations about the U.S.'s duplicity, how it had denounced imperialism but embraced expansionism: same concept, different words. My parents talked about how the U.S. branded itself a democracy, but oppressed its own people and supported dictators in Latin America and the Caribbean, oppressing entire populations in favor of its own interests. There was an understanding that the problem of white supremacy reigned not only over the U.S., but the globe.

What this meant for us, my parents would tell my brother and me, though not in the same conversation, was that we were going to have to work twice as hard as our white peers. *You are going to have to be better,* they would say, referring to school and education. *You are going to have to be mindful of how you present yourself.* The message: White people can be average and get ahead. You have to be exceptional.

They tried to make it easier on us, starting with our names.

My parent's names, Lucía and Wilfrid, were not easy for white people to say. People often pronounced my mom's name "Lu-chi-ah," the Italian pronunciation, rather "Lu-see-ah," the Spanish version. My dad was often called Wilfred—people missed the fact that it was "frid" not "fred." So my parents gave us common, easy-to-say standard English names—Alison and Christopher. They were clever, though. My middle name, Mariella, is a blending of my grandmothers' names, Marie and Ella, and my brother's full name—Christopher Henri—is an inversion of the name Henri Christophe, a key leader of the Haitian Revolution. It was subtle, but also right under your nose if you knew your history. White people didn't, so my brother's name was deemed safe.

As a result, I didn't have to repeat my name three times to teachers. Presumably, on college and job applications, my name didn't scream "Black" or "child of immigrants" and therefore offered me a chance of getting an interview. While my parents spoke Kreyòl and Spanish with various relatives and friends, they chose to speak only English to us. They didn't want my brother or me to have an accent. White people would often tell me how articulate I was and how smart I sounded, which, years later, I realized was a microaggression rooted in the surprise that came from not expecting as much from a Black girl.

What my parents didn't prepare me for—how could they?—was that I would be expected to speak for the entire Black race.

This first happened in sixth grade at Dwight-Englewood, a private school in the highly segregated town of Englewood, New Jersey. If you went through Teaneck's Black neighborhood, you'd roughly end up in

Englewood's Black area. From there, if you hopped the railroad tracks and went a bit farther north, you'd cross the color line, arriving in the land of country clubs, mansions, and one of the best private schools in the area, Dwight-Englewood School.

My presence at Dwight-Englewood was, at its core, about preparing me for the white world as best as my parents could. But I ended up there because I started hanging out with the Black kids. It went down in fifth grade, when students from the various elementary schools merged in middle school. Suddenly, I was in a class with not just one or two other Black kids, but as many as five or six. There were three African American kids, a Trinidadian, a kid from Jamaica, a girl from Puerto Rico, and me. I loved it. We all sat together in the front right corner of the classroom, save for the Jamaican kid, because he was afraid of getting in trouble. We were disruptive at times. We were louder. We liked to talk. And for this we were labeled the troublemakers. Once, on the way out to recess, my teacher pulled me aside. "I wouldn't expect this behavior from you," he said. "This is not you. You're too bright, too smart." Except it *was* me. I loved the energy of the group. I loved having a contingent of kids who looked like me in class. But it didn't last. The teacher redid the seating chart and separated us. So we convened at lunch and recess instead.

At a parent-teacher conference, my teacher told my parents that I was socializing with the "wrong crowd." These kids, my teacher said, were going to pull me down. I was so annoyed. Why was hanging out with the Black kids—the kids I wanted to be around, was happy to have after years of playing with mostly white kids—bad? The low-performing white kids were not kids I was supposed to stay away from, but the low-performing Black kids were a "bad" influence? It was the first time, but not the last, that I saw how race and class were often conflated in the United States and how the kind of Black I was (middle class) was somehow seen as exceptional, but in danger of being "contaminated" by the kind of Black (working class) some of my class-mates were. My immigrant parents were well aware of racial dynam-ics. Still, education was everything to them. I had the highest grades in class, and when they heard my grades might suffer, they were alarmed.

Compounding the moment was the fact that my brother had also made Black friends. He and his friends all wore the fashion of the day: sagging jeans and big puffy coats. There was nothing inherently wrong with the style, but this was the '90s and the look, popular among hip-hop artists, had been criminalized. My parents weren't so much wor-ried about my brother's friends as they were about how the combination of his wardrobe, skin color, and friends could be interpreted as trouble by the police. The risk of my brother being profiled for doing some everyday act like walking down the street was too real. I understood. Once, a manager at CVS had told me to leave the store for no reason other than laughing with my friends, but those girls, both white, weren't asked to leave. Private school, they reasoned, would help protect us and give us the best educational opportunity available.

I'm grateful for my parents' sacrifices, but they inadvertently put us into a whiter white space. Dwight-Englewood wasn't exclusively white, but with only a dozen or so Black kids across all grades, kindergarten through twelve, it felt that way. More often than not, from sixth through twelfth grades, I was the only Black student around, and so my white classmates viewed me as the "representative." When some-thing big happened that involved Black people, my classmates wanted to talk with me about it. Take the murder of Tupac. Who did I think shot him? Was Biggie Smalls involved? What was his best album? Which was better anyway, East Coast or West Coast rap?

I had no idea. My parents had only let us listen to classical music until recently. I'd only just bought my first tape, TLC's *CrazySexyCool*. My brother had just bought one by Nas. But suddenly, I was expected to be an expert. I stumbled through some answer, pretending I knew what I did not. When the rumors began that Tupac might be alive, my classmates assumed I was following the case and looked to me for answers. They assumed I knew the lyrics to all rap songs and understood slang. *What does* yayo *mean*, they wanted to know, *and* cush? One boy came up to me with his fingers all tweaked and his elbows out. I looked at him in confusion, having no idea it was a Crips hand signal (or was it the Bloods?).

One Halloween, there were rumors that members of the Bloods and Crips were in New York City, and there was a threat of violence, both in the city and around Englewood and other areas with Black neighborhoods. My classmates wanted to know what colors to avoid wearing on Halloween, because I apparently knew the Crips were associated with blue and the Bloods with red. All I knew was that I was dressing up in a poodle skirt. That's right, I was going trick-or-treating as the white woman from the movie *Grease*.

Another moment that stands out: A boy approached me between classes and started performing a song by the rapper Mase. He swayed and popped, waiting for me to join in, which of course I did, faking my way through. Afterward, I went home and studied the lyrics. I had to. As the arbiter of the Black race, I had to put on a good show. White kids could know things or not know things, but I believed I had to have all the answers. As my classmates' vision of a Black person, it was my responsibility to present us as knowledgeable, informed, and in the know. It was stressful, and exhausting.

By eighth grade, I wanted to let my classmates know that I was just me, Alison, not a symbol of Black people they could use to "understand" Black people. So when we were assigned to write our own version of Martin Luther King Jr.'s "I Have A Dream" speech as part of a lesson on civil rights, I wrote about what it was like to be treated as a Black person rather than as me. I wrote about the burden of it, the weight it put on me. I wrote that I'd rather be accepted as an individual with unique interests, that I could not speak for the entire race in the same way that one of them could not speak for the entire white race.

I won an award for that essay. My classmates told me it was "soooo good." But nothing changed. When Jay-Z came out with the album *Vol. 2 . . . Hard Knock Life*, they asked me if I thought Jay-Z could now be considered the Best Rapper Alive. Is he better than Biggie? Better than Tupac? What did I think?

Every year, one of the final projects in eighth grade was called the Living Wax Museum, in which students dressed up as historical figures or famous people. The entire school looked forward to the wax museum as a fun break from the regular school day. I'd been to many in years past and kids had typically dressed up as Marilyn Monroe, John F. Kennedy, or Pablo Picasso. I knew immediately who I'd be. Ota Benga, an African man who was kidnapped from his home in the Congo and displayed with the monkeys in the Bronx Zoo in 1906.

Since the model town project in elementary school, I took every opportunity to disrupt the white spaces I was in. I knew an entire history my white peers (and it seemed my white teachers) had no knowledge of. And so I decided that I could be instrumental in educating them. I also wanted the opportunity to humanize Ota Benga. When I first heard his story in one of my mother's classes, I was struck by the blatant disregard for him as a person. *They put a human in the zoo?* Ota Benga was a man of short stature, with sharpened teeth, as was the custom of his people, but rather than consider that there was a culture in which sharpened teeth was normal, even beautiful, whiteness treated him as an aberration, not unlike how I was treated. I wasn't in a physical cage, but I was performing for my white peers, trying to be the Black person they expected me to be. In my retelling I could show Ota Benga, and perhaps myself, through my eyes, as a person deserving of kindness and respect. Maybe, in a small way, this project could course correct history.

I dove into research on his life and experience and learned that when Black clergymen in Harlem protested his treatment and demanded his release, whiteness hid behind "science" to justify white supremacy. The nation's leading biologists and ethnologists insisted that the Black race was a separate species. A "degraded and degenerate race," as Harvard professor Louis Agassiz put it in the years leading up to Benga's capture. Others argued that Black people simply did not have the same educational opportunities as white people. The science of the time said that the differences between the races were such that education was moot. "The black, the brown, and the red races differ anatomically so much from the white . . . that even with equal cerebral capacity they never could rival its results by equal efforts," said Daniel Brinton in the late 1890s, the outgoing president of the American Association for the Advancement of Science.

Later, I'd learn that the nation's leading newspaper, the *New York Times*, published an op-ed saying that Benga could not be suffering because "Pygmies are very low in the human scale, and the suggestion that Benga should be in a school instead of a cage ignores the high probability that school would be a place of torture to him . . . The idea that men are all much alike except as they have had or lacked opportunities for getting an education of books is now far out of date."

For the assembly, I wore tattered clothing and "sharpened" my teeth by blacking out parts of them. My cousin found a bunch of thick sticks, six feet tall, and built a cage. I stood inside of it in the gymnasium as students from K through twelve, as well as teachers and administrators, walked around.

When they stopped at my station, I grabbed the bars of my cage and, as the character of Ota Benga, told my life story. I spoke of the beauty of my home and people, of the injustice of being put in a cage for white people's amusement, and of the shame and humiliation this caused me. I spoke of how colonialism and white supremacy made the act of treating a Black person like an animal seem normal, even appropriate, and how the ideology of white superiority allowed well-esteemed white people to think that I, Ota Benga, belonged in a zoo. I shared that at one point, the pain and sorrow became too much, and I shot and killed myself.

My teachers were impressed with my choice. Some of my classmates seemed affected by the story. Others thought the cage was cool. But no one seemed to see the larger picture. They viewed Ota Benga's treatment as a moment in history, the result of misguided white folks at the time, rather than seeing that we weren't very far removed from how white supremacy was affecting me. I was, it seemed, alone in my understanding about race. White people were naïve and ignorant about race, unable to see the white supremacy all around us.

B y the time I was in high school, I knew I was at the wrong school. The majority of the kids were white and wealthy. I was Black and middle class. The white kids wore $300 jeans and were driven to school in Mercedeses and BMWs. The idea of $300 jeans made my parents laugh (though I convinced them once to buy me a pair). My parents dropped me off in a Volvo, which made me feel poor and ashamed that my parents didn't have more money. So to fit in, I became the Black celebrity, the "exceptional" Black girl, the one everyone loved but didn't truly know.

The building of this persona began a couple of years earlier, in Mr. Anderson's math class. Mr. Anderson was Jamaican, Black, with a thin face, glasses, and short, curly hair. He dressed in a suit and tie every day. We sometimes teased him for being nerdy, but we also loved him because he was fun. He'd grab the notes we tried passing in class and read them out loud, shaming us in a way that said he was in on the joke. He was the only Black staff member, other than the maintenance staff, and he took me under his wing.

Every year during Black History Month, we would have an assembly where the story of Martin Luther King Jr. would be told, and we'd do the we-shall-overcome dance and pretend racial tension ended in the '60s. One day during rehearsal, Mr. Anderson, who knew I took singing lessons, said "Why don't you sing for us?" I don't remember what song I sang—Michael Jackson or something from the Jackson 5?—but I remember slipping easily into the music, swaying as I sang, not worrying about how people saw me. My classmates' faces changed when they realized how good I was. It was validation. It was recognition. I could survive here by being good at everything.

Mr. Anderson helped me get my math scores up. He encouraged me to go out for track. When I lined up that first day for a 100-meter time trial and beat all the girls on the team, I looked over at Mr. Anderson, who was the coach. We smiled at each other—mine in amazement, his out of pride. He had a deep belief in me that I could be good at anything. Not because I needed to be twice as good, but because I was a gifted person. Mr. Anderson saw me as an individual, not a race, and he encouraged me to draw out all the talent inside me.

By freshman year of high school, I already had a reputation as the smart, talented Black girl, and I ran with it. I played soccer and ran winter and spring track, all varsity, and earned myself a letterman's jacket. I was captain of this and president of that. I was in all AP classes. I sang in a band. I performed for my classmates. I was always upbeat, always happy, always "on." Senior year, I was voted "Most Likely to Succeed" and "Most Likely to Be President." Everybody loved me. "Hey Ali D.!" folks would shout in the hall.

This was a genuine part of who I was. I had natural leadership ability. I was generally an upbeat person. I was studious, and I liked being busy—pye poudre, powdered feet, like my dad had nicknamed me. But it also felt necessary. My white peers moved through the school with the ease that came with knowing they belonged there. Their presence was inherent. Mine felt conditional. I wasn't white and we weren't wealthy, but dammit I was smart and talented. It was proof that I deserved to be there.

It was also essential validation in a world that kept reminding me I was separate from it—reminders that came at me almost every day. My white peers told me I "talked white." They were confused about why a Black girl didn't speak "Black." A few Black students on campus told me that I "sounded like a Valley girl"—i.e., talked like a white girl, implying that I was doing so because I thought I was better than them. The Black students were associating me with whiteness, something that I, too, was being harmed by. The white students had such strong stereotypes of Black people, it never occurred to them that we were a diverse group, with different accents and language depending on where we grew up. It was painful. I was just speaking the language I'd been surrounded by my whole life, in the voice that came naturally to me, and people were telling me I was pretending to be something else.

In the halls or on the bus coming home from away track meets, students would be talking about whatever their parents were talking about or what was in the news. This was the '90s, so Haiti and Colombia were in the headlines. Then someone would shout, "Hey Alison, aren't you Colombian?"

"Yeah, my mother's Colombian and my father's Haitian."

A cry would ring out. "Oh, Haiti, gross, AIDS comes from there."

"Is your family connected to Pablo Escobar?"

"What do you know about cocaine?"

"Everyone must be doing drugs down there."

"Such a violent place."

My classmates didn't see me. They didn't see that they were making

a caricature out of my people, out of *me*. They didn't see they were echoing stereotypes and messaging propagated by white news, white curriculums, and white supremacy.

I didn't say anything to my classmates directly. Rather, I took solace in naming the problem. Junior year, we had to recite a poem to the class. Most of the students picked works by Sylvia Plath. I read a piece by African American activist Jayne Cortez called "There It Is." It equated white supremacy to Legionnaires' disease, a disease sprayed on people, poisoning minds with a lie about their superiority, that their way was the right way. The poem allowed me to say words and phrases like "ruling class," "Ku Klux Klan," and "penises" out loud. I loved the discomfort my teachers and classmates seemed to feel when faced with language and ideas we were not supposed to use. In composition class, I wrote an essay about not being seen as a reflection on the poem "Harlem (A Dream Deferred)" by Langston Hughes. I read Maya Angelou's *I Know Why the Caged Bird Sings* and wrote about how I, too, felt caged by the white forces around me. I couldn't be me, I had to be the white version of me. I wasn't considered beautiful. Beauty was white, thin, and with long, straight hair. White people dominated our book lists, our history subjects. Our greatness, our achievements, weren't reflected in the curriculum. With no classes that explored Black history, Black literature, or Black culture, there was no warmth, no recognition.

What I craved was a sense of belonging. I wanted my heritage, the color of my skin, the beautiful aspects of Black culture, and the contributions of Black people to be a part of the story. I wanted to be seen as a person, not a race. None of my classmates knew how I felt. There was the appearance of fitting in, but I had no sense of belonging. I read somewhere, years later, that fitting in is shaping yourself to try to match the space or people around you. But belonging is being yourself, being accepted for yourself regardless of the space you are in or the people you are with. Belonging is being embraced and valued as your authentic self.

I experienced such connections only as pockets of time, stolen experiences. It was how I felt sitting with the other Black kids back in public school and in the presence of Mr. Anderson in middle school. In high school, I found it among the maintenance staff, who were majority Black—African American and Afro-Caribbean immigrants like my parents. The men (they were mostly men) took their break on the steps leading up to the lawn, and I'd watch as students and faculty walked by without acknowledging them, as if they were invisible, not even there, and I'd break the silence.

"Yo, what's up?" I'd say.

"Alison!" They'd grin back.

Carl was a Jamaican man who did landscaping; Jim, a short, jovial African American man who fixed things. I'd ask them about their kids. They'd ask about schoolwork. We students often left our bookbags outside in piles on the lawn when we went in for lunch. Whenever I came out of the building, Carl would be there holding my bag for me.

I was particularly close to one man, Bud, a six-foot African American man with a stocky build and an easy laugh who worked as the school's security guard. There was no shortage of times I would forget a book in my locker and return after hours when the buildings were locked. Bud and I would hug like old friends, he'd let me in the building, and on my way out, we'd catch up. He had a daughter who was a very talented softball player, and he'd show me photos from his wallet, tell me when her championship games were coming up. He'd tell me about the latest incident with one of the white parents, how they ignored him, treated him like they didn't have to listen to him. I'd shake my head, blown away by the complete disregard. He was always puffing me up. "You're going to be somebody someday," he'd say. "Don't forget me," he'd say. I could breathe in these moments. These men, by the simple act of seeing me, created space for me on campus. They told me that despite the surroundings, the white space, I did belong.

4

Lost

A few years later, I found myself at Columbia University surrounded by Black people. *Surrounded* is relative. I'd selected Columbia primarily because it was near my home and I'd be in the city, which made me feel like a grown-up. The school's racial makeup wasn't part of my decision. In fact, Columbia is a PWI, a predominantly white institution. The core curriculum is dominated by white people and white thought. Walking around campus, I'd bump into Thomas Jefferson and Alexander Hamilton, statues white people might see and think, *founding fathers*. I saw enslavers. Standing in front of Butler Library, I had only to look up at the list of white men's names etched into the stone façade to be reminded that whiteness reigned over the campus; it was part of the buildings, permanent, living in the walls.

But there were more Black people on campus than I'd encountered before. I could walk around and see Black people every day. It was a revelation. Also, for the first time in my life, my heritage and history were represented in the curriculum. While classes on the Haitian Revolution and Latin American Culture were not part of the core curriculum, it felt important that these topics were included at a prestigious institution. It was, to me, an acknowledgment of the inherent value and worth of our perspectives and experiences, a different story from the one typically told.

There was also a feeling of inevitability to being at Columbia and living on the blocks so close to where my father had worked in Harlem and where I'd gone to music school as a child. The neighborhood itself was familiar. Living in the city, on these streets, felt like freedom, and I took full advantage. I skipped class to go to street fairs, chose to eat at places like the Heights or the West End instead of the cafeteria, and sat for hours on the steps of St. John the Divine and people-watched.

I briefly walked on to the track team. I went to two or three practices and learned that coaches stationed trash cans at both ends of the track; the idea was to work out so hard you'd throw up. I'd invested so much time and energy into being involved in everything in high school and found I had zero interest in working that hard, so I stopped going. I partied and drank, a lot. I went to class, but just enough to pass the tests. I did give myself the one activity that brought me joy, singing, by joining an a cappella group, which is where I met Sean.

Sean was Trinidadian, with a bald head and big smile, and he'd just arrived in the United States to attend Columbia. When he auditioned for the group, our shared Caribbean heritage connected us immediately. We went to H&M and I helped him buy his first winter coat. Sean told me how strange it was to be treated with caution and alarm or suspicion here, because Black people are the majority in Trinidad. The country is 40 percent Black, 40 percent East Indian, 18 percent mixed, 1.2 percent Chinese, and 0.6 percent white. He knew whiteness, of course; Trinidad had a colonial past. But growing up in a country with Black presidents, Black legislators, Black business and civic leaders, and Black kids in private schools, Sean's racial identity was one brimming with deep pride in Blackness, one that was not contested at every turn as mine seemed to be. *What a concept*, I thought, *to have lived in a place that viewed you as normal.*

Friendship with other Black people was pure joy. Like with Bud and Mr. Anderson, I was at ease. When Sasha, a first-generation American whose parents were Jamaican, joined the a cappella group, the three of us became A.S.S.: Alison, Sean, Sasha. Sasha and I bonded over the similarities of our Caribbean parents, their strictness about education and the many times we got in trouble simply for sucking our teeth or rolling our eyes. She, too, had been one of the only Black students at a majority-white private high school. She, too, had been at the top of her class, president of every club she joined, had excelled as a means of survival.

Sometimes we spoke in patois, using shared words from the creole languages of our parents' respective countries, languages born out of necessity, out of bondage and resilience. We'd say things like "wah gwaan" and "mi soon come" and "mash up" and be transported back to family. When we were together, we didn't have to be the best or the brightest for acceptance; we could be silly, sometimes ignorant; we could let loose, just be normal.

Normal was also how I felt when I got a marketing internship junior year at Bad Boy, Sean Combs's (aka Puff Daddy's) record label. I was doing everything possible to get as far away from whiteness as I could, and Bad Boy seemed like the other end of the earth. I applied and got the job. The office was a human-resources nightmare. People had sex in conference rooms and came in hungover from the night before. When four o'clock rolled around, the Crown Royal came out, found easily in the bottom drawer of most employees' desks. I loved it.

Everyone at the label was Black, from the mail carrier to the CEO. It was the first time I had experienced this, and I wanted desperately to fit in. I wanted to be fun, and I thought "fun" was being drunk and the life of the party. Being part of the club scene was part of the unwritten office culture, and late nights became the norm. I'd skipped classes before; now, I went only when I had a test.

One afternoon in the office, one of the executives, Ashton, came over to my desk and began chitchatting—where was I from, how did I like working there. He was six feet tall with a caramel complexion and dark black hair. Fine. Very fine. He invited me out. I was nineteen. He was thirty-six. I fell hard.

Ashton's job was to "break" new records, meaning make them famous. He'd hit the clubs at night, give the DJs the latest recordings, and then try to build up enough hype and demand in the club scene so that radio stations would start playing the songs. When Ashton walked into a place, people looked at him, and so they looked at me. He knew every club promoter, door guy, and the hottest DJs at the hottest clubs. When I was with him, I didn't need to whip out my fake ID and hope for the best. We didn't even wait in line. We simply walked to the front and were greeted with hugs and kisses and drink tickets.

I put my entire self-worth in the hands of Ashton. It shocks me now to think how desperate I became for his attention. My concentration fell, along with my grades. Once, I drove through the Lincoln Tunnel to get to his house in New Jersey. I was drunk and fell asleep and hit ten cars before my car stopped. When the cops came, I took the gum out of my mouth, smushed it onto my fake ID, and tried to stick it behind the seat. The officers found it and added an extra charge to the DUI. My parents were in Cancún, so I spent the night in jail, waking up on a cot wearing the tiny skirt and tank top I'd had on the night before. I immediately reached inside my pocket to find my phone. All I wanted to know was if Ashton had called. My phone, of course, had been confiscated, and so I sat for hours in the cold cell waiting for the judge to see me. I had no guilt or shame, just sadness that I hadn't made it to Ashton's house as planned, and anger that jail had derailed my ability to see him.

Then, out of nowhere, Ashton stopped calling. A few weeks later, I interviewed for an internship at MTV for senior year and dropped by the Bad Boy office to see him. I chitchatted with folks, tried to get his attention. He wouldn't look at me. I pulled out my Sidekick and messaged him on the AOL app: *Hello! What's good?* I watched him look at his phone and put it back in his pocket. He would not look my way. I left and hurried out to the sidewalk, trying to catch my breath. I started walking around Midtown, hyperventilating, having what I'd later realize was a panic attack. Frightened, I called my mom, and told her I wanted to come home.

It would be difficult for me to ascribe a single factor that led to my depression. It was a layering that began with the constant hum of racism, of whiteness. There was no name-calling, no overt anti-Blackness, simply the fact of existing in white spaces where the real me was invisible. The persistent feeling of not belonging, of feeling deficient, and not being seen was always inside me, just below the surface. Ashton, who didn't see me, either, brought it all to the surface, pushing me over the edge.

My mom slept next to me that first month home, holding me. My cousin, who lived with us at the time, helped me make a sock puppet with her photograph on it. I carried that puppet with me to school all spring and summer semester to help me feel less alone. Somehow, I managed to graduate alongside the rest of my class.

But I never fully recovered. When you walk around the world feeling like you don't belong as a baseline, life hits you differently. Everything feels like a failure, which is how I felt after graduating and having no idea what to do with my life. My degree in history (with an emphasis in Latino studies) hadn't been a career path; it was selected because it was a friend's major, and likely also due to my parents' influence. I floated through jobs. I worked for a few months at a law firm that helped a pharmaceutical company get out of compensating elderly people who'd been harmed by their drug, but quit over disgust at defending profit over people. I left a job at a charter school in Harlem because the place was more of a training ground for young, white teachers, rather than a positive learning environment for Black kids. I tried separating the idea of work and purpose and took a job as a party planner in Manhattan. But weddings and birthday parties for rich white folks? Couldn't do it.

From a very early age, people had told me I was going to be "somebody," and since I was not, failure became another layer to a deepening depression. Drinking offered the easiest means of avoiding my life. Concerned, my parents bought a condo in Fort Lee and allowed my cousin and me to live there. I was five miles from Harlem, but it might as well have been one hundred. With no need to go to the city, I drifted away from friends. Embarrassed, I talked to Sean and Sasha only infrequently.

I didn't know how to pull myself out of depression, but I tried by returning to Columbia for a master's degree. I chose Latin American and Caribbean Regional Studies because despite how intentionally my parents had raised me, I still felt rootless. I was Caribbean American but felt neither Caribbean nor American enough, which lent itself to a disorienting in-betweenness. So I focused on the scholars and writers with dual heritage like mine. I studied the work of Michel-Rolph Trouillot, a Haitian American anthropologist whose writing called into question dominant paradigms of history, and whose interest they serve. He solidified what my parents had been showing me: History is told by the people in power, but that does not make it the truth. Who chooses what is good and worthy is a product of worldview, not fact.

I thought about the "literary canon" at Columbia, filled with largely white authors. If a Black author was there, Toni Morrison, for example, there had been a sense that her work was on the periphery. Is Shakespeare really the best playwright to have ever lived? Hardly. He is given prominence in curriculums because of who makes the decisions.

I took solace in the fiction of Edwidge Danticat, a Haitian American novelist and short story writer. Her book *Krik? Krak!* strung together stories of Haitian struggle and survival. I loved finding my family in her words. There was a realness to her work that let me know I, too, could make my mark on the world for being authentically me.

I saw the deep humanity of my people in these Haitian Americans' work, the joy and the pain, and how it conflicted with the messages I'd received that Haiti was "bad." When it came time to write my thesis, I chose to expose how the narrative of Haiti in the U.S. was an intentional project of white supremacy. I wrote how Haiti has been portrayed as poor, diseased, and without a future, because it was the only successful revolt by enslaved people, and it will be paying the price for that radical act forever. If Haiti had become a thriving country, what would it have signaled to other enslaved people, other nations under colonial or imperial rule? *You can unseat white supremacy.* That was not something the world wanted anybody to think.

The program was clarifying and grounding, but it wasn't a solution. The answer to belonging was not in a degree, a job, or a relationship. I needed to go internal, but I couldn't see this yet. I felt an overwhelming sense of failure, of doom, that was compounded by comparison. I couldn't see how lucky I was to have an apartment paid for by my parents, parents who were trying to give me the space I needed to find my way. All I saw was that I was living with my cousin in New Jersey, with no job, no prospects, and a new boyfriend who was as toxic as the last.

Another layer: my father's decline. The dementia had begun with delusions when I was an undergrad. My mother had called and told me to meet her at the emergency room. I went uptown to 168th and Broadway, where I stood with my mother and father, waiting for him to be called. "Do you see all these people?" my father asked. "Do you see all these homeless people?" There were no homeless people. Over the course of six years, the dementia worsened, and he stopped making sense. I remember once when we were dressing my dad to go to my graduation for my master's, he started crying because he thought we were dressing him to go to the firing squad.

He needed around-the-clock care, and it was my responsibility to provide that care when my mother worked. At the apartment, I remember lifting him from the bed to the toilet, feeling resentful that this burden was mine, and then ashamed of my resentment. Sometimes he would pass out and I'd have to lie him flat and make sure oxygen was getting to his brain. He could appear dead, and I'd be crying, thinking he was going to die, then he'd wake up again and his eye would catch mine and he'd smirk and shrug as though nothing had happened.

Everything came at me at once. Seeing my father frail. The glaring failure of my professional life. A lifetime of not belonging. The layers became too heavy. I started taking NyQuil. But if my mind was racing, NyQuil wouldn't knock me out. My mom was on Xanax for her own depression, and when I was at my parents' house and she wasn't looking, I would open her dresser drawer and take as many pills as I dared from the bottle. Back at the apartment in Fort Lee, I'd take one, fall asleep, then wake and take another. A year later, I started running.

5

―――――

A Marathoner

After the tune-up half marathon in Fort Lee, something shifted. I began to call myself a runner. Up until that point, running had been a means to an end, a path back to living. Now, out of the fog of depression, a new identity formed. Calling myself a runner gave me a positive identity, a purpose, something I was passionate about, and I embraced the label with a beginner's eagerness, reading articles online to learn more about what runners do. The ones on sports psychology spoke to me the most. I read about staying in the moment, the idea of running the mile you're in, and about the power of a totem, the idea that you can imbue an object with meaning and it can have a positive impact on you.

I reached for a necklace my uncle had given me with two circular charms engraved with images of the Virgin Mary. I wasn't religious, but the feeling of the two charms bouncing on my chest as I ran, when they synced with my breathing, told me I was stronger than I thought. I read about visualization, how it can prepare you for the task ahead, so I pulled up a preview of the course in San Diego, closed my eyes, and tried to imagine myself running along the route, feeling good, doing it. This was where the lessons of running crossed over into life for me: the ability to see myself in a future I was planning for and to trust in my ability to get myself there.

Small lessons kept coming as I ran:

Focus on what is in your control.

Stay in the present.

Life has meaning.

It seemed as if some higher power were handing me wisdom, but it was movement.

There is a reason to live.

The reason to live is simply to live!

Running told me I could enjoy life. I could accomplish goals. During a sixteen-miler along the West Side Highway, I wondered if I could finish it. I hadn't slept as long as I would've liked, just six hours, and my pace group was assigned to do a few miles at marathon pace, which I was concerned I couldn't maintain. *What if I fall behind?* Then I'd realize I was not falling behind, I was feeling strong, so why worry about it? *Run the mile you're in!* Then fatigue did hit. *Oh, I'm tired.* But I'd been there before, on the last long run, and learned that I could in fact handle it.

I read a quote about how once you make a change, it's hard to imagine what your life was like before. That's how I felt one night at home, dropping pasta into a pot. *Were there really days when I didn't leave my bed?* I thought. *Were there really days when the only thing I could do was shut out the world with sleep?* I could not wrap my head around the idea that that had once been me.

Three weeks before the marathon, we did a twenty-miler, our last long run. A group of us headed out of Central Park and ran up the West Side Highway to the George Washington Bridge, crossing over into Fort Lee and Palisades Park, where we'd done the half marathon a few weeks earlier. My body felt strong. I took the hills without worrying about my ability to climb them and have enough energy for the remaining miles. I was ready to suffer a little, a far cry from the committed track runner I'd been in high school. Back then, we did thirty-minute workouts, and while they involved hard efforts, I never felt exhausted. I used to watch the distance runners (all white kids) return to campus with their faces twisted in fatigue and think, *No, thank you.* As I descended the hill, I felt a pull. My hamstring. I hobbled on it for a few miles, but the pain was too great. I got in the sweep van, devastated and worried that I wouldn't be able to run the marathon.

"No, no, you have the time on your feet," our coach said when I went to his physical therapy studio. He diagnosed a Grade 1 tear and told me not to run for two weeks. I protested. "Just rest," he said. "The hay is in the barn. Your fitness is there."

"How do you know that?" I asked. "How do you know that will be true for me?"

He explained that was how training worked. Fitness is stored in the body and will be there on race day. "It's simple: if you run on it, it will get worse. If you don't run on it, it will get better," he said.

My instinct was to run anyway. My depression had lifted, but I still believed I had to do every workout in order to finish the marathon; I had to do everything right. But I remembered what he said—*if you run, it will get worse*—and convinced myself that not running was in fact doing it "right."

I didn't run, save for once on an anti-gravity treadmill at the coach's physical therapy office. The week before the race, I put in two easy, pain-free thirty-minute runs. I wanted to cry with relief.

traveled to San Diego with an avocado. The Team in Training coaches had instilled in us all the things you should and should not do race weekend, and their advice reverberated in my head. *Nothing new on race day*, they'd said. So tucked gently among my tights and singlet was my pre-race breakfast: gluten-free bread, Justin's classic peanut butter, and that avocado. I walked around the expo rejecting sports drinks and bar samples. *Don't try anything new.* After an hour, I realized I was still on my feet. I went back to the hotel and put my feet up. I didn't want to mess my race up. I didn't come this far to only come this far.

I didn't sleep well the night before but didn't worry about it. *Sleeping two nights before the race is what matters.* I boarded a bus at five in the morning with other runners and we drove through the dawn, disembarking in the middle of Balboa Park. There were thousands and thousands of runners. I scanned the crowd for Black people but with limited sight in the dark, my search turned up empty. I was with a small group of Team in Training runners, all of us decked out in our purple and white. I couldn't stop posing for pictures. When one of the race photographers walked by, I lifted up my throwaway shirt to reveal my bib number and posed for the camera. An award I could've won: the corniest first-timer ever.

The blare of the starting horn sounded and we were off. Just like that, I was doing it. I was running a marathon. All those hours of training and sacrifice were culminating in this moment, which was, when I thought about it, somewhat mundane and ordinary. We'd paid all this money to run down a public street with thousands of other people to participate in what was essentially a solo experience. We were running, but we weren't engaging with each other. My mind wandered to the runners around me. I wondered how many of us were running a marathon for the first time. I wondered what had brought them to the starting line. I wondered if their training experience had saved their lives like mine had. We left downtown and the neighborhood transitioned to a more run-down area with bodegas and liquor stores. I knew this was the Black/Latinx part of town. I'd left the white area, with its wealthier houses on tree-lined streets next to a beautiful park. The predictability of this country was so disappointing.

The early miles of a long race were critical, I remembered my coach saying. You have to run them smart; that is, not too fast, or you'll blow up at the end. But I was already at the 10K mark when I first looked down at my watch and saw that my pace was fast. *Shit.* Exactly as coach had warned. The starting line adrenaline could propel you into a quick pace and then you might never recover. *Slow, slow, slow,* I thought, letting the word take over my mind as I dialed back my pace.

I had rejected the "go team" mantra throughout the training because it seemed lame and I hadn't felt a bond with anyone. But in the excitement of the race, whenever I saw another purple TNT singlet, I shouted, "Go, Team!" making the seemingly unconscious decision to embrace the notion I'd heard so many times in training: that we were all in this together—that the marathon was an equalizer, a place where differences disappear. *We're all just runners on the road,* I'd heard someone say. Rhetoric like that didn't normally land for me because it simply was not true. But I was grasping for anything that would give me a sense of connection and community.

At mile sixteen, I thought I might not make it. A man carrying an American flag passed me, and I couldn't imagine how he was running with the extra weight. At mile seventeen, a Team in Training coach offered me a McDonald's salt packet. "No," I said, "I didn't do it in training." She insisted, so I opened the packet and downed it like a shot. My body immediately perked up, or maybe my mind had. I spent the next mile wondering if the salt had impacted me physically or if it was a placebo effect, but what did it matter?

At mile eighteen, I fell apart again. The course detoured away from the finish line here, a mental challenge. There was nothing to be done but run, so I kept going. When I saw the finish line, I started crying. All of the work I'd done over the past sixteen weeks had gotten me to this point. All of the early morning runs. The commitment to remaining sober and abstaining from Xanax. The Alison who was once glued to the couch in a depressive fog—what would she say if she could see me now? I had defied every negative thought. I had accomplished something that so few people ever would. The tears were cathartic, almost like a shedding of so much of the pain I'd been carrying for so long.

I was not expecting to see anyone I knew, but my mom had gotten in touch with a distant cousin who lived in San Diego and sent her a picture of me. She found me at the finish line. "Alison," she said, "I know you don't remember me, but I'm your family. I know your mother." We hugged and she took a picture of me crying.

We walked around Balboa Park before I finally needed to sit down. I snapped a selfie, smiling, medal in hand. That's the picture I would

look at later. The one that reminded me that running had brought meaning back to my life.

I went to the after-party that night. After filling the tub with cold water, adding ice, and sitting in it for ten minutes (*ice baths aid recovery*), I put on jeans and a white tank top, placed the medal back on my chest, and walked to the restaurant lounge. At first, I didn't recognize anyone. I had only seen these people in running clothes, sweaty with salt stains on their faces. I saw balloons and a lot of commotion at the back of the bar, and then a few Team in Training signs came into view. I walked around the party, noticing just how cozy everyone was. People were doing shots together. Couples were making out. I realized I could disappear and no one would notice. So I did. It was a relief, really, not to have to perform for these white people.

I went back to my room, changed into my pajamas, and with my medal still around my neck, closed my eyes, replaying the 26.2 miles I had just conquered. Maybe Team in Training wasn't my place, but I knew without a doubt that running was.

PART

TWO

6

Outside

When I finished my first marathon, I felt like I had cracked the code to human existence. There was no shortage of runs that started with a problem that somehow got resolved over forty-five minutes of pounding the pavement. There were runs when I zoned out and thought of nothing, filling me with rare and unexpected moments of freedom. There were runs fueled by anger at past mistakes, my arms and legs charging forward so fast that I felt as though I were chasing myself, chasing my life.

Running taught me how to be embodied, to feel at home in myself. I saw now that I had been a weather vane, moving around in the wind, letting myself be tossed about. Running was an anchor to a sense of self. And while the direction I was going wasn't entirely clear, the course I was on was mine.

So of course I kept running. I found a job at the Team in Training office working in runner services, helping folks fundraise. It was a relief to have money coming in. It also felt like a way to be connected to this sport that had saved me. Sometimes I still couldn't believe running had pulled me out of my depression. The word *magic* kept returning to describe running, and helping bring more people into running seemed to be an ideal job. But I quickly realized that was not what I was doing. I was looking at forms, seeing how much money people had raised, and offering strategies on how to raise more. It wasn't the warm fuzzy part of getting people into running, but it was a job.

The office was downtown on Twenty-Third and Park, a new neighborhood for me, and I ran after work by myself, exploring the expansive and iconic streets. It felt like a scene out of a movie. I'd run and marvel at structures such as the Waldorf Astoria, the Pan Am Building (now known as the MetLife Building), and Grand Central Terminal. I had to remind myself to stop craning my neck to admire the tall structures and to look in front of me to see where I was going.

Other times I took the train north and ran a loop in Central Park, now familiar to me after so many training miles. The east side of the park always felt cold, not temperature-wise, but in its energy. The west side was more familiar, and I had things to look forward to, like Harlem Hill, which felt sort of like home. Having running as a regular part of my life was a gift, but when I saw groups running together I longed for comradery, someone to share a high five with when I reached the top of the hill.

I loved experiencing how the choices I made affected my running. Eating fruits and vegetables instead of processed food made me feel full and light, and I ran lighter. I experimented with tempo workouts and fartlek runs and saw how two weeks later, the same workout felt easier. *Do the inputs to get the outputs.* I loved the simplicity of that.

I raced whenever I could. A half marathon. A 10K. A 15K. I traveled to Philadelphia to run the Rock 'n' Roll Half Marathon, where I unexpectedly knocked nearly twenty minutes off my time. I surprised myself with a strong 5K in Delaware, feeling the effects of speed work in the ease of my stride. I scrolled through the New York Road Runners website to see what was on the racing calendar, and competed in a half marathon in Brooklyn and various distances in Central Park. I even ran at the Armory, running the 800 in 2:44.

At each race, I scanned the crowd for other Black people. Rarely did I find more than a dozen or so of us, even in places like Philadelphia and Washington, DC, cities with large Black populations. That distance-running culture was white was something I knew when I started Team in Training, and while I hadn't expected that to change, I was struck by how obvious it was that the sport was a white space, particularly in Black areas like DC. I had a sense of being an observer more than a participant, someone outside the culture looking in.

Running's whiteness wasn't only evident at major events; it permeated the sport. On every running website I went to—for shoes, for clothing, for advice—I saw white models in the ads and stories. At the Team in Training office, I'd flip through someone's issue of *Runner's World* and find one, maybe two, people of color; more often than not, I'd find none. Once, I counted three Black people, but it included my own face in an ad for Team in Training. *There just aren't a lot of us here*, I thought.

B ut why? Why was that?

Before I started running distance, I hadn't given much thought to why white people ran distance and Black people ran track. But the question surfaced as I noticed the dearth of Black bodies in distance running. Why didn't we run distance? In high school, I never once considered running cross-country or the 1500 meters because I'd never seen a Black distance runner before. The images I was seeing in the media and in the running industry were of white people, which showed who could be a runner and who the industry thought distance running was for. My perception only shifted once I saw my friend's post on Facebook. Consequently, when I started the Team in Training program, I hadn't felt welcomed because I was outside of white culture.

These thoughts were true, but they didn't fully explain why I thought distance running was for white people. Or why Mr. Anderson suggested I run track instead of cross-country. If white people were seeing themselves in distance running, where were we? Who was a runner to us? A Black runner was Jesse Owens, Jackie Joyner-Kersee, or Carl Lewis. They were Flo-Jo or Allyson Felix. A Black runner was a track star.

The summer after running my first marathon, I watched the 2012 London Olympics and, as usual, I tuned in for my favorite events: the women's 200 meters, 400 meters, 400-meter hurdles, and relays. These events were familiar because I ran them in high school and because they were dominated by Black women. I'd once dreamed of making the Olympic team; ultimately I knew I didn't have the work ethic it would've required, but I was fast and felt connected to these women.

I watched Allyson Felix win gold in the 200 meters and Sanya Richards-Ross take it in the 400 meters. I screamed at the screen during the 4 x 400 as the United States blew Jamaica out of the water. It never occurred to me to watch the 800—a distance event. But as a marathoner, I watched the women's race for the first time and recognized Shalane Flanagan and Kara Goucher as women I'd read about in *Runner's World*. I concluded that there must not be any elite-level Black American distance runners or Black running groups; that the divide between track and field and distance running must have occurred decades ago.

Indeed, whiteness had told us that track was where we belonged.

"The brute caricature portrays black men as innately savage, animalistic, destructive, and criminal," wrote sociologist David Pilgrim, Ph.D., founder of the Jim Crow Museum at Ferris State University. Many believed Black men were uniquely capable of excelling at sports that required strength and power—boxing and track and field, and later, after integration, football and basketball. Eugenics, despite being unscientific and deeply racist, further propagated the idea that Black men were biologically predisposed to sprinting.

"I think power is the key to the Black athlete's success," U.S. Olympic coach James E. Counsilman told a reporter for *Sports Illustrated* in 1971. "For instance, in 1968 the eight Olympic finalists in the 100-meter dash were all Blacks. In the U.S., the Black athletes dominate the sprints and don't do as well in the distances . . . The Black athlete is more adapted to speed, and that accounts for his superiority in sports. Football, baseball, boxing, basketball, sprinting, high jumping, broad jumping—these involve speed. I'm not saying the Black man is inferior or superior. I'm just saying that he is better adapted for speed and power." Black women were equally stereotyped, painted as masculine and aggressive, animalistic and highly sexualized, qualities that "explained" their talent in track and field.

Black people were stereotyped as being *only* good at power sports, limiting the definition of what we could do in a way that did not apply to white people. White people could head toward distance or track, whichever their particular body type was better built for, or where their interest lay, while Black Americans were marginalized, pushed to occupy a space dictated by whiteness.

Martin Beatty, the head track and field coach at Middlebury College in Vermont for many years, said that growing up in the 1960s and 1970s, "the thought never crossed my mind to run distance. I never knew anything more than the 400; it was never made available to me." I joined track instead of cross-country in high school because, as Beatty had experienced, that's what Black kids did.

One day at the Team in Training office, some of my coworkers were talking about this runner named Prefontaine. I was still relatively new to running, and whenever my coworkers used a word or talked about someone I didn't know, I secretly googled it. It was how I learned about fartlek workouts and VO2 max, and that foot strike was a thing. I don't remember why people were talking about Prefontaine (only that I thought his name was Pre Fontane). But Google told me that Steve Prefontaine was a running legend—a white guy with a '70s mustache who competed for the University of Oregon and said things like "To give anything less than your best is to sacrifice the gift." *Nice*, I thought.

I also learned that he was part of the "running boom." I had no idea there was a "boom," so I followed the Google links and learned that running used to be "jogging." I also learned that in 1963, a man named Bill Bowerman started a running club in Eugene, Oregon, an event that marked the beginning of the running craze. He was the University of Oregon's track and field coach (which included Pre), a coach for U.S. Olympic teams, and four years after the running club began, he published the book *Jogging*, which went on to sell a million copies and introduced the whole country to running as a recreational sport for the masses. An organization called the Road Runners Club of America began hosting two-mile fun runs in the mid-1960s, and a medical doctor named Kenneth H. Cooper published the book *Aerobics* in 1968, which sold millions and promoted jogging as an ideal form of aerobic activity.

I kept reading and learned the story of Kathrine Switzer. She ran the Boston Marathon in 1967, when women weren't allowed to run, and the race director famously tried to pull her off the course. The images of the scuffle pushed the women's running movement into the mainstream. Switzer, I learned, went on to advocate for women's inclusion in distance running. She helped start a series called the Avon International Running Circuit to bring more women to the sport, which eventually led to the women's marathon being added to the Olympic Games in 1984.

I was reading about the boom, seeing only white bodies in the old photos, and noting the dates. 1968. Wasn't that the year Martin Luther

King Jr. was assassinated? I looked it up and confirmed it was. We'd only gotten the right to vote a few years earlier, in '65. In '67, if a white woman running—Switzer—was seen as problematic, a Black woman would not have had a chance. I also knew that Switzer's marathon in '67 and subsequent advocacy wouldn't have signaled to Black women that she was advocating for them.

The origin story of the running boom began in 1963, when Bowerman invited people to join him at Hayward Field, in Eugene, Oregon, to "jog." I'd never been to Oregon, knew nothing about the setting, and so, curious, I turned to Google again to better understand the context of that first run. Oregon, in 1963, was not unlike the rest of the United States at the time: intentionally segregated. But while other states separated Black people from white people within a city and state, Oregon had declared the *entire* state white. In 1857, white people who had colonized the territory approved a constitution that barred Black people from moving to the area. They also made it illegal for Black people already living in the territory to vote, own real estate, make contracts, or use the legal system. When Oregon became the thirty-third state two years later, it was admitted to the union as the only state with a Black exclusion law. In the 1920s, Oregon had the nation's highest Ku Klux Klan membership per capita, and had you looked north on Willamette Street in Eugene, you would've seen large white KKK letters on the hill.

By the time Bowerman formed his running group, the exclusion law had only been repealed for thirty-seven years. Black people couldn't own property until the state's Fair Housing Act passed in 1957, six years before the running group first met. Eugene's population in 1963 was only 0.4 percent Black, or 220 of nearly 51,000 people. The University of Oregon had a small percentage of Black students, but it wouldn't approve a Black student union until 1966.

When Bowerman invited people to join him for a run, he had just returned from New Zealand, where he himself had started jogging. At the encouragement of his friend, local coach Arthur Lydiard, he joined a couple hundred people—men, women, and children—for a few miles in a park while he was there. Up until that point, Bowerman's routine of running and walking about a quarter mile a few times a week hadn't prepared him for distance, and he struggled. But he came to learn from Lydiard and his running group that slow, steady running could have a powerful impact on the health of not just athletes, but everyday people as well. Bowerman ran nearly every day for the rest of his time in the country and returned home ten pounds lighter and more fit than he'd been in years. When he got home, he issued an invitation via the local paper, the *Register-Guard*, for anyone who wanted to try jogging to come to Hayward Field that Sunday, February 3, 1963.

I tried to place myself in 1963 and imagine what Black people would've thought about the invitation to jog at Hayward Field, if they even saw it. I could not know for sure, but I did know from experience that when you have been excluded from a place and seen harm come to people for entering it, you take precautions. Just because the KKK sign no longer sat on Skinner Butte and the state law had been updated to read that "anyone" can come does not make the space suddenly safe. If Bowerman had wanted to encourage the city's Black residents to jog, the call in the newspaper would have needed to say "Negroes welcome."

As it turned out, about two hundred white people showed up at Hayward Field that first day. Over the course of weeks, Bowerman's group runs grew to a reported two thousand people, and the publicity helped jogging spread to towns across Oregon.

The running boom sprung from lily-white Oregon, so it was in fact coded white, this confirmed, from its very conception. Feeding the boom were high school and college cross-country teams—white boys and men—and the white men who competed in the then-niche sport of marathoning. When mainstream media reported on the emerging sport of jogging, it almost exclusively featured white people. White runners appeared in *Newsweek*, the *Washington Post*, and the *Chicago Tribune*. Senator William Proxmire (D-Wisconsin) was one of the runners featured in the *New York Times Magazine* in 1968, along with Senator Strom Thurmond (R-South Carolina), another white man—and the Southerner who stood on the Senate floor for twenty-four hours and eighteen minutes to protest the Civil Rights Act of 1957. The *Times Magazine*'s story ran on April 14, 1968, ten days after Martin Luther King Jr. was shot to death on the balcony of his hotel room.

I thought about these facts as I ran sometimes. Not about the boom, but about how this wasn't my history. We weren't talked about in the origin story of running. It was as if Black people weren't there, didn't even exist. Maybe I was wrong, but as I kept reading, all I found were stories that centered and celebrated white people, the image of distance running I had grown up with: white, male, thin, college-educated.

I learned about Frank Shorter, a twenty-four-year-old Yale graduate who won marathon after marathon in the 1970s, and Bill Rodgers, who took over winning in the late 1970s. Shorter won the Olympic marathon in 1972, and Rodgers won the New York City and Boston marathons repeatedly. Prefontaine was setting records in the 5000 and 10,000 meters before he tragically died. These men defined the sport, showed who belonged, and as the number of runners rose to 25 million during the 1970s, people who looked like them were largely the ones who joined the jogging craze. White women were running, and despite what happened to Switzer, it seemed they pretty quickly found their place. The New York Road Runners launched the Crazylegs Mini Marathon in 1972 to bring more women to the sport; Switzer launched the Avon International Running Circuit for women; and later, seeing a business opportunity, Nike and others put on multiple women-only races, from 5Ks to marathons.

As I read this history, I noted an assumption among runners that anyone who wanted to run could run. *All you need are running shoes! Just show up*, and *It's simple and accessible* were common phrases. I recognized it as the same sentiment in the marketing materials at Team in Training: running was "for everybody." But the "everybody" running called to, through its media, its marketing, and its image, didn't include us. It was a clear example that white people lived in one world and Black people lived in another. Black people have to know the rules of the white world and our own world, while white people don't even have to know there is another world. "White privilege," wrote feminist scholar Peggy McIntosh, Ph.D., in the journal *Peace and Freedom* in 1989, "is like an invisible weightless knapsack of special provisions, maps, passports, codebooks, visas, clothes, tools and blank checks." It is carried by every white person, and allows them to be seen, centered, and feel normal at all times. It allows them to run.

White people, then and now, were not accounting for the forces of racism, discrimination, and bias; hostility that could come along at any time. "I'll be running along and a car will come alongside me," said one Black runner of the early days of the boom. "The cat inside will roll down the window and I know what he's going to say. 'N——!'" Later, I'd read about a young Black man who listed *Don't run in public* as a rule for Black men learning to navigate white culture and white spaces. A story in the *Michigan Chronicle* in 1997 summed up the risk: "If you're driving, walking, or—God forbid—running (jogging), and you simply look like an African American, you are subject to a stop and search."

When I lined up the dates of the boom, the Civil Rights Movement, and beyond into the 1970s and '80s, they moved along parallel tracks, meaning we were fighting for our basic human rights while white people were starting to jog. There was 1963, the year

Bowerman started his running group, the same year as Project C, the civil rights campaign in Alabama, when peaceful protesters in Birmingham were attacked by police dogs and sprayed with fire hoses. The whole decade was marked by the fight for our rights, met at every turn by fierce opposition by white people who used violence against us: The bombing of the 16th Street Baptist Church in Birmingham, killing four little girls who were found in the basement rubble. The bombing of the bus of thirteen people—Black, white, men, women—known as the Freedom Riders, met by a mob of white people, who attacked them. Students who protested at lunch counters were spit on and harassed by white people, while Black students trying to exercise their right to education were heckled by white adults and kids. White teenagers patrolled parks in Chicago and terrorized Black kids who dared enter "their" territory.

During the '50s and '60s, civil rights lawyers filed multiple lawsuits in attempts to desegregate state parks. But rather than open parks to Black people, South Carolina shut down its entire parks system. Georgia opted to lease a dozen of its parks to private operators, circumventing the legal system. The message from white people was clear: *We don't want you in our spaces and we will do everything we can—including extralegal means—to enforce it.*

Black families trying to move to white neighborhoods were met with threats by "good" white people defending the color line. This particular strain of violence even had a name: move-in violence. White people hurled rocks through a window of the home of the Wade family in Shively, Kentucky, with a message attached: "Nigger Get Out." The police, acting as agents of the state, did little to dissuade these acts or hold any of the perpetrators accountable. In fact, police contributed to the violence. Between 1932 and 1968, white police officers killed 123 Black people in Jefferson County, Alabama, alone; in 51 of the killings, officers shot victims in the back while they were fleeing. "We can never be satisfied as long as the Negro is the victim of the unspeakable horrors of police brutality," Martin Luther King Jr. said to the crowd gathered for the March on Washington. He would be assassinated five years later.

Wow, I thought. We were being killed in the streets while white people were taking to the streets to run. We couldn't use a state park while white people were starting to jog in them. It was as Gil Scott-Heron wrote in his 1970 spoken word poem:

"No hot water, no toilets, no lights.

(but Whitey's on the moon)."

I went to a race in Central Park and stood in the corral surrounded by white runners. I was quiet, uncomfortable, and kept to myself. White people like to think the world changed following the Civil Rights Movement, but it didn't. Neighborhoods and schools eventually became more integrated. The signs in the South were taken down. But white supremacy remained intact as the ruling structure of the nation, and the same was true of running. The sport was not separate from the rest of the nation. Intentionally or not, running was built on the same system and operates within the system. The archetype of a runner was still a thin white man who ran fast. The secondary figure was a thin white woman. A Black woman among them was on the outside.

So I began to play around with the idea of what a place for us, by us, could look like. What if I could rewrite the rules so that Black people like me could know they did belong, even if conventional wisdom, whiteness, and media said otherwise?

7

A Place for Us

White supremacy has pushed Black people into segregated corners of America for centuries, forcing us to carve out spaces for ourselves. But my favorite thing about us? We can make a way out of no way. There is no shortage of examples where our culture, beauty, and resilience have resulted in some of the most incredible gifts to the world. The Harlem Renaissance, every Black college and university, the Greenwood District, Seneca Village, jazz, hip-hop, and civil rights.

Running was no different. The desire for space and place led Black runners in Atlanta to create the South Fulton Running Partners in 1979. A couple of friends, Jim Lemon and Jerry McClain, began walking around a high school track for fitness in the city's Southwest neighborhood. The walks became runs, and they took their workouts out onto the neighborhood streets. Eventually they ran local 5Ks and 10Ks and were surprised to see so few Black people. "In Atlanta!" Lemon said in a 2011 story in *Runner's World*. The two men connected with a few other Black runners at the races and formed the South Fulton

Running Partners. They hosted a 5K and supported other clubs that were forming, like the South Dekalb Striders, a majority Black group that formed in Atlanta in the mid-80s.

Other groups followed. The National Black Marathoners Association, founded in 2004 to bring more Black Americans to the sport. Black Girls Run in 2009. Black Men Run in 2012. In 2013, I didn't know about any of these groups. All I knew was that I loved long-distance running, yet didn't feel part of the community. So I decided to start a running group in Harlem.

There was never any question of where. Even before I lived there through college and graduate school, Harlem had always felt like the center of the universe to me. It was a place where Blackness was celebrated. Streets were named after Black people—Malcolm X, Martin Luther King Jr., Adam Clayton Powell Jr. I could walk the neighborhood and see statues of historic Black figures like Mother Clara Hale. It was a place imbued with our history, where thousands of African Americans moved during the Great Migration to escape Jim Crow; where many immigrants, including my parents, landed from the Caribbean and Africa. Malcolm X spoke on the corner in the 1960s. James Brown and Aretha Franklin performed at the Apollo. When I was a child, my parents brought me to Harlem on the weekends for music lessons, and afterward, we'd walk around the neighborhood getting ice cream. Sometimes when we were at home, I'd stare at the black-and-white photos of my mom and dad hanging out at the Cotton Club and Smalls Paradise, wondering why they ever left—wishing I had grown up there, wishing I could be transported back to that place and time.

I took photos of my friends Sean, Sasha, and Kristin running and created a flyer: borrowing my father's nickname for me, Pye Poudre, I called it the Powdered Feet Run Club. *Monday nights, 6:00 p.m., meet at Harlem Yoga Studio, 44 W. 125th Street.* That first night, one person showed up, but never came back. Then, no one came. For weeks, then months, I stood on 125th between Malcolm X and Fifth, scanning the street for people dressed in running clothes. After a half hour, I'd sometimes call my mom. "I'm doing this for nothing," I said.

"No, you're building a presence," she countered. "People won't come if you're not there. Your consistency matters."

I was frustrated, but also convinced that everybody was watching and waiting for this running club to happen. So I worked on marketing. I printed business cards. I reached out to other groups in Harlem, like the Marcus Garvey Park Alliance and Harlem Park to Park, to let them know about the new running club. I posted flyers at different yoga studios, cafés, and the online community board at Columbia. Then on Monday nights, I stood in front of the yoga studio and waited. Henry, the barber on the second floor, would strike up a conversation. He wanted to know what I was doing and worked hard to convince me to get my next cut from him. The security guard at the lingerie shop next door started waving hello when he saw me, as did the owner of a Jamaican juice spot down the block. Their acknowledgment was encouraging. *Hello sister*, it said to me. *You're welcome here.*

Often, I set off running on my own. I crossed Malcolm X Boulevard and went over to the West Side Highway. I ran from park to park—St. Nicholas to Jackie Robinson. I passed Harlem Hospital and thought of my dad. There was such beauty in Harlem: the old porches of Astor Row; the brownstones and tree-lined streets; the greenery of Marcus Garvey Park; the stately image of the Frederick Douglass statue and Duke Ellington beside his grand piano. I had run in Harlem a couple of times during Team in Training, but I had been mostly focused on getting miles in. Running the streets now, I was more aware of the space around me. I was running outside for the sake of being outside and running. My mind wandered, caught new things. I wondered about the people who lived on Astor Row in the '20s and '30s, what their lives were like. I ran past the Harriet Tubman statue, which depicts her striding south to help more enslaved people come north to freedom, and reflected that slavery seems to be considered only our history, our roots, and not white people's history as well. I wondered, why are statues of Black icons only in Black neighborhoods? Why are our icons not American icons? Why, I wondered, does Frederick Douglass Boulevard, or Malcolm X Boulevard, run only the length of Harlem? Why do they not extend down into the rest of Manhattan?

Little kids abandoned their game and ran with me, pulling me out of my musing. The stoop dwellers yelled:

"You're slow, run faster!"

"If you keep running, you're gonna lose your ass, sis!"

"You're getting faster every time I see you!"

"Keep running and you're going to lose your uterus!" a Black man yelled once, reciting an old trope he knew was bullshit. We both laughed.

One Monday night in early 2014, I spotted a woman walking down 125th Street toward me. "Are you Alison?" she asked. Christa was tall, wore glasses, and, yikes, she was white. I had wanted the running club to be a place for Black people. I believed there were lots of people like me who had no idea running could be a powerful way of life, and I wanted them to know this space was theirs. White people could come of course, but a white woman wasn't who I saw when I pictured Harlem Run. Still, I was grateful someone had finally showed up, so I smiled and said, "Yes, I'm Alison. Welcome."

Christa and I ran what would become known as "the Classic" at Harlem Run because it was my favorite route and the easiest to describe. We went west on 125th Street, turned down Malcolm X Boulevard, and entered Central Park. We climbed Harlem Hill and made our way across to the 102nd Street transverse before returning via Malcolm X.

Christa told me her father was a runner, and that running together had brought her closer to him. She also shared that she would be undergoing surgery in a few months; I got nervous for her, but also for me. Would I lose my first member as quickly as she came?

I didn't. She returned the next week, and the week after that. Monday nights ceased to be a terrifying hour of embarrassment and became my favorite day of the week. Later, I dubbed Christa the OG, the original gangster. It was ironic, but also perfect.

I continued to post on Instagram and Facebook and stumbled on the hashtag #werunharlem, used by a running group that met every third Sunday at a Baptist church on 116th Street. I was the furthest thing from Baptist—somewhere between atheist and agnostic—but I was curious to see who this other person in my neighborhood with the same idea was. I went to a run and met the founder, Amir Figueroa. He was warm over DM, but in person he seemed standoffish. Only one other person showed up, a woman who talked about her running life the entire 5K. Amir and I just nodded. Mostly, I struggled to keep up with the pace.

After that first encounter, I was surprised to see Amir at my run the following week. By this point, my friends Sean and Sasha were running with us, so counting the OG, we were a group of five. Amir came intermittently, texting to ask for the route when he couldn't make it. A few months later, both of us were still only getting a handful of people, so we talked about combining our groups. We decided we didn't want a religious affiliation to deter anyone, so he folded his group into mine.

In these early days, my most pressing question was: how do you grow community? I knew I made people feel comfortable and included, but how did I get people to show up to do a potentially daunting physical activity? I reached out to a few other groups that at first glance seemed to share my vision of a running space that was for us and by us. I sent emails, tweets, and messages to the Black and brown male leaders of these groups (there were no other women-of-color-led groups in NYC at the time) to see if there was a possibility of networking or supporting each other. I got no response. I didn't think much of it, but made it a point to attend the runs of these groups, as well as others. I wanted to see what those other communities looked and felt like, and get a feel for the running scene in general.

I learned about a number of groups through social media, and one Saturday morning I headed over to Seventy-Second and West Drive in Central Park to meet a group with a decades-long history in the city. At the dot of 8:00 a.m., a narrow white man stood atop a tree stump and told the group—mostly white men—that we'd run the six-mile park loop and meet back here. The next thing I knew, everyone was racing off toward Fifty-Ninth Street, leaving me alone in the back, running my 9:30 pace. The "Everyone Welcomed" on their web page must've been meant for fast folks.

One Monday night, instead of running in Harlem, about seven of us from my group took the train north to join a group that started at 8:00 p.m. The start time came and went and we stood there, wondering what was going on. Finally, around 8:20 p.m. two men announced the run details. No one moved; everyone kept talking, seemingly unbothered by the delay. I looked at my watch when we finally took off; it was 8:45 p.m. As we followed the other runners, a member of my group muttered under their breath, "Will we be home by midnight?"

Besides the group's loose organization, the vibe felt more cool kids/ night club than a welcoming space for everyone, a place where you could just show up and feel like people were glad you came. It was the same at another Black/Latinx crew that met downtown. They talked on social media as if they'd invented running; the hubris was worse in person. The leaders told the crowd that they were not like the "losers" of other running clubs. No "running nerds" were allowed. I shared a glance with the three runners from my club who joined me. Then we were told to "expect the unexpected." What this looked like in reality was running in fits and starts, through oncoming traffic, stopping whenever one of the cool kids decided there was something worth stopping for—a photo op by a bridge, a gallery show they heard was happening—never knowing when the run would be over. As soon as I recognized landmarks indicating we were back at the start, we got out of there.

What I learned by running with these groups was that the New York City running community was male-dominated and exclusionary at best. At times, it bordered on hostile. The beauty was that these experiences taught me something about what kind of community and culture I wanted to cultivate. My model until that point had only been Team in Training. What I appreciated about that experience was that we'd started on time, pace groups had ensured no one was left behind, and workouts had a clear structure you could count on.

At Team in Training, what would my experience have been like if someone had said hello that first day? If an effort had been made to make all of us feel like stars, not just the fast or experienced runners? I didn't want anyone to feel invisible. I wanted to build a community that would be open to a wide range of paces and abilities. I wanted to create a sense of security and stability, meaning people would know what to expect. I wanted to build a community that would extend beyond my ego; a place that was not about me, but about us. A place where the sum of the parts was greater than any individual input.

And so I was intentional. As runners showed up, I greeted them. Other regulars like Amir did the same. Then we'd form a circle and the first words I spoke were: "Welcome to Harlem Run. Great to see so many people out here. Is anyone here for the first time?" We were getting one, maybe two, new people each week. If someone's hand went up, the group applauded and welcomed them. I added icebreakers to create connection. In a circle, we went around answering the question of the day: *What's your favorite ice cream, movie, song?* It allowed each person to know someone, to actually have spoken to a fellow human and shared a bit of information about themselves. It was fun, and felt both silly and intimate. Finally, I ended each workout with a lunge matrix I learned at Team in Training—a series of lunges in different directions to stretch and strengthen the legs, but mostly to add clear structure and a sense of routine to end every run.

I continued doing in-person, neighborhood, and social media outreach, but little came of it until I met Mary Arnold, the community manager for the running store JackRabbit. She'd bought the domain HarlemRun.com, thinking it would be useful someday if a store ever opened up in the neighborhood. But when she heard about my group, she said, "Oh, you're the person who needs this." She transferred the domain to me and just like that, Powdered Feet Running Club became Harlem Run.

The name changed everything. Now, when people searched for "running" and "Harlem," Harlem Run came up. We grew quickly after that, getting twenty people, then thirty and forty. Our numbers got too big for a circle and an icebreaker, so I had everyone turn to the person next to them, introduce themselves, and answer the question of the day. I asked everyone not to wear headphones so we could engage with our community, and to run two by two on the sidewalk; I'd witnessed groups take off as a mob, clogging traffic, endangering runners and pedestrians alike. When we ran, we made sure there was room on the sidewalk for others, recognizing that we all shared these streets. I also plotted our routes to showcase Harlem's historic monuments and places. In these ways, Harlem became a member of Harlem Run, and we became custodians of the neighborhood.

Running with other Black people was exactly as I'd pictured it, better even. Harlem Run had members who were white, Asian, and mixed, but Harlem Run was decidedly a Black space—warm, welcoming, centering us. People seemed to love the runs and routes and vibe as much as I did, and we often hung out in front of the yoga studio or headed to a local bar, staying out until 10:00 p.m., talking and getting to know each other. It was exactly the joy I'd anticipated, not unlike the experience of finding Black friends in college when, suddenly, I'd felt normal. But I lived in New Jersey, and felt a nagging sense of disconnection. How could I claim Harlem when I wasn't a resident? I found a tiny studio on 129th Street between Lenox and Adam Clayton Powell and made it official. I was once again a Harlemite.

Another reason I moved: I had started a two-year master's program at the Teachers College of Columbia University in counseling psychology. I was drawn to the program in part because of my own experience with depression, and in part because of running. Running had shown me the link between our bodies and our minds, and I wanted to understand how it all worked—how we heal. And while Harlem Run and running were in many ways becoming my life, or at least my love, they weren't going to pay the bills. What did I want to do? I still didn't know. Counseling offered a path.

I selected this particular program at Columbia because it approached counseling through a social justice lens. All counseling looks at issues through a particular point of view or theoretical perspective—psychodynamic or cognitive, for example. The approach informs the way you interpret a client's behavior, thoughts, and feelings and ultimately how you develop the treatment plan. Social justice counseling puts the individual within the context of society, meaning it doesn't look only at what's going on with you; it explores how what's going with you is influenced by social forces like racism, sexism, white supremacy, transphobia, ableism, capitalism, and so on.

The program spoke to me because my own life had been shaped by living as a Black woman in a world that centered whiteness. Some of the feelings of self-loathing and worthlessness that led to my depression came from feeling like I didn't fit a white ideal. The counseling program, I thought, could provide me with some much-needed insight.

One morning, as Harlem Run was growing—we were at sixty or so people now—I set off from Harlem in the early morning to attend the group workout of a running crew that everyone was talking about. The group had multiple chapters across the country, had been featured on the cover of *Runner's World*, and was characterized as something special, so I was curious to check it out. I ran southeast, weaving through the city, with Amir running with me. For a while after combining our groups, Amir had been a run-and-done participant. But since he'd broken off a relationship, he'd joined our post-run gatherings, and we'd become friends.

The group met at Carl Schurz Park on the East River, where the mayor's house was. As we approached, a large group of white people at the tops of the steps on the promenade were jumping up and down and shouting. I immediately looked around, taking in the scene. It was barely light and these people were yelling within steps of the mayor's house? We couldn't do this. Imagine the attention fifty or sixty Black people would garner if we were on the lawn near the mayor's house, screaming "Fuck yeah." I imagined a passerby wondering what the "hoodlums" were up to and calling the police. But this group seemed not to be worried at all, not the slightest bit. *This is what it's like*, I thought, *to be white and move freely in the world.*

One of the coleaders caught my eye but looked away. There was no *Welcome*, no *Hey, are you new?* The weird noises and call-and-response continued. I glanced at Amir. He was jumping at barely a bounce, looking hesitant. Curse words rang out, more screams, then a final call-and-response, and the rally cry was over. The ritual was odd, and alienating; without welcome or instruction, we'd had no idea what was going on or what to do.

The leaders then divided us into groups and Amir and I were separated. We were supposed to do what seemed like icebreakers or warm-up exercises, but the assumption was that everyone would be comfortable performing for others. One exercise called "star jumps" required you to jump with outstretched arms and legs while yelling "I'm a star!" I took a pass. Then there were "hoistees": a partnered exercise that requires coordinating with another runner, in my case, a stranger. The proper way to do it is to face your partner, sneakers touching, sit your butt to the ground, and hold hands (crossed). Then you hoist each other up and yell "hoistee!" It was absurd and odd to me, exposing ourselves in this way with a group I had no trust with. I took a pass on that one, too.

The rest of the workout couldn't be over fast enough for me. At the end, we gathered for a group photo on the steps. Before the shot was taken, one of the leaders asked if it was anyone's birthday. A few hands went up and the runners were called to the front and made to dance while the leaders sang "Happy Birthday." What was fun and welcoming about rituals rooted in humiliation, discomfort, and being on display? Whiteness, I knew, could be genteel, as in a country club, like the Team in Training vibe with a dose of cold-shoulder aloofness. Or whiteness could be this: a couple of frat-like boys controlling the group, the entitled feel of bro culture.

Amir and I left quickly, running the forty blocks back up to Harlem, laughing. What the fuck was *that*?

arlem Run grew steadily over the next six months—70 people, then 100. I added pace-group leaders to share the responsibility of both leading the runs and creating an inclusive culture, what we would eventually call the Harlem Run Way. One night, 150 people came. It was unbelievable, but we were ready. We'd mapped out the routes, had the leaders and logistics in place, and had mentally prepared for the energy necessary to manage and motivate such a crowd.

That night, it seemed to me, we set the world on fire. We ran the Classic and made a cheer tunnel for folks as they made their way back to home base. It felt like the high fives were endless as the last runners and walkers made their way back.

After that, every Monday night felt like a special event, a reunion. For a brief moment at 6:45 p.m., I would worry that no one would show. Then, suddenly, people would be coming from every direction

and the space would be filled with predominantly Black and brown runners, people with large bodies and small ones, older adults as well as parents with jogging strollers and school-aged kids. People were talking to each other and greeting each other, and the magnitude of what I created hit me. I thought: *I have created a space where Black people feel comfortable, a place people want to come to, a place where people are forming connections and friendships. A Black space, a place for us. These runners would never have to wonder if running was for them because we'd created a space that was.*

After the group assembled, we were off, moving through the neighborhood. The pace leaders pointed out the history. That's where Malcolm X spoke. That's where Louis Armstrong played. That's where Langston Hughes lived. Sometimes, we'd have scavenger hunt runs where runners stopped at historic places and took a photo: You and the bronze bust of MLK Jr. You and the abolitionist Frederick Douglass.

You and the towering figure of Harriet Tubman. Each week we set off into the neighborhood. Everywhere we went, history was alive in the present. There was so much comradery and excitement. It felt like we were doing the most important thing in the world for Black people, in the most important city in the world for Black culture.

And then there was this: No matter where we ran, white places—the West Side Highway, Central Park, the New York City Marathon—became our places, too. With every stride, we were in a community. This was the power of the third space, a sociocultural term used to describe a transformative place where oppressed people plot or find their liberation. A place of unity. A place where folks like me can exhale. A place where we belong.

8

Reframing

One night after a run, I was home journaling about different parts of my identity. Journaling wasn't a habit of mine; this was an assignment, part of the two-year master's program in counseling psychology I'd started. The assignment was for a class called "Foundations." Its purpose was to explore the fundamentals of counseling, and ourselves. We studied topics like identity, bias, and "social constructionism," a theory that views characteristics believed to be immutable—like race, gender, class, ability, and sexuality—as social constructs shaped by culture and history.

What poured out of me as I wrote were unresolved feelings of alienation and resentment toward the white kids at my high school. I'd been harboring a sense that the white students were somehow better, both because of their wealth and their race. The goal of journaling was to try to reframe the narratives you'd been told, so as I wrote, I questioned the ideas I'd been fed, and a light bulb went off. I had internalized the idea that being white and wealthy was right, somehow better. I had believed I was ugly and unattractive because I had consumed white beauty standards. I had believed wealth made people worthy, that it was a sign of how hard you'd worked, how good and deserving you must be. The narrative I'd been given was false and rooted in white supremacy.

My upbringing had taught me that white supremacy existed, but up until that moment I hadn't really understood how it was directly linked to me. I knew white supremacy was in laws, education, and other institutions, but I hadn't connected the dots to how white supremacy had impacted my feelings about myself and my sense of self-worth—that white supremacy existed *in* me.

My class notes:

White supremacy—belief that the white race is the superior race—the belief system that drives racism, racial discrimination.

Patriarchy—an enforced belief in male dominance and control—is the ideology. Sexism is the system that holds it in place.

As I journaled, I saw that all the feelings I'd been fighting—of being unattractive, out of place, worthless—had not simply been "my feelings." Rather, the forces of white supremacy and patriarchy were feeding me those messages and I had swallowed them, turning my own inner thoughts against me. As clinical psychologist Tasha Brown, Ph.D., notes, "In your formative years, if your identity development is formed with this lens of racism, it impacts how you think about yourself and what you think you can do, where you think you can go and how you navigate the world."

I was not the problem after all. There was nothing wrong with me. The problem was society. The problem was that I am a Black woman living in a patriarchal, white supremacist country that devalues me.

After the class was over, it was running that helped me sort through the pieces that bubbled up. I'd run alone along the West Side

Highway, and as it had when I first started running, movement delivered wisdom. This time, it was in the form of questions:

Do I hate white people?

Or do I hate white supremacy?

Is there even a difference?

To what extent are individual white people responsible for upholding white supremacy if they, too, are ingesting and internalizing the same messages?

When does it become their responsibility to recognize that they are upholding white supremacy and the status quo, and they should change it?

How, though, could white people have been complicit in this for this long?

Running didn't deliver the answers. And while it often shook out some of my anger, my resentment toward white people kept resurfacing. It was boundless. I resented that I was made to feel like I had to speak on behalf of the entire Black race while made to believe that I was less than. I resented that white people could go for a run with little regard for the space and place they occupied and a lack of awareness around their race. I resented white women who talked about feminism when what they were really talking about was white feminism. I resented that white people didn't see the entitlement and privilege that comes with being white—and ultimately, that the racial work of our nation falls on the shoulders of Black people.

Some of this resentment came to the surface in a class called "Race Lab." It was the kind of class where white people cried and Black people tried not to roll their eyes, but everybody left transformed in some way. We did an activity that asked everyone to line up in a semicircle according to skin color, lightest to darkest. Everyone in the class got up and began assembling themselves, except for a dozen or so white folks. They stood there, flummoxed by the whole affair. "I don't know where to go," a white woman said. *Oh for fuck's sake*, I thought, just get on the end. White people are so uncomfortable with race that they pretend not to know the color of their own skin.

So we had a conversation about this. What is it like for each person to arrange themselves according to race? This was where white people's feelings on race surfaced. White people felt "bad" that Black people had to line up as "dark." It was ridiculous. I don't feel bad about the complexion of my skin. *You* feel "bad" for me because you're projecting your biases about Blackness as "bad," "inferior," and "other" onto me.

Faced with their own biases for the first time, some of the white women began to cry. I could hardly contain myself. This was of course the whole point of the exercise; not the tears, but the awareness. Nothing more had been said other than to line up according to complexion. Everything else, all the feelings and thoughts that came, were what you made of it, or rather what you had been taught and socialized to make of it.

Later, we got into a conversation about work and wealth, and the white people in the class insisted that their parents were self-made; that the sole factor in their family's wealth was hard work. My white peers refused to acknowledge that race affected the school they'd gone to, the loan or funding they'd received, the promotion they'd landed at work. *Of course* their parents had worked hard. But their skin color had also given them advantages that we did not and do not have. These two facts coexist.

For several months, I grappled with rage and anger at white people. Sometimes when I ran, the anger would leave my body, only to have it rise again later. I walked down the street thinking every white person was racist and evil. I wanted nothing to do with white people; I shut myself down to any friendships or even the possibility of friendly banter with anyone who was white. I avoided, as much as possible, the white runners at Harlem Run.

Finally, I went to my professor's office and shared my anger with her. Dr. Riddhi Sandil is a woman with a big heart and a clear-eyed view of racial complexity. She answered the questions I'd been asking. "You don't hate white people, Alison, you hate whiteness and white supremacy," she said. I felt so relieved. She was right. I'd worried that if I did in fact hate white people, that would mean that I was prejudiced and a bad person, but Dr. Sandil had solved that for me. I wasn't prejudiced against white people; I was being harmed by white supremacy. White people's ignorance and privilege angered me. That didn't change. But what I hated was white supremacy, and the way it had made me think, the way it made other people think. I hated the racism it spawned, the racist system it had built. I hated that white supremacy and racism were a way of life in the United States.

Once I saw the underlying problem of society's white supremacist culture, more running and thinking showed me that I was still fighting the white supremacy in myself. My own ideas on perfectionism stemmed from the internalized belief that "perfect" was possible and something we should all strive for. The need to show and prove myself through my education was a product of believing my worth rested in my degrees, my productivity; as well as the notion that as a Black woman, I had to be twice as good as my peers to be accepted.

Through the subtle yet powerful ways whiteness operates—sanitizing civil rights leaders, whitewashing history, labeling us as dangerous and criminal—I realized that I, too, had prejudices against Black people. I'd bought into stereotypes about African Americans, accepted the party line of "hard work" as the ticket to the American dream. I'd measured my looks, my success, and my worth off a racist system that refused to value me. On more than one occasion I had looked at homeless people on the street and thought they must've done something to deserve it. These were ugly truths to confront. I'd work for years—I still am today—to root out the white supremacy in me. But simply being aware of it was liberating. It allowed me to recognize when I was seeing myself in relation to whiteness and create space for me to see myself for who I was: a smart, beautiful, powerful, and complex Black woman.

I didn't enter the counseling program to get a better understanding of myself, exactly. But that's what happened. In the second year of the program, I took a class that required us to participate in fake counseling sessions in which sometimes you were the client and other times you were the therapist. These sessions weren't really make-believe, though, because we were all processing our own issues. One day I was working with another student, a white woman with long brown hair. I'd shaved my head a couple of years earlier for practical reasons and almost immediately, people started assuming I was a lesbian and militant. So, imagine a Black woman with a low cut sitting across from a white woman with wavy brown hair falling down her back. The white woman decided to bring up that she was thinking of cutting her hair for charity, but she was struggling with the decision because she thought women with short hair were ugly.

Every association I had with hair and beauty reared up. I sat there trying to think of ways to curse her out in a manner that would be suitable in an Ivy League classroom. Dr. Sandil must've seen my rage because she jumped in. She suggested we analyze the moment from an interpersonal lens. Dr. Sandil offered that in the role of therapist, I might find myself triggered by what clients are saying, and that learning these triggers is imperative to the work. She commented that in this situation, my white classmate was regurgitating the beauty standards we all receive in white supremacist culture. She, too, had grown up being fed a lie about what was considered acceptable and beautiful, even as a white woman.

Seeing how white supremacy could damage white women was another step toward releasing my resentment. They, too, experienced overlapping systems of oppression and privilege. This, I learned, was intersectionality, a framework for understanding how interlocking systems of oppression impact our lives. The term was coined by Kimberlé Crenshaw in 1989 to expose how the law was blind to the multiple layers of discrimination experienced by different groups of people, particularly Black women. For example, when a court looked at "racial discrimination" and "sex discrimination" as two separate buckets, it failed to see that the double burden of racism and sexism on Black women is different than the singular burden of sexism on white women or racism on Black men. Every identity—race, class, sexual orientation, body size, ability—either adds privilege or disadvantage to a person's experience. A Black queer woman. An undocumented, disabled Latinx man. An obese white man living in poverty. An African American girl who'd grown up with a single mom who struggled to make ends meet.

Understanding our intersecting identities and talking about it in class made it clear I had many privileges. I was able-bodied, cisgendered, and heterosexual. I had grown up in a middle- to upper-class environment, with two parents in a stable, loving home. I had access to education and the opportunity to pursue not one, but two master's degrees.

It also made this clear: Only cisgendered, heterosexual, able-bodied white men with money can really pull themselves up by their bootstraps. They were handed the straps by way of gender and skin color and simply needed to pull, i.e., apply themselves. That's not to say they don't work hard or face barriers; it's to say their gender and skin color grant them privileges based on these characteristics alone. Other forces like racism, sexism, ableism, and homophobia limit a wide range of people to differing degrees. And while talent is distributed equally among all people, opportunity, resources, and privilege are not.

There's a cartoon that illustrates this beautifully. A white man and a black woman are on the starting line of a race. The white man's lane is clear, save for a few hurdles he can easily maneuver around. She's on the starting line with a ball and chain latched to her ankle. Her lane is littered with hazards and barriers—barbed wire, a crocodile, a broken brick wall. He's speaking to her. The caption: "What's the matter? It's the same distance."

"What's the matter?
It's the same distance!"

Add a white woman to lane three. Her lane has fewer barriers than the Black woman's and there's no weight on her ankle. The middle-class Black man in lane four would have similar hurdles as the white man— but ones that cannot be easily walked around—plus the ankle weight. The Black man in lane five, who came from a family living in poverty, might have weights on both feet, plus a couple of hurdles and a wall. Lane six is empty because the obstacles were insurmountable for the disabled Black woman.

I thought about the opportunity I had been given from my parents alone. They knew English well enough that they could read my essays and help me with them. For students whose parents don't speak English or have a formal education, they might not get that kind of support; not because they don't have good parents, but simply because those are the circumstances.

I processed all this on a run later and I saw that white supremacy harms everyone, even cishet white men. A culture rooted in dominance and hierarchy—where your identity exists in opposition to those you are made to believe you have power over—is exhausting and toxic. It puts you in the position of constantly having to prove your superiority, or another's inferiority. A deep belief in the dominance of white people over Black people can explain why white people often make decisions that go against even their own self-interest to maintain the color line, for example, voting for a president who was racist but against healthcare, the very healthcare so many white people living in poverty desperately need; or policies that make voting access more difficult for everybody in an effort to disenfranchise Black people. It's counterproductive, but it's real.

In the end, what I came away with was less self-pity and more empathy for myself and others. There are no Olympics for oppression, no gold medal for the most suffering. There are layers of privilege and layers of oppression. Every experience is different, and every experience is valid. What's up to us is what we do with our privilege.

My schoolwork was positively influencing how I showed up in the world. I was more confident, no longer willing to bend myself to the will and expectations of others. There were consequences to this shift. The same groups that I had reached out to when I first started Harlem Run—the Black and brown male leaders of other crews who had initially snubbed me—began supporting Harlem Run now that it was successful. But they wanted me, the woman, to fall in line, kiss the ring. One group in particular, with multiple male leaders, expected me to run my plans about Harlem Run's events by them—the dates, the times, the locations—before proceeding. This wasn't about making sure our events didn't conflict. They wanted control over the running scene and expected me to ask permission. Why would I do that? They were my events.

One of the group's leaders showed up to Harlem Run one night, which was great—it showed support, I thought. Except that when he saw a friend in a Harlem Run shirt, he asked me when I'd be giving him one. "The shirts are fifteen dollars," I responded. "I don't pay for shit," he said. And poof, his support, along with the others', vanished. I was shut out of the "inner circle" of other founders and leaders of color. I understood now: despite having Black and brown leadership, these men saw me as a threat to their position and authority within the patriarchy. It was another way that the running community mirrored society at large—patriarchal values means leaving Black women behind.

A similar situation happened in group therapy class. There were about twelve of us in the room. Myself, one other Black woman, a Mexican guy, and the rest white men or women. The early phase of group work is when members sort out issues of power and control—who leads, who follows, who takes charge and delegates, etc. Once this is established, the group can function and be productive. All of us contributed initially, but there was a sense that my classmates expected more from me. I wasn't interested in giving it. It was unconscious at first. I was tired. Managing Harlem Run, which was now two nights a week plus events, helping care for my father, carrying a full course load, and processing all the emotion that came with these classes had taken a toll.

But then the conversation became about my refusal to participate. The group expected me to take charge, in part because I'd taken charge in these settings before. But as their insistence that I lead the group intensified, it became clear that their expectation stemmed from the white idea that Black women are supposed to save and serve. For centuries, we were mammies and nannies, the magical Negro, the office pet. I refused. *I am not here to serve you,* I thought. *I'll do what I need for myself, even if it makes you uncomfortable.*

There were long awkward silences, and then folks commented on the long awkward silences, and everyone looked at me. My resistance infuriated them. We never got past it. The teacher's assistant eventually stepped in. I didn't care. I was not going to budge for other peoples' convenience. I had honored myself in that moment. Later, I talked over the experience with Dr. Sandil. "You never have to do or be anything for anyone," she said. "There will be consequences for those choices, but those are outside of your control."

The experience gave me permission to be myself. I was aware that how other people saw and experienced me would always be something I'd be up against, but I also knew that I was not responsible for other people's stereotyping, opinions, feelings, or actions. *I will inhabit my body. I will take up space in the world. And I will do it in a way that centers my own comfort and joy.*

9

Purpose

As the master's program was changing me, it was also changing how I viewed the work I was doing at Harlem Run.

After finishing college and my first master's program, I had no real understanding of what I wanted to do with my life. But the program in counseling psychology began fitting together pieces of a puzzle I hadn't known I was assembling. I enrolled in the counseling program because of my experience with depression and anxiety, but my interest in actually being a therapist was half-hearted. What I loved was running, and what I wanted to do was have a positive impact on the world. But I didn't know how.

That began to shift when I traveled to a conference in New Orleans. This was during Harlem Run's early days, just as the group was growing and getting big, and right before I started the master's counseling program. At the conference, I met a Black woman who was pursuing her Ph.D. in counseling psychology at Temple University. We got to talking and I told her about Harlem Run, describing it as a means of improving people's mental and physical health. "Oh, but what you're doing is about so much more than that," she said. "Movement can be a movement."

She told me about a program in Philadelphia that uses cycling to aid women transitioning from prison to civilian life. The women are getting fit, she said, but they're also getting access to reliable transportation, addiction treatment, life skills classes, and social support they otherwise would not have access to. She explained that the program was a form of social justice—the view that everyone deserves equal economic, social, and political rights and privileges. The goal of social justice work is to open the doors of access and opportunity for everyone, particularly those in greatest need; programs like the cycling group and Harlem Run are part of the solution.

I immediately saw her point: Harlem Run was opening up the benefits of running to Black people in Harlem, centering those who had been historically and presently excluded from distance running.

On the plane ride home, I reflected on how true that was, based on the stories Harlem Run members were always sharing about how running was changing their lives. One woman struggled with her weight and body image all her life and really wanted to be thin. But once she started running, she experienced the power of her body. Running opened her eyes to the truth that her body was so much more than its form and her focus became what her body could do, where it could take her. She was able to confidently reject that lie that patriarchy had fed her and create her own narrative.

Another woman had been in an unhappy marriage for twenty years. She stayed because she didn't have a vision of what a different life could look like; being in the shadow of her partner was the only role she knew. Once she began running with us, she found that there was so much more to her, and that she could create a new life. Thanks to Harlem Run, meeting new people—a new network of support—was as easy as showing up on Monday nights. Changing her life would be painful, but could be done by taking a series of small steps.

Other people changed careers, ate healthier, lowered their blood pressure, and found confidence and a sense of self. Harlem Run was sending a message: *I can transform into a better version of myself.* I saw that these personal transformations were part of the larger work of social justice. Black people at Harlem Run were accessing opportunities to move and recreate that were historically not available in their neighborhood, defying the statistics you often hear about—higher rates of obesity, heart disease, and hypertension than white people. Daily hypervigilance due to racism and microaggressions is one reason for higher disease rates and increased stress levels in Black people, which leads to premature biological aging, a phenomenon known in the medical world as weathering. Each personal transformation over time would help address health disparities in New York City by changing the neighborhood's health statistics, and those of Black people at large.

By providing access to a free activity that reduces stress and improves health, Harlem Run was helping manage the toll of discrimination. And in the simple act of running as Black people, we were showing the Harlem community that distance running was for us.

started the master's program shortly after returning from New Orleans, and its view of the role of a therapist was what made me look at Harlem Run differently. Traditional counseling views the therapist as a change agent only within the walls of the counseling room, while a social justice approach sees the therapist as a change agent both inside the counseling room and out in the larger world, as an advocate for changing rules, laws, and conditions that impact clients' lives. A social justice approach asks, What are the conditions in the world that contribute to my client's mental health symptoms—such as racism, food insecurity, and sexism—and how can I as a therapist work to resist and dismantle those conditions in order to help my client?

This approach made it clear to me that it was my job to push back against oppressive systems, and that Harlem Run could be part of that. We were literally running through and among the cumulative effect of years of redlining, divestment, and NIMBYism. If we ran east on 125th Street to Lexington Avenue, we'd be confronted with an over-saturation of drug treatment facilities placed in Harlem due to poor implementation of "fair share" criteria, which allowed the city to take advantage of the neighborhood. Harlem has nearly 20 percent of the city's drug treatment and homeless shelters—most concentrated within 0.4 miles of 125th Street—with the majority of patients in the treatment facilities commuting from other neighborhoods. A neighborhood that makes up only 4.3 percent of the city's population carried a burden far greater than its own. When we ran through the area, we slipped into single file in order to avoid the bodies sleeping on the sidewalk and community members panhandling on the corner.

Some nights we headed south and would be met by the floodlights at Martin Luther King Jr. Towers, placed there by the city to improve the lighting and reduce crime. Floodlights were part of the city's overall approach to the neighborhood. It didn't respond to Harlem's needs with what white parts of the city have: resources. Instead, it added more police and big mobile floodlights. The beams were so bright that we'd stop mid-run for a photo op. Each time we ran through the lights, I thought about the city's failures in our community. The lack of funding, inadequate housing, poor maintenance, from trash collection to the condition of our schools to over-policing. (Sometimes, we'd be gathering for a run at Marcus Garvey Park and a patrol car would drive right through us. This wasn't happening in white neighborhoods.) What could Harlem Run do? We could use our community to address the failures of the city.

We began organizing trash pick-up sessions around Harlem and participated in park maintenance and clean-up events hosted by other groups like the Marcus Garvey Park Alliance. The parks commissioner,

Mitchell Silver, started running with us (this was a big deal, and we always made sure to assign a person to run with him), and so we lobbied him for better lighting in Marcus Garvey Park, where we'd started staging our weekly runs. He in turn invited us to be present whenever meaningful change in our community was happening, like a ribbon cutting for a new park on Lenox Avenue that had replaced a deteriorating pile of equipment that had long been an eyesore. We collected items for those in need: a toy drive and school supplies for Take Care of Harlem, an organization that helps provide for underserved kids and beautifies the neighborhood with trash collection and landscaping. Two Harlem Run members worked at the Rikers Island prison, so once we collected tampons and pads, which were often in short supply for incarcerated women.

One of the primary ways we worked to address decades of histori-cal and present-day injustices was fundraising. Some of our fundraisers were informal. We simply announced at the beginning of a run that we'd be taking donations for a particular organization and asked people to pull out their phones and donate if they could. Then we'd head out for our run. We ran the New York City Marathon as a team fundraiser for Harlem United, a group that provides a wide range of services (hous-ing, healthcare) to unhoused populations and people who are HIV pos-itive. And we partnered with local bars for happy hour fundraisers.

Our biggest undertakings made us into race directors and event planners. In 2015, for example, an opportunity to hold a race on Fa-ther's Day in Marcus Garvey Park fell into our laps and we took it. We brainstormed about the best way to approach a race that was in line with the principles of social justice, and decided our goal was to hold an event that would benefit the community at large. So what did that look like? We knew we didn't want to hold a race that focused on speed and fast runners; the city had plenty of those and they could be intim-idating. We also wanted to ensure that families and non-runners felt welcomed. So we created the Harlem 1 Miler. One mile was an acces-sible distance for most folks, and in our marketing, we said people could "run" any way they wanted: walk, skip, hop, jump, crawl, or run. We offered free entry for kids under twelve, and scholarships for those who needed them.

We also ran multiple heats: a family heat where some men ran with kids on their shoulders; a youth heat for little kids; and age-group cat-egories for older kids. One boy, Aubrey, who ran in the 11–13 age group, had always played basketball. His mom was a Harlem Run member, and after the race, he started running regularly with us. He was shy when he first came. He ran with his mother, but quickly got faster than her and became confident enough to run with his own pace group. He loved running. When he went to high school in the Bronx, he joined the cross-country team, and he now wants to run in college. For decades, Black kids have grown up thinking that distance running was only for white kids; Harlem Run showed Aubrey it was for him, too. We'd changed the trajectory of a kid's life through the simplest of means: existing in his community.

What we were doing mattered. I understood this fully about a month after the Harlem 1 Miler, when an editor at *Runner's World* reached out to do a story on Harlem Run and me. I did the interview over the phone and a photographer joined us on a sticky day in August for a photo shoot.

The piece ran in the print edition of the magazine and online in October, one month before the 2015 New York City Marathon, which I was running with six other members of Harlem Run. The day before the race, the television station NY1 aired a segment on us.

Both media stories emphasized the inclusive nature of Harlem Run, though neither talked about why inclusion was newsworthy—I didn't put it in racialized terms then myself. But what the media coverage made clear to me was that what we were doing in Harlem had national importance. The coverage was an acknowledgment that using running for personal transformation and social change was significant. And media was a means of amplifying our message beyond Harlem and impacting the broader story of distance running.

As marginalized people doing something that disrupts the status quo, we'd become a pathway to something larger. In the simple act of running, we were sending a message that we were here, working to normalize Black people running. White running groups could be about fun, training, health, and community, which is great. But as a Black group, we had an added element of shifting how society sees Black people and how Black people see distance running. In this way, Harlem Run was a political act, an act of disruption, an act of social justice.

'd run the New York City Marathon the year before, but this year felt more important. When I first founded Harlem Run, all I wanted was people like me to run with. Now, as the seven of us, all decked out in Harlem Run gear, boarded the Staten Island Ferry race morning, our presence in the race felt meaningful.

A bus met us off the ferry, but it broke down, leaving us scrambling to get to the starting line, and we ended up joining a later wave. We stood in the corral, embracing and singing aloud to Frank Sinatra's "New York, New York," going wild when the DJ transitioned seamlessly into Jay-Z and Alicia Keys's "Empire State of Mind." We were so wrapped up in the moment we hardly noticed anyone else in the over-crowded corral.

We gradually moved our way toward the front and over the starting line. Different paces and goals eventually separated the seven of us. Yet what I remember thinking as I ran was that we'd created a space within a space. Scattered among the field of mostly white runners from around the world were Black people from Harlem. Each of us was a force of disruption, shaking up the status quo, inviting others who looked like us to join in. North in Harlem, thirty or so Harlem Run members were handing out water and cheering folks on, and I ran feeling the antici-pation of running there, of getting to the place that was home.

In the early miles, I removed my long-sleeved shirt and tied it around my waist, revealing a sports bra with my name on it. A man from Italy came up behind me and asked, "Is it you?" referring to the woman he'd seen on the NY1 broadcast. I said yes and leaned in so he could take a selfie. At mile nine, the Brooklyn Tabernacle Choir was singing with so much joy and enthusiasm in front of Emmanuel Baptist Church that I almost stopped. But I found myself instead speeding up from their energy, then reining in my pace. I couldn't lose steam before Harlem.

I passed the hipsters in Williamsburg with their beards and funny signs with messages like "You're running better than the government," and used the quiet in the stretch through a Hasidic community to gather my strength for the big climb up to the Queensboro Bridge into Manhattan. Once on the bridge, the wind whipped me and I drafted off a slightly taller and broader runner until we dropped into the thick crowds on First Avenue. Their screams overrode all other sounds, even those of my own thinking, but I was able to make out screams of "Ali-son!" by strangers reading my sports bra.

I ran knowing Harlem was close; I could almost feel it. I made my way through the quiet stretch in the Bronx, waved to my high school English teacher who was cheering with his running club, then popped over the Madison Avenue Bridge and into Harlem. I smiled. My body felt both relaxed and rejuvenated, like the feeling you get entering your house after a long day at work.

As I ran down Fifth Avenue, my stride was loose and light. I hugged the right side of the street to take in the high fives and cheers offered by people in the neighborhood. As I approached our cheer station, everyone started chanting, "Al-i-son, Al-i-son." Other runners looked at me trying to figure out who I was, and I soaked it in.

That burst of energy carried me all the way down Fifth Avenue and into Central Park for the finish at Tavern on the Green. I crossed the finish, got my medal, and took the subway to Harlem, joining my group. I cheered on runners, screaming and pointing to my medal, "Go get yours!" then collapsed two hours later.

It was powerful to see our presence on the course. Before Harlem Run, Harlem was a neighborhood that runners briefly dipped into in order to get from the crowds on First Avenue to the hills of Central Park and the finish line. But as we cheered runners on, it was clear our presence on the course made Harlem a part of the marathon and a fuller part of the marathon experience for all runners. Now when you ran through Harlem, we were there to carry you with our energy, staying late until the night, past the time of the sweep bus, to cheer in as many people as we could. Harlem Run and what we stood for—community, inclusion—was represented. We were changing people's lives, helping our community, and shifting the narrative and culture around distance running—exactly the work I wanted to be doing.

All this time, I thought I was just starting a running group; instead, I was finding my purpose.

10

Puzzle Pieces

The path of social justice made so much sense once I saw it. I'd sometimes wondered how people knew what they wanted to do from a young age—be scientists, doctors, teachers, carpenters. But I realized I'd known, too. It was there in my interest in listening to my parents talk about history and world events, and in my instinct to do the model town project, dress up as Ota Benga, and write about the damage of white supremacy on Haiti for my thesis. What I was doing then was trying to center our stories, reveal historical wrongdoings to help my classmates see the world more fully. I just didn't have the language for what I was doing back then, but I had it now: Activist. Advocate. Disruptor.

Still, a question lingered: how would I make a living?

I knew I didn't want to monetize Harlem Run by charging for it as so many people suggested. Keeping Harlem Run equitable and accessible was a nonnegotiable for me. But I was using student loans to pay my bills, and that was unsustainable, a recipe for lifelong debt. An answer, or rather, the beginning of one, came when a member of Harlem Run learned that the apparel company Under Armour was moving into the running space and looking to sponsor run crews. Under Armour also had a history of partnering with the underdog: Misty Copeland, for example, the first African American female principal dancer with the American Ballet Theatre, was one of its athletes. We decided that we could be influential in helping Under Armour grow its running category, and so we put ideas down on paper.

I sent in a pitch emphasizing our community and social justice approach, as well as our accomplishments—gathering hundreds of people together to run each week, hosting a one-mile race, raising more than $100,000 for our community, racking up media coverage about it all. I also noted that we'd done this with no outside funding or brand support.

We were one of four crews selected. The contract was for Harlem Run, not me—that would come later—but it was a big moment of increased visibility, both for Harlem Run as a movement and me as an important voice and leader in the running community.

As an official Under Armour–sponsored crew, our leadership team was regularly gifted all of the latest and greatest gear from head to toe. We were invited to Under Armour VIP events—sneaker release parties in the city and basketball games at Chelsea Piers. We were models in marketing campaigns, and Under Armour elevated our own content and stories on its social media platforms. Three of us were selected as leads in their "Run With Fight" campaign, which, coincidentally, was photographed in East Harlem. We loved that this global photo shoot was happening in Harlem, in *our* backyard. We spent the day in hair and makeup, moving between trailer and set, running as we chased a taxi with the photographer hanging out the back to get shots of us in agony. "Run with fight!" he'd scream whenever we slowed down. The photographer proposed that we chug bottles of milk so he could capture us vomiting at the end of a run. We were so eager to please we would've done it. But the Under Armour team thankfully vetoed it; they didn't want us to ruin the clothes we were advertising.

It seemed like we'd found a partnership that would help us get the word out that running was for people like us, for Black people. That we belonged here. And we had. Under Armour's promotion of us and other crews inserted Black bodies and Black joy and strength into the running space. While the relationship was imperfect—their promotion of us slowed, and we wanted compensation along with gear—what it gave me was insight into the industry. Since starting to run, I knew running was a business—the shoes, the clothing, the events. But working for a brand showed me the industry's power. It was a big machine that shaped the culture of running. Brands had a look and feel that they wanted, and if you fit their look, you were highlighted. I understood that the industry—the brands, the media—decides who is elevated and visible, who receives funding, who is presented as a runner, and how they are presented. It was the industry who defined who a runner is.

I n 2016, Under Armour hosted an event in Colorado for the four crews it had signed. Two or three leaders from each crew were flown out, put up in a fancy cabin resort, and fed catered meals for four days.

While the experience was structured as a running camp—there were three or four workouts a day—its real purpose was to create marketing content for the brand. We had the opportunity to pick some of our experiences—like a yoga session or a massage—but others were required, like morning runs and recovery sessions. We never knew how long a run would be; the Under Armour team wouldn't tell us. But we were into it. We suited up in the latest gear, ran up trails, down mountainsides, through snowstorms, all while maintaining the tough and intense facial expressions Under Armour was known for as video rolled and cameras clicked.

It was fun. And I learned a lot. I learned that trail running was a thing, and that I liked the grandness of being in nature. I also noticed running on dirt was easier on my body. I learned about cool new running technology and techniques, including a "sound bath" (think wind chimes and ocean waves to put your body in a tranquil state). But the best part was experiencing all this with Amir.

Only a day before we left for the trip, Amir and I became official. We'd been spending a good amount of time together and found ourselves wanting to spend even more time together, but for a while, we stopped it there. We could not date, we insisted, because we had to put Harlem Run first. We thought dating would somehow ruin it, along the lines of not mixing business with pleasure. If our relationship went sour, what would happen? We told ourselves that the group was bigger than us, and we couldn't risk it. Mostly, we took ourselves too seriously.

It was nice to finally stop fighting the feelings we shared and be open as a couple. Amir signed up for different workouts, and as a faster runner, he was at the front of the pack, while I was pushing myself in the middle. But we were both thriving and supporting each other in a way I'd never experienced before in a relationship. All the men I'd dated up until that point had been assholes (there's no other word): selfish, self-centered, insecure, and needing to be in the spotlight. Amir was none of those things. He was happy to do his own thing. He was thrilled to see me shine. He didn't feel threatened by my success. Instead, he bolstered me whenever he could.

Amir and I, along with everyone else, were all sore and exhausted by the time we did our final workout at a famous amphitheater outside of Denver called Red Rocks. The workout took us five miles up a mountain, then five miles down, combined with running the stairs and doing burpees and squats in between. When it was over, it felt like we'd run a marathon.

That night, Amir had the bright idea to "recover" with some edibles he'd purchased at the dispensary earlier in the day. My good sense told me it wasn't such a good idea. We had a dinner with everyone that night: the other crews, the photographers, the big Under Armour executives. I did it anyway. I took a bite of the gummy. An hour later, I felt nothing, so I ate the other half. As we loaded onto the bus for dinner, time slowed down. I felt heavy, weighted. Walking was like moving through molasses. At dinner I was a bumbling mess. Amir would look at me and we'd crack up, unable to breathe with laughter. Some part of my brain told me to "act normal," but words did not compute.

Everyone knew we were high. I was embarrassed, though mostly I felt connected to Amir. We were in our own ridiculous world. We spent the rest of the night back at the hotel eating, and I showered three times, trying to feel less high. Nothing helped save for sleep, which we finally succumbed to at three in the morning.

I was awakened a few hours later by a call from my mother. She was direct.

"Alison, it's your father," she said. "He's dead."

I stopped being present after that. We spoke a little more and hung up. I somehow went from the hotel to the airport and boarded the plane. Once inside, I broke down, crying hysterically. We were not sitting next to each other, but Amir sat next to me anyway, hoping to switch seats with whomever's seat he was in. A woman arrived and refused to switch. But a man across the aisle stood up and allowed Amir to have his seat. We shuffled the row around and I laid my head in his lap the entire flight home.

The next day, Amir arranged for friends to visit me at his apartment, sharing love and condolences. It was Saturday. I had planned a thirty-one-mile run around the perimeter of Manhattan on Sunday for my thirty-first birthday. I went to sleep that night not knowing whether I had it in me to run the next day. But I woke and decided that I would do it in honor of my father.

Amir and I jogged over to the start on the West Side Highway where a handful of Harlem Run members were waiting. Amir had planned it all. We set off heading south. Amir ran by my side the entire time, as other runners came and went. His presence was reassuring. As I ran, I didn't allow myself to feel. I relied on the physicality of the day to express what was inside. My father had just died, but in a way, he'd been gone a long time already. I had grieved little by little over several years for the loss of the father I had known. His body in the end weighed 120 pounds; this passing was a final letting go.

I was surprised by how good my body felt, how strongly I was able to move and push as we made our way around the city. There was no thinking, just running.

The next night, Monday, at Harlem Run, we ran the Wilfrid Désir Run in honor of my father. Amir put together a route—Harlem Hospital, where he'd worked; my parents' old apartment on Lenox Avenue; Columbia Hospital, where I was born.

If you'd asked me then, I would have told you that Amir and I weren't forever. We were so new and I had not quite allowed myself to see beyond the moment. Though in truth, I was adjusting to a new me—one that knew she deserved better. I had not valued myself enough until then to be with someone who valued me. Over the next several months, I would sign with Under Armour as an individual sponsored athlete and take part in a global campaign called "Unlike Any," alongside Misty Copeland and Natasha Hastings. The words of Aja Monet would define my purpose:

"I move,

I am a movement.

I lift and carry sisters

I am most free running for freedom."

Along the way, Amir's support would never waver. We'd become a unit, and when he dropped to his knee on Ninth Avenue in front of Chelsea Market a year after the Colorado trip, another puzzle piece slipped into place. We'd marry a year later.

11

Meaning Thru Movement

Here's a space I never imagined I'd be: in a rented van filled with the stink of five runners, inching down a road in the pitch of night. Two people wearing headlamps ran down the road. The three others slumped in the seats, knocked out, or trying to be, anyway. We were sixty-seven miles north of Philly, but we could've been anywhere. From my seat in the van, all I could see was the fifteen feet of road our headlights illuminated in front of us, and the bouncing reflection of our two runners. I was up next, so I tried to sleep. I adjusted the pillow between my head and the window and closed my eyes. But sleep didn't come. I was too tired, too excited, my mind filled with the women I was running for. We'd only run 35 miles. We had 215 to go.

After the 2016 election, I found myself thinking a lot about the future of our country and about the ways in which the forces of racism and sexism play out on both a national scale and a personal one. Since founding Harlem Run, the sexism I'd experienced in the running community had been painful and disheartening. Because I chose

to manage Harlem Run in my own way, without bowing to the pref-
erences of the Black and Latinx male crew founders in the city, and
perhaps because of the overwhelming success and media coverage of
Harlem Run and me, they'd shunned me. I had imagined they'd be
proud to have a Black woman emerge in a sea of only male leaders in
New York and collaborate to bring more of us into the fold, but it
seemed the lure of dominance, or maybe jealousy, was too great. When
the groups collaborated on events, the men left Harlem Run and me
out. The leaders trash-talked us on social media and in person, to anyone who would listen, saying things like *Harlem Run is a bunch of college
kids, we don't fuck with them*; language intended to somehow make us
appear "less cool" and create division.

In many ways, the man entering the White House operated in the
same manner—name-calling those who didn't agree with him or follow in line with his bidding, stoking division to gain power. It was terrifying to imagine that this person would set the agenda for our nation
for the immediate future. His mindset was "win at all costs" and he
pushed a nationalist (read: white, cisgendered, able-bodied, Christian
male) agenda. I was frightened for my people. His laws and policies
would further marginalize those already marginalized, Including Black
people, the LGBTIQ+ community, undocumented people, Indigenous
people, and women. The incoming administration was already discuss-
ing rolling back reproductive rights. Any cuts in funding and changes
to reproductive rights would disproportionately affect women of color.
Where rights and access are concerned, we're the first to be negatively
impacted and the last to be considered. Our agency over our bodies was
on the line.

All of this was on my mind in December 2016, when Amir and I
had a long conversation with a friend of his who worked at the White
House during the Obama administration, and his partner, who we'd
gotten to know. I told them about my work with Harlem Run, how it

was a political act in the sense of claiming space, advocating for our community, and centering the experiences of Black people and other people of color. Amir's friend was enthusiastic, as he believed communities like Harlem Run were deeply important in the larger political theater. He also emphasized how damaging the new administration's policies would be, particularly to people in neighborhoods like Harlem. "You have a powerful voice and powerful community," he said. "You could really do something impactful, using movement."

My mind jumped to the history of movement as protest, to Martin Luther King Jr.'s civil rights marches. More than 200,000 demonstrators rallied together in the March on Washington in 1963 to demand equality. In 1965, thousands joined the fifty-four mile walk from Selma to Montgomery over a five-day period, with 25,000 people walking the final leg to the Alabama State Capitol. These collective actions reminded me of the power we have when we speak with one voice to demand the rights we deserve.

How could I use running in the same way?

Our friend brought up the Women's March planned for January 21, 2017, the day after the inauguration, which was shaping up to be one of the largest marches of our time. His partner added, "You could run there?"

Amir and I looked at each other. My mind was already racing, thinking about the way the endeavor would bring together all these threads—movement, protest, running, and community. After turning it over for a couple of hours, I asked Amir what he thought about me running solo from Harlem to Washington, DC—not just to do it, but as a fundraiser for Planned Parenthood, timed to arrive the morning of the Women's March. "Oh, yeah," he said in his understated way, implying this was a foregone conclusion. "I'll drive alongside you."

I pulled out my phone and calculated the distance—250 miles. Would it be possible for me to complete the mileage by myself? I had done one ultramarathon in celebration of my thirty-first birthday, and I was in the best shape of my life. But I knew that many miles, even if spread out over the course of a week, would be painful at best. So I called Talisa Hayes, a pace-group leader for Harlem Run and the only ultrarunner I knew, and threw out the idea of a relay to her. She's a ride-or-die kind of person, and after we hung up, she emailed within minutes: "I'm in."

It was exciting, but was it possible? We decided we'd add two more runners to make the distance manageable, and I created a GoFundMe page—(Four Women) Run For ALL Women—trusting that the logistics would work out and we'd find two other women to join us. I posted the link on Instagram and Facebook. Twenty-four hours later, more than one thousand people had visited the GoFundMe page and we'd raised $1,000.

Everything accelerated after that. I received DMs from Kim Rodrigues, runner and fashionista, and Quita Francique, a well-known runner, community builder, and high school teacher; and just like that, our team of four was complete. Planned Parenthood's CEO tweeted about our effort, and the organizers of the Women's March said they were pumped for our participation. More than one hundred women reached out wanting to take part in the run. Like me, they were worried about the rollback of reproductive rights, particularly because we'd learned the new administration would likely withhold federal funding from Planned Parenthood, making our effort more urgent both in dollars and in principle. My friend Mary, who gave me the Harlem Run domain, jumped on logistics and created a spreadsheet that broke down the run into four-mile segments, with times and locations so people could sign up to join us.

Eight days into our fundraising, we went viral. We broke my initial fundraising goal of $44,000 (in honor of Barack Obama, our forty-fourth president), with donations coming in from people around the world. Our sign-up sheet was so full we told people not to worry about signing up and to just show up! They could follow us on Twitter and Instagram for location updates. I started fielding calls from news outlets in Canada, Ireland, and Australia. Stories ran online on *Glamour*, the *Cut*, *Bustle*, *Essence*, and more, all linking to the GoFundMe page, all discussing the threat to women and our desire to raise awareness and money for Planned Parenthood.

It felt bananas, but mostly surreal to stand on the corner of 145th and Lenox in Harlem on Wednesday, January 18, 2017, two days before the inauguration and three days before the Women's March, surrounded by two hundred supporters ready to run the first four miles with us. NBC, ABC, and CNN had their cameras rolling. I wondered if this was what it was like to be a professional runner on the starting line of a big-city race: all eyes on you, and anticipation riding on your performance. I disassociated a bit in order to manage the magnitude of what I was responsible for; it seemed at times that I was watching the action rather than living it.

A little before 6:00 p.m., our start time, I stood to address the crowd. A couple of days earlier, I'd spent time reflecting on why the run was important, and I shared that in my speech.

I began by acknowledging that it was easy to turn on the news and fall into despair; I'd heard it said that if you want to become depressed, you should just turn on CNN. My own concern about the state of our country was compounded by the loss of my father, and how helpless I'd felt in the face of his disease. What I'd learned, I told the crowd, was that I could focus on the helplessness, or recognize that I could, in fact, do something. We are not powerless in the face of injustice; there is always something you can do. I didn't have lots of money, political power, or tons of followers on social media, but what I did have were running shoes, two feet to put them on, and enough passion and drive to organize. It was as basketball coach John Wooden said: "Don't let what you cannot do interfere with what you can do."

And then we were off.

The four of us—Talisa, Quita, Kim, and me—led with Mary right behind us, her bright headlamp lighting our path. As we traveled up Adam Clayton Powell, my nerves settled and I took a moment to appreciate the spectacle of it. People on the streets watched and cheered as our group of two hundred passed. I made eye contact with an old man with a cane. "All right now, that's how we do it!" he shouted. I threw up a fist and he threw one back at me, smiling.

We took a wrong turn and two hundred people had to course correct with us, a flock turning en masse through the streets. Our group seemed to grow as we ran north through Washington Heights, and soon we were twenty people wide, stopping traffic and taking up every inch of space available. This was not how I usually ran with groups, but the relay was a moving protest; disruption was part of the point. The community loved it—they were cheering for us, blowing horns and flashing lights to show their approval.

We made our way to the base of the George Washington Bridge and ran up the ramp. A few people had run ahead and cheered as we passed, the masses stopping there and waving us on. The bridge was busy at night, but the pedestrian path was clear. There were only about fourteen of us now, including Amir and a friend who'd agreed to be our videographer, and we ran energized. Crossing the bridge, I felt invincible, like I was floating, not even aware of my footfalls. We were doing it.

Off the George Washington Bridge, we turned left into Fort Lee, New Jersey, where we met our van and the first of multiple drivers (provided by a generous donor) and put our plan in motion: one to two people running with supporters, the others resting in the van, which followed the runners as closely as possible. It was around 7:30 p.m., and according to our plan, I wasn't running again until after midnight, so I settled in and watched the other women run. I felt proud that our four leaders were Black women. Black women don't come to mind when people think of ultrarunning or epic running events and yet here we were, taking up space that was largely the domain of white men. It felt radical, resistive, disruptive.

We made a pit stop at a gas station and almost left Quita behind, and I worried about the challenge ahead. The running was only one piece—in a way, the easiest. Put one foot in front of the other, keep going. But making sure everyone was in the van, meeting the drivers, meeting the people en route, and doing it all safely was already harder than I'd imagined.

We switched runners every four miles. Someone climbed in the van; someone climbed out, switched on her headlamp, got moving. On foot, you see a place in a way you don't in a car: close up, more intimately, particularly at night. With so much of the world asleep, I felt the world around me more easily. I sensed energy shifts as we moved through each neighborhood. The well-resourced neighborhoods like Edgewater—quiet, clean, well lit—felt light and weightless. Newark was in the shadows, poorly lit, and the energy was heavy as we kicked needles with our feet. Black folks were on the stoop, playing dominoes. Streetlights flickered. Years of redlining, housing discrimination, and other structural violence were captured in the topography.

In the van, I munched on a granola bar; Quita on premium jerky— runner food—while Alma, a fifth runner who'd wanted to join us, unwrapped arroz con gandules y pollo. The van erupted in laughter. "What?" she said, confused. I told her I'd expected everyone would bring food you typically eat during an ultramarathon: bars, bananas, peanut butter. But like everything else about running culture, those foods had been selected according to a white palate. It was refreshing to have the rules disrupted.

Westfield, New Jersey. 2:00 a.m. While so many people had signed up to meet us and said they'd be there, I was still amazed each time to arrive at our next four-mile segment and see people on street corners, in parking lots, in front of gas stations waiting for us. We were ahead of our estimated pace and tweeted out updates, unsure if folks would make it. But they did. They tweeted back, *On our way!* and left whatever they were doing to greet us.

In a New Jersey suburb, I spotted a collection of neon lights, like the halos and light sticks kids carry on New Year's Eve or at a rave. A group of women were waiting for us in reflective gear. The women—six white, one Black—were the Union County chapter of Moms Run This Town. They'd arranged childcare, enlisted their partners' help, and taken the next day off from work to join us. We piled out of the van for hugs, then got the run underway. Quita and I ran among the group as we talked. They told me that they didn't feel called to protest in events like the Women's March, yet they felt strongly about reproductive rights and shared our concern for the damage the new administration could do. When they learned about the event, they had to come.

The Black woman and I ran side by side and she said that she saw herself in me: it was only because the event was led by Black women that she had rearranged her life so she could participate. I was touched by this and thanked her, letting her know how much it meant to me that she felt represented.

Eight miles later, we all hugged goodbye. Talisa and Kim pulled on layers and hopped out of the warm van and Quita and I climbed in. I tried to sleep, but couldn't. My mind wandered to the conversations I'd just had with the Jellyfish, the nickname we'd given the women because of their glowing neon vests. Running had provided them with an avenue for action and protest. I smiled at that. I thought about the Black woman in particular, who came out only because this run was Black-led. I thought about the Black women who had been the same for me. Harriet Tubman making nineteen trips on the Underground Railroad, traveling 116 miles each time and risking her life to bring people to freedom. Her movement an act of life and death. Marylou Jackson, Velma Jackson, Ethyl Miller, Leolya Nelson, and Constance White, Black women who, in 1928, cycled the same 250 miles we were running for the simple joy of cycling.

I thought about all of the ways that Black women have been disembodied, forced over the course of history to give our bodies in service of others. Our milk used to feed white babies. Our bodies taken at the pleasure of white owners. Our corpses dug up and stolen for science. Our reproductive systems manipulated to further gynecology research at the hands of Alabama doctor James Marion Sims, the so-called father of gynecology. He conducted painful experimental surgeries on Black women without their consent and without anesthesia, forcing them onto the surgical table with physical force, enslavement, and opium. For his actions, he was celebrated with a statue in Central Park. Henrietta Lacks had her cells stolen in 1951 by doctors at Johns Hopkins Hospital. Her cells, known now as HeLa cells, led to medical breakthroughs in the polio vaccine and AIDS treatment (and later, the coronavirus vaccine). She never knew or consented to her cells being taken, and her family was never compensated.

Black women have not only been used; we've been disregarded in ways big and small. For me, it was the Black male leaders in New York City dismissing my leadership. Before me, it was the women of the Civil Rights Movement whose efforts were overshadowed by men, all while experiencing gender discrimination and sexual harassment within the movement. Olympian Wyomia Tyus who became the first person, male or female, to win back-to-back titles in the 100 meters—yet no one knew her name, and media in fact often credited Carl Lewis for the accolade.

I felt familiar anger rise up, an anger captured by Malcolm X in a 1962 speech: "The most disrespected person in America is the Black woman. The most unprotected person in America is the Black woman. The most neglected person in America is the Black woman."

What we were doing, then, was an act of reclamation, a reclaiming of body and voice for Black women, then and now. All women would be harmed by the new president's attacks on women, and that meant Black women and women of color in particular. We're more likely to rely on Planned Parenthood's services, in part because more Black women live in poverty than white women. If wealthy white women need an abortion, they have options. Many Black women don't. When women cannot access healthcare—from basic checkups to birth control to an abortion—or make decisions for themselves, terrible consequences follow. Education opportunities can be lost, affecting future employment. A woman's health, the health of her family, and therefore the health of her community all suffer. Our bodies, running through the night, were a declaration that we will not be silenced or controlled. We will run and we will fight.

January 19. Philadelphia. 10:00 p.m. Fatigue caught us twenty-four hours in. We were running and meeting and greeting, and sleep was impossible. I was a zombie, a bundle of nerves, elated, exhausted, irritable. People would meet us super excited and want us to be energetic, too. All I could think was, *You realize we've been in a van for twenty hours, right?* We braced ourselves for Philadelphia, where the crowds were supposed to be overwhelming. We pulled up to Independence Hall to the sound of people screaming. "Is this real?" I asked myself aloud as I stepped out of the van. It felt like a concert and I was Beyoncé.

The crowd was 250 deep with runners from Black Girls Run, No-vember Project, City Fit Girls, and Run215, to name a few. I screamed greetings and thanks—no matter what I said, people cheered back. I wasn't even sure I was making sense. Adrenaline rushed through my body and I felt alive. The crowd wanted to see us, so the four of us plus Alma moved to the middle of the street and smiled for what seemed like hundreds of flashing cameras. Then we set off down Market Street, occupying the entire roadway—screaming, laughing, high-fiving. For those few miles, the streets were ours.

January 21. Washington, DC. The rest of the 140 miles went by slowly and quickly. We were revived by a kind stranger who fed us soup and let us shower at her house. We were scared, briefly, by white men chasing us down the street. We watched as they sprinted, juggling con-tainers in their hands, trying, we finally realized, to bring us coffee. Email notifications came in alerting me that donations were coming. Most were $10 to $25, from regular folks from all over the world. But

every now and then a donation would come through from someone like John Legend, who was a friend from college, or the DJ Elvis Duran from Z100, who had heard about us when we went viral. I'd scream and share the news to hoots and hollers from everyone in the van.

In Baltimore, the crowd was equal to Philadelphia—large, loud, supportive. Multiple police officers on motorcycles escorted us through the city, which I'd later regret. Freddie Gray had died in police custody in Baltimore; the idea that we were aligned with the police was not the message I'd intended to send.

We ran into DC in the early morning, the last four miles escorted by the District Running Collective. Soon, the dome of the Capitol building came into view. The four of us moved up to the front to be together when we arrived. The streets were quiet. The barricades for the march later that day were already up. We maneuvered around them and made our way up the Capitol steps, screaming, laughing, high-fiving, taking in the beauty of the building, illuminated by a warm

glow of light. We had covered 250 miles in sixty hours. I'd run 84 miles myself. Never would I have thought that possible. In total, we raised $104,000, which would help ensure women would have access to health-care regardless of the new president's actions.

I was already nostalgic about the run, the purpose it had served, the community that had come together to make it happen. While the others went to the march, I rushed across town to the MSNBC studios with Amir to appear on Joy Reid's show. I remember sitting in hair and makeup and then being rushed into the studio, but the only memory I have of the conversation is the feeling of speaking confidently in front of a global audience—millions of people—while also feeling like I was just talking to a single human being. In the back of my mind, a voice kept telling me, *Don't F——— this up.*

The following night, we all took the bus back to Harlem. As we rode, we couldn't get over the fact that we'd just run this very route. I wanted to tell everyone on the bus, "Hey! We just ran this!" but I stayed quiet. I sat in my seat inspired, hopeful, proud, exhausted. I felt part of a lineage of protest and disruption, of claiming and reclaiming, of power and voice. I knew that what we had done mattered. I knew my voice mattered. What I knew as the bus pushed into the night back home to Harlem was that when it came down to it, I could do big things.

12

We Were There

I n February 2017, I was on a panel for the running organization New York Road Runners, which puts on the New York City Marathon, the largest in the world. The event was at the organization's Run-Center in Midtown. There were four of us up front. Myself, plus two other Black people who led running clubs in the city: a coleader from Black Men Run in Brooklyn and a founder of the Quicksilver Striders, a club in Queens. The three of us were the modern counterpoint to the panel's historical focus. February is Black History Month, and to be honest, I was so busy at the time that I hadn't paid attention to the topic. I'd spoken to enough media and had been on a few panels for Under Armour that I knew what I was going to say. What I didn't know was that what I would hear would completely change my understanding of the running boom.

The fourth panelist was historian Pamela Cooper Chenkin, the author of a book called *The American Marathon*, which traces the rise of the marathon as a competitive event. Chenkin was a petite white woman with a serious look, and, frankly, I wondered why she was on a panel for Black History Month. But then she started speaking, and I was riveted.

The first question posed by the moderator was about Ted Corbitt, and in her answer, Chenkin told the crowd that Corbitt, who was a Black man, was in many ways the father of American distance running. *What? Who?* He was the first Black man to represent the United States in the Olympic marathon (Helsinki 1952), and a national marathon champion in 1954. He set American records on the track in the 100-mile and twenty-four-hour run—distance events!—and was legendary for his two-hundred-mile training weeks. *Wow.* Corbitt was also responsible for standardizing road race distances by bringing the calibrated bicycling method to the United States. And he was the first president of the New York Road Runners.

One of the men in the audience started sharing a story about Corbitt, but I missed it because my mind was processing. *A Black man represented the United States in the marathon in the 1950s? A Black man was the first president of the New York Road Runners?*

The panel continued, and Chenkin began talking about a little-known club called the New York Pioneer Club. The club was founded by three Black men in Harlem in 1936, she said, as a counterpoint to the elite-level athletic clubs at the time, which wanted fast, ready-made athletes. Three businessmen in Harlem—Joe Yancey, Robert Douglas, and William Culbreath—decided to open a club that would let anybody run.

The team trained in the winter at the Armory near the Harlem River. The rest of the year, they ran at Macombs Dam Park across the river in the Bronx, a popular training ground for distance runners. At the time, athletic clubs were segregated, but white runners began joining the Black runners for training sessions. Yancey, a local civil rights leader who fought for full integration of Black people, decided to explicitly open the Pioneer Club to all people (men), and in 1942, the group changed the constitution to welcome everyone, "regardless of race, color, or creed," Chenkin said, reading from notes.

The move made the Pioneer Club one of the first integrated athletic clubs in the country, amateur or professional—not just in running, but any sport, preceding the integration of the national football, basketball, and baseball leagues. Pioneer Club members were African American, Jewish, Irish, Italian, Caribbean, and Puerto Rican. Yancey had never intended for the club to be competitive, Chenkin said, but it was. By the late 1940s and early '50s, the club was producing top athletes in both track and field and distance. Its most prominent member was Ted Corbitt, who represented the Pioneers at the 1952 Olympics.

The origins of the New York Road Runners, she said, can be traced to the New York Pioneer Club.

My jaw dropped (not literally; I managed to keep a straight face). *The New York Road Runners started in Harlem?* Chenkin had an academic air and was sharing this information matter-of-factly, so I thought, *Did everyone know this and I hadn't been paying attention?* She seemed to hedge a little in her language, as if nervous about giving three Black men credit for laying the foundation of what became one of the most important (white) running clubs in the world. What would the old-timers from the New York Road Runners in the audience say? But she dropped enough details to make it clear that this club in Harlem had been a key player in the foundation of the running boom—and in fact, had preceded Bowerman's club by decades.

I walked home to Harlem, fiftysomething blocks, that night thinking, *Of course, Harlem Run wasn't the first. How could I have been so naïve? How could I have missed this?*

After the panel, a Black man, the leader of a running group in the city, had given me a sweatshirt he'd made modeled after the Pioneer Club's logo—dark blue with "NEW YORK PIONEER CLUB" in big bold white lettering. It rested over a chair when I started googling "Ted Corbitt" and "Pioneer Club" the next day.

I didn't find much. There were obituaries in the *New York Times* and *Runner's World* after Corbitt's death in 2007. Neither piece mentioned the Pioneer Club, but I learned that Corbitt was born in 1919 on a cotton farm in South Carolina, where his grandfather had been enslaved. He ran track in high school, and continued in the shorter distances at the University of Cincinnati. I learned how, later in life when he had moved to New York City and was working as a physical therapist, he racked up two-hundred-mile training weeks, running to and from work every day, covering twenty or thirty miles each time, sometimes adding distance by detouring twenty or thirty miles—holy shit!—through Westchester.

The only place that had any depth of information was the website tedcorbitt.com, created and managed by Corbitt's son, Gary. The site was a treasure trove of data: "Black Female Marathon History." "Black Running History Timeline (1880–1979)." I loved learning about the "Pedestrian Era" in the 1880s—who knew?—when people walked hundreds of miles on a track as a spectator sport, and that Black people dominated. After a six-day event at Madison Square Garden in 1880, Frank Hart, one of three African American competitors, covered 565 miles to win the race, setting a new world record. *Talk about epic!* The two other Black men, William Pegram and Edward Williams, took second and seventh. The headline in the paper the next day read "The Negroes Lead the Walk." The three men had been born when slavery was still legal, and, as one paper said, during the race the men circled the track together in a show of solidarity, demonstrating "their constitutional right to walk in public, without regard to any previous conditions what[so]ever."

It blew me away to see the names of so many Black distance runners. Moses Mayfield had led the first New York City Marathon in 1970 and had won the Philadelphia Marathon that same year in a record 2:24:29, becoming the fastest African American marathoner. There was Bill Lucas, an NCAA cross-country champion. And Lou White, described as "a renaissance sportsman," with national titles in 15K and 10 miles in 1950 and 1951. Arthur Hall won the Penn Relays Marathon in 1975 and ran 2:22 at the 1978 Boston Marathon. Herman Atkins ran 2:11:52 at the Nike/Oregon Track Club Marathon in 1979, the fastest marathon by a native-born Black American. (Nathan Martin would set a new record by running 2:11:05 at the Marathon Project in 2021.)

There was so much data on Ted Corbitt, it was overwhelming. World records and American records and so many firsts: first Black man to represent the U.S. in the Olympic marathon, first Black man to win a national marathon championship, first president of the New York Road Runners, first person to win the Cherry Tree Marathon at Macombs Dam Park in the Bronx in 1959, a precursor to the New York City Marathon. Over his lifetime, Corbitt ran 223 marathons and ultramarathons. He ran the Boston Marathon twenty-two times, finishing

sixth three times and third for Americans five times, and running under three hours nineteen consecutive times (1954–1972), tying the record with Clarence DeMar.

I found the names Marilyn Bevans and Ella Willis on the women's
page, and dug around for more information. Marilyn Bevans was a leading marathon runner during the running boom. She took second behind Kathrine Switzer at the inaugural Maryland Marathon in 1973,
and went on to win the marathon twice. In 1975, she became the first
African American woman to run under three hours in the marathon,
running 2:55:52 at the Boston Marathon and placing fourth behind
Liane Winter of West Germany and Americans Kathrine Switzer and
Gayle Barron. That same year, she became the first African American woman to win a marathon: the Washington Birthday Marathon in
Greenbelt, Maryland. She also took second at Boston in 1977, becoming the first African American woman to medal in the race.

There were no girls track or cross-country programs at her high
school, so Bevans began running on her own. In college, she caught
the eye of Coach Vern Cox, who invited her to train with the school's
men's distance team. Over the course of her career, she ran twenty-
three marathons, winning three and taking second in five. In 1977, Bevans was the tenth-fastest female marathoner in the world, despite the
racism she faced. "When some runners ran, there were cheers," Bevans
told *Runner's World* in 2013. "When I ran, you heard crickets. I was
called the N-word sometimes."

Ella Willis was Bevans's contemporary. Willis followed up Bevan's
historic first marathon win with a victory of her own at the 1975 Motor
City Marathon in Detroit, becoming the second African American female to win a marathon. Willis achieved the fastest time run by an
African American woman in 1989, which she held until Michele Bush-
Cuke ran 2:37:41 at the California International Marathon for second
place in 1991.

I knew the traditional (read: white) telling of the running boom, the one I'd read about, the one featured in the film *Free to Run* that highlights Frank Shorter, Steve Prefontaine, Kathrine Switzer, and others as the architects of the sport. The film celebrates the freedom of the 1960s but frames it as the summer of love and women's lib, not civil rights. Corbitt isn't mentioned, and neither is the Pioneer Club. I stared at the screen a moment, then sat back in my chair. *We were there,* I thought. We were part of this, and I didn't even know it.

I kept going. I felt a responsibility to know the stories, to know our history. I learned that in 1909 Black men were winning marathons. Wait—I read it again. Yes, Black men were winning marathons. Howard Hall won the Pittsburgh Marathon and Charles Burden won the New Orleans Marathon. In Burden's case, the white folks who'd put on the race couldn't comprehend that a Black athlete was, one, competing in the race, and two, had won it. When they learned that "Burden was colored, the promoters almost had fainting spells," the *New York Age* reported. The article ended with this line: "The promoters of the race are not yet over Burden winning." A decade later in 1919, Aaron Morris became the first known Black man to run the Boston Marathon.

I learned that the Pioneer Club was a civil rights organization as much as it was an athletic one. Its mere existence as an integrated club, hosting integrated meets, challenged the status quo of segregation. It took on the Amateur Athletic Union (AAU), which governed the majority of amateur sports at the time and sanctioned quietly and openly racist meets; they did nothing to aid Black athletes in an era when they couldn't eat or sleep in the same places as their white teammates.

In 1946, for example, the Pioneer Club boycotted the national championships in San Antonio, Texas. The AAU, eager for the Pioneer Club athletes to compete, sent a representative to New York to talk to the club, trying to persuade the team to attend. The club refused on principle. Four years later, the Pioneers took a stand against the national championships being held at the University of Maryland, which did not allow Black people in the dorms. To make a point, the eighty-five athletes, Black, brown, and white, stayed at Lincoln University, a historically Black university in Pennsylvania, ninety-three miles away.

The New York Road Runners, I learned, grew out of the Pioneer Club. In 1957, steeplechaser Browning Ross, a 1948 and 1952 Olympian, published the *Long Distance Log* (circulation 126), the only means of communication among distance runners at the time. Ross had trained under Yancey. He had watched the New York Pioneer Club challenge the system. Like Yancey, Ross was a populist who wanted to open distance running to more people. So, in the August edition, he proposed forming a new organization that would get the sport out from under the age and gender restrictions set by the AAU. He wrote that the new organization "could exercise full control of our branch of the sport."

Response was positive, and the Road Runners Club of America (RRCA) launched in February 1958 with its first meeting at the Paramount Hotel in New York City. Corbitt—Ross's teammate at the 1952 Olympic Games—missed the meeting, opting for a thirty-mile training run instead. A couple of months later, Ross convinced Pioneer Club member John Sterner to launch the RRCA's New York chapter by quoting Corbitt: "You cannot sit back and complain all the time. Organize and do something about it." And in June 1958, the New York chapter—which would later change its name to the New York Road Runners—was founded with forty members, half from the Pioneer Club, with Corbitt becoming its first president.

The establishment of the RRCA and the New York Road Runners changed the future of distance running. Like the Pioneer Club, its existence upended the system. The RRCA started holding national championship events in multiple distances and did away with age and gender restrictions, welcoming women, teens, and kids into the sport. By 1963—the year Bowerman formed his club in Eugene—the RRCA had thirteen districts across the country managing and promoting road races. The number of marathons began to rise, with new races emerging each year, like the Labor Day Marathon in Missouri, the Windy City Marathon in Chicago, and the City of Lakes Marathon in Minnesota.

Corbitt established a course-measuring system to standardize distances nationwide—before he brought the calibrated bicycle method to the U.S., a marathon could be 25.9 miles or 26.8. Corbitt also instituted age-group categories at New York Road Runners' events, a model for the country. The RRCA's fun-run series followed, with events across the country. By the 1970s, when millions of people began running, the infrastructure for the sport was in place.

I was floored by this. We were not only there; we helped build the sport. But our participation had been erased, buried. While the New York Road Runners, the RRCA, and the sport as a whole evolved into a white sport, it was clear to me now that the running story is not only a white story. It is a Black story. It is a civil rights story. It is a story of our talent and resilience. It is a story of creating space for Black people. The idea of an inclusive distance-running culture—the democratic, anybody-can-run ideal running wants to be—traces its roots to 1942, with three Black men who embraced and fought for integration and inclusion. Said simply, the first chapter of the modern running boom began with Black men in Harlem.

For a while, I was angry. How could Black people have been left out of the story? Why weren't our historic firsts celebrated alongside the historic firsts achieved by white runners? Ted Corbitt had been inducted into the inaugural National Distance Running Hall of Fame in 1998, along with Frank Shorter, Bill Rodgers, Joan Benoit Samuelson, and Kathrine Switzer. But Corbitt was not celebrated in any meaningful way on the New York Road Runners' website, and the organization didn't acknowledge its Pioneer Club roots. If Corbitt was as integral to running as the white legends and icons, why wasn't he a known actor in distance-running history? If the Pioneer Club was foundational to the boom, why hadn't I heard of it?

I knew the answer to these questions. History was told through a white lens, from the perspective of those in power. But as I ran that summer, I thought about the Pioneer Club, Corbitt, Bevans, and all the others, and I wondered how much the course of history might have changed if Black people had been rightfully included in the running boom story. What if Bevans (the first African American woman to win a marathon), Willis (the second African American woman to win a marathon), Mayfield (eighth at the inaugural New York City Marathon, two-time winner of the Philadelphia Marathon), and others had been celebrated more in the popular press for their achievements? What if Corbitt and the Pioneer Club had been held up alongside Shorter and Rodgers? How might running have evolved differently if the New York Road Runners had celebrated Corbitt and the Pioneer Club as much as it celebrated Fred Lebow (cofounder of the New York City Marathon and its race director for twenty-two years)? If the Boston Marathon had listed the firsts of Black runners along with firsts by white women and men? If we knew we were there from the beginning, would I and millions of other Black people have turned to running sooner? Would I have seen myself in the sport? Would I have felt like I belonged?

What I knew now was that distance running was ours. We are part of the story, the heritage. And damn, we started it.

Late that summer, I couldn't shake the feeling that Harlem Run had all been fate—that we were destined to pick up the torch of our incredible legacy of long-distance running. And that it was our responsibility to correct history, to let people know we have always been part of distance running. An idea for how to do that came when we held our annual New York City Marathon singlet design contest. One of our members, a white man actually, emailed us suggesting we honor Corbitt and the New York Pioneer Club by creating singlets in the Pioneer Club style. *Oh, snap*, I thought. *That's it.*

We had them printed, and on marathon day, fifty runners moved through city streets with "NEW YORK HARLEM RUN" across their chests. I was at our cheer station at 124th and Fifth Avenue, and I watched as a group of them ran toward us, imagining Corbitt and the Pioneers running down the street, imagining what Harlem looked like when these were their streets.

That December, I ran the Ted Corbitt 15K for the first time. I can't remember if I knew about this race before I was on the panel, but what I did know was before this, I'd had no idea who Ted Corbitt was, and had little interest in running a race in the winter. There was nothing to draw participants. There was no medal offered, it was cold, and it was also only a month after the New York City Marathon; runners were still recovering.

When I saw the race on the New York Road Runners' calendar after the panel, the fact that the race existed seemed significant at first. I appreciated that it started and finished near 102nd Street, closer to Harlem than New York Road Runners' typical start and finish around Seventy-Second Street, a small but important gesture. But the more I learned about the race, the more it became apparent that the race was marginalized. Why would the race honoring one of the club's founders and its first president, a champion, a pioneer, the man who gave us precise race distances, not have a medal, or be given a significant place on the racing calendar? This is what the white lens does. It diminishes our importance, places us on the margins, and then pats itself on the back for recognizing us at all.

At the race, I ran with the Pioneer Club–inspired singlet over a long-sleeved shirt, jogging in place to stay warm in the corrals. As the gun went off, about four thousand of us moved off the line. It began to snow, making for slippery conditions. I barreled forward, feeling surprisingly good, high-fiving folks along the course.

Afterward, I bumped into Mary Wittenberg, former CEO of the New York Road Runners. Mary and I had met a couple of years earlier at a group workout in the city, when she was still New York Road Runners' CEO and Harlem Run had just gotten big. She came to a race we put on, the Harlem 1 Miler, and had been a supporter ever since. I'd started a podcast that summer, *Find Meaning (On the Run)*, as a way to reach more people with messages that were important to me by getting behind-the-scenes takes on what it means to be "successful," uncovering stories that hadn't been told. When Mary was launching a global sports program with Virgin Sports, I had her on as a guest.

Mary has a high-energy, sometimes frenetic way about her. When she saw me, she asked with urgency, "Do you know Gary Corbitt, Ted's son?" I shook my head no. "You two have to know each other," she said, taking my arm. We walked westward across the transverse toward an elderly Black man with soft, kind eyes, who wore a Black Men Run T-shirt and a purple cap to guard against the cold.

Gary and I greeted each other with a hug. I pointed to my singlet and told him that it honored his father. Soon, other New York Road Runners staff members were around us, including Michael Capiraso, the CEO at the time. I got the sense that the New York Road Runners crowd knew exactly how significant Corbitt was to their organization and to running, and yet they were indifferent to the way they approached the race. I was grateful that Black Men Run honored Corbitt by creating custom medals for the race.

Before leaving, I mentioned my podcast to Gary and asked him to be a guest. I wanted to use my platform to carry on his father's legacy. We connected a few months later.

"My father didn't throw anything away," Gary told me. Training logs, newsletters, correspondence. It was as if he knew someone—his son?—would need to preserve the history, to uncover it so that it would not be forgotten, which is exactly what Gary did. After his father died, Gary spent the better part of a decade going through those documents, piecing together the history about his dad, both his known achievements and the more intimate parts of his story.

One of my first questions to Gary was about his memories of his father as a runner. "Well, he ran to work a lot," he said, and we laughed at the understatement. "He would leave at six in the morning and would do a twenty- or thirty-mile workout. He would run north up to Yonkers to McLean Avenue past Woodlawn Cemetery and back into the Bronx, then make his way down the East Side Drive to his workplace at Twenty-Third Street and First Avenue."

Gary told me he grew up watching the sport grow. A big race in the 1960s, he said, had thirty-five people. There were twelve people at the start of one of the New York Road Runners' early races. "My dad was the editor of the [RRCA] quarterly newsletter," Gary said, "which was a six-to-eight-page newsletter that was printed at our kitchen table." His dad, he said, felt he had an obligation to help further the sport, but he always preferred training and racing over a meeting.

Gary and I stayed in touch after the podcast, and I learned more about his dad, his life, his legacy. I learned, for example, that Gary turned three the day his father became the first Black man to win a national marathon championship in 1954. Corbitt passed race favorite John J. Kelley in the final miles to win in 2:46. (The Pioneer Club won the team championship.) The next day, the U.S. Supreme Court ruled school segregation unconstitutional.

I was struck by the fact that Corbitt accomplished all that he did during the same period that lynchings and other forms of terrorism were happening regularly to Black people in the United States. I knew the vigilance we ran with today; how did Ted Corbitt find the physical and psychological strength to run during a time when the U.S. was more blatantly racist and violent? "My father was a quiet man," Gary told me. "Soft-spoken and said little about the problems he faced." But he knew his father had been harassed at the Olympic Marathon Trials in Yonkers in 1952; Corbitt estimated that he'd been stopped by police more than two hundred times. In his father's papers, Gary learned his dad joined the Alpha Phi Alpha fraternity in order to have a place to stay when traveling to races. Sometimes Corbitt would miss a competition because he couldn't find a hotel that would rent him a room. After college in the 1940s, Corbitt sometimes chose not to travel to meets out of fear of what he'd encounter, and it cost him. The times he ran in time-trial workouts on his own would have challenged competitors: One workout in 1942 translated into a 48.2 for the 400 meters and would've been a top-ranked U.S. performance. In 1944, Corbitt ran two miles in 9:06; the American record was 8:58 by Don Lash.

Sometimes I'd go to the website tedcorbitt.com and reread the mantras Corbitt used, to keep them in my mind.

"I will be relaxed and free of all restrictions."

"I will feel buoyant and strong while running."

"I will run hard and enjoy the effort."

Occasionally, Gary would reach out when he learned something new, or just to share another anecdote. Like how on his epic runs to and from work, Corbitt sometimes passed Malcolm X speaking to a crowd on the street in Harlem. Or how much Gary loved finding a letter a young Black runner had written to his father, saying that he wished he'd known about him when he was in school, when his coaches had steered him away from distance toward the sprints. I thought again about how I learned marathoning was for me: by seeing a Black man training. Corbitt, too, was first inspired by Jesse Owens and Ralph Metcalfe—seeing Black men excelling in the sprints told him what was possible. He only turned to distance after seeing a photo of Boston Marathon champion Ellison "Tarzan" Brown, a Narragansett Indian. "He intrigued me because he wasn't white," Corbitt told *Runner's World* in 1976. "At the time I thought he was a negro, but later found out he was an Indian."

Our stories have to be told, Gary said. He spoke emphatically about how his father always said that he wasn't alone—that there were other great Black American distance runners, that even Ted didn't know just how rich our history was until he'd started to look into it. History is "fragile, easily lost, forgotten or distorted," Gary said. "But young Black runners need to know they have many role models and are part of a rich history."

Gary's comment about history stayed with me when I ran. White runners see themselves, not only in mainstream narratives like those of Prefontaine and Switzer, but in everyday advertising, articles, and images. I had to actively work to uncover my history, and every run since then has been a reclaiming of our place in distance running. I was carrying the torch the Pioneer Club had lit. Harlem Run was holding the flame, too, and every Black runner was reaching into the past and bringing it forward. With each step, I felt like I was doing exactly what I was supposed to be doing. I felt like I was in exactly the space I belonged.

13

Inclusion/Exclusion

Every runner has a race that sits in their memory for one reason or another. Mine is the 2016 Brooklyn Half Marathon. I ran 1:39. The time was memorable, but it was more the feeling that came during the race that stayed with me.

I lined up exhausted after two hours of sleep. Amir and I had taken a night train back to the city from Baltimore after attending Preakness Stakes, the horse race, with Kevin Plank, the CEO of Under Armour. The brand had a long-standing tradition of hosting a hospitality tent at the race, all you can eat and drink. We wore the fancy hats, ate and drank all we could, feigned interest in the horses' names so we could join in the cheering, the whole shebang—a perk of sponsorship that cost us precious pre-race sleep. I had no grand plan for the race and stood at the start thinking I would just need to survive it. We lined up with a dozen or so Harlem Run friends. "Run with us," Amir said, referring to the fast group he would be heading out with. "No, no, you go," I said. He nodded and the other runners wished me a good race.

I started at an easy jog, settling into a rhythm. A Harlem Run friend who had started behind us caught me a little way over the start. "What are you going for?" he asked. "I'm trying to survive; running ten-minute miles," I said. That worked for him and so we ran. I kept the pace comfortable, but at mile two, my watch told me we were on 8:30 pace. The fatigue I'd felt at the start had disappeared. I told my friend I was going to push a little; he nodded, and I took off. Mile three came and went. Then miles four and five. It seemed like I was pulling the ground away, grabbing pavement and putting it behind me, the miles rolling by without me even noticing. I'd never moved so intensely before.

Soon, I was out of Prospect Park and shooting down Ocean Park-way for five miles toward the finish at Coney Island. The stretch is a subtle downhill, and it felt like there were no limits to how fast I could go. I was powerful, in control. I pushed, picking up the pace even more, and crossed the finish in 1:39, besting my half-marathon time by six minutes. I caught up with Amir and the others, who'd all finished ahead of me in 1:35. We hugged and high-fived. "Dang," I said. "If I'd stayed with you all from the beginning, I know I could've run that fast." Joe, one of the runners who was also a running coach, said, "If you keep training, you could qualify for Boston."

It was an in-the-moment comment that I didn't think much about until that summer, when I was debating whether to run a marathon for time. I had never set time goals other than a vague desire to run under four hours in the marathon. Speed had come simply with experience and play and exploration with my body and movement. If I could run a 1:39 without thinking about it, I could qualify for Boston with a little effort. The question was: did I want to?

That was easy: Nope. Boston was not a city I cared to go to. It's a racist place, more than other cities and towns in the country. It's in the air, a product of the city's history. Not just in the fact that segregation originated there in 1838, when the Eastern Railroad started segregating cars between Boston and Salem before the end of slavery, but also in the city's pride in colonialism, and how lower- and middle-class Irish Americans resented middle-class Black people, believing they were taking economic opportunity from them. It's in the way Boston fiercely fought school integration in the '60s and '70s, and how Black parents were still fighting for equal resources for their kids, for the end of police bias and brutality, for the end of Jim Crow. On top of that, the Boston I knew and had been to was Dorchester and Roxbury, two neighborhoods with large Black populations. But those neighborhoods weren't part of the Boston Marathon, because the majority of the race doesn't actually go through the city of Boston. It travels through predominantly white suburbs and finishes in a predominantly white part of the city.

The Boston Marathon's reputation was also a deterrent. The race is viewed as the holy grail of our sport, the most sought-after event. If you've run Boston, you've somehow "made it" as a runner. But Boston's "specialness" stems from its exclusivity. The race is open only to those who can run fast enough to earn a spot, unless you run for charity and can fundraise thousands of dollars. Speed makes you "worthy" of Boston. I had no interest in participating in an event that valued exclusion. What is white supremacy, ultimately, but an ideology of exclusion, of thinking you're "special," above all the rest? In my mind, the Boston Marathon epitomizes this thinking, and I wanted no part of it.

But six months later, an email landed in my inbox from Hyland's, a Boston Marathon sponsor that makes creams to help with leg cramps. It was putting together a team of female "changemakers" for the 2017 race and had invited me to join the team. I thought about it. Being seen as a changemaker was validating, but I did not want to run Boston. The race was celebrating the forty-fifth anniversary of women running Boston, which was really a celebration of Kathrine Switzer and white women breaking running's gender barrier. I knew now about Black women like Marilyn Bevans, and I also knew that she would not be celebrated similarly for breaking the color line, for becoming the first Black woman to place at Boston, and for making way for women who looked like me. Could my participation be meaningful, even disruptive? Running Boston would be significant in terms of representation; I could pick up Bevans's baton and carry it forward through history. So I said yes. I'd go, represent my community, and see what the race was like for myself.

I didn't train much because I couldn't. I'd run eighty-four miles in January during the relay and my hamstring was giving me problems. I put in a few miles during the week, but only ran one thirteen-mile-long run. It was frustrating knowing I'd have to suffer through the miles.

Hyland's set up a private Facebook group for the women's team, and I connected with the other women there. There were fourteen of us, all white save for myself, another Black woman, and a woman who ran in a hijab. Most of our online chatter was training-related, but at one point, some of the women began posting that they were receiving pushback from other runners about their participation at Boston—people who were frustrated that we'd gotten into Boston without qualifying, implying that we did not deserve to be there.

This seemed wholly ridiculous to me. The qualifying times were arbitrary, made-up times to support the race's "exclusivity." The idea that only certain people who "worked hard" deserved to be there is a harmful line of thinking emblematic in our society of the "pull yourself up by your bootstraps" myth of the American Dream. You can work hard in construction, in the service sector, or as a teacher, and you can work hard in upper management, as a CEO, or a stockbroker; but one group's hard work is rewarded more, both monetarily and in cultural currency, creating a country of haves and have-nots. Those who have, so this line of thinking goes, must have worked harder. Two thirty-year-old women can train equally hard; one will run 3:29 and qualify; the other will never hit 3:30, but that doesn't mean her effort was any less.

The dialogue was my first introduction to how much runners buy in to the Boston Marathon myth of exclusion. Our participation as sponsored athletes seemed to threaten these runners' perception of the race's specialness, and therefore their own specialness. They suggested we'd cheated the system. But the idea that a system is inherently right and we all have to abide by it is problematic. Why not change the system to welcome more people? Why not have a dialogue on ways to expand the race experience to more runners, rather than shrink it?

I traveled to the race with a friend who was also on the Hyland's team, Candice Huffine, a supermodel and body positivity advocate; her husband, Matt; and Amir, who had qualified for Boston at the Miami Marathon. Matt drove as we all scream-sang '80s and '90s classics. But the mood shifted for me when we walked into the fancy hotel Hyland's had put us up in—think mahogany walls, overstuffed chairs, paintings of white hunters on horseback headed out to chase a fox. White places like these remind me of the risks around me, and the historical treatment of my people. Fifty years earlier, Black people wouldn't have been able to enter the front door of a place like this. I found myself taking deep breaths, trying to push away the feeling of the walls closing in.

Hyland's did a great job of creating hype and fanfare around our participation. We'd received press in *Outside* and *Women's Running* in the lead-up to the event. On site in Boston, we did live podcasts at the expo and were featured on social media. The other women in the group seemed blown away to be there, awed by the idea of Boston. When they made comments, I bit my tongue. I wasn't there on my own terms and didn't want to seem ungrateful, so I expressed my frustration to Amir.

As I moved through the weekend, I found myself at times in a tug-of-war between experiencing the excitement of a big-city race and resisting the impulse to buy into the notion that this experience was something only a select few deserved. I got that feel the first night when Amir and I attended an invite-only pre-race party hosted by a major running publication. It felt cool to have been invited. But as we smiled and laughed our way through the party, the atmosphere rang of entitlement and privilege, and it occurred to me that I was welcomed in this space only because the powers that be had decided I could be. I was the same person I'd always been. The only difference was that the publication now saw me. It was almost like we were the kids who had been allowed to sit at the grown-up table.

I left the party with an acute awareness of how easy it is to fall for the feeling of exclusivity—how good it feels to be included, to think you're special. It came up again the next day when Candice and I bumped into Mary Wittenberg at the expo. "Oh, Alison," she said, "you must meet Kathrine Switzer." The three of us got in line, and when it was our turn to meet Kathrine, she was enthusiastic and gracious, hugging us and asking about our work. We took a bunch of photos, then Mary, Candice, and I went out to the finish line, a blue-and-yellow line painted on the street. People were posing, taking photos, giddy, as if we were on the red carpet at the Academy Awards. Mary, Candice, and I lay down on the finish line and took photos. I took one alone with my bib and found myself thinking, *Wow, I can't believe I'm here.* Then I stopped myself. *Wait, what is the big deal? What is special about Boston? Why is this marathon the marathon of all marathons?*

Boston's stature seems to stem from the fact that it is America's oldest continuous marathon, founded in 1897 after the running of the marathon at the first modern Olympic Games in Greece. Its qualifying standards were introduced in 1970 to keep the field size down. In the 1970s, Boston likely saw itself as the "Olympics" of marathoning in the U.S. at the time. The distance was not yet a mass participation event; the majority of people running marathons in the early '70s were fast men, mostly white, who were participating in what was then "amateur" athletics. But as participation grew and the marathon became a distance for all runners, Boston did not evolve. Other big-city marathons like New York, Marine Corps, Chicago, London, Berlin, and Tokyo all chose a lottery system to manage participation. Boston went through multiple changes to its qualifying times rather than doing the obvious—switching to a lottery system. It chose to be elitist rather than democratic.

Standing on the finish line, I glanced down Boylston Street to see if I was missing something. Nope. It was just a street. It wasn't twinkling or covered in gold.

Yet everywhere we went—the parties, the expo, the finish line—the idea that Boston was special was being sold. People were wearing previous Boston Marathon jackets and talking about past races—"Remember that year the weather was so hot? Remember when it was freezing rain?" The point wasn't remembering; it was to let you know that they'd been there before, that they were repeat members of the elite Boston club. I wanted to hold a mirror up to them: Can't you see we are back in high school, when we thought a varsity jacket made us more special?

I was at once excited for a marathon and frustrated and repelled by the mentality of "better," the uppity attitude that permeated the Boston scene. I appreciated being able to talk about my ideas on running being a vehicle for social change and activism at one of the sport's biggest races. It was fun having a marathon experience paid for. But I rejected the idea that we should be grateful for being allowed to participate at Boston. This was so salient to me that I skipped the conversation with Boston's longtime race director Dave McGillivray. The only thing I wanted to ask him was how he reconciled the cognitive dissonance of celebrating the joy of running for everybody when his race was only for a select few.

Hopkinton, where the race began, was to me almost a make-believe place. It was the quintessential colonial town, the kind depicted in snow globes and fairy tales. As Candice and I waited in our corral, I looked around for other Black people. We were starting with the charity runners, and I noted that there were more diverse body types than would've been expected in a fast-runners' race. Still, I could count the people of color on two hands.

The wave in front of us took off. We walked toward the starting line, and then we, too, were off. Boston's first miles are downhill, and as we started running, I thought how easy it felt, how I might actually enjoy this race. Maybe I was just being a hater; maybe there was indeed something transformational about Boston. But as we ran, the energy I felt didn't come from the race but from running with Candice. Everyone seemed to know Candice. People on the course, runners and spectators, would say, "Oh, are you Candice Huffine?" And then they'd see me and say, "Oh, are you Alison Désir?" She had included me in a campaign called Project Start, which followed the lives of a few women and how they'd gotten into running. We were mini celebrities, which kept my spirits up, fueled my ego.

But I grew uncomfortable as the race wore on. The course runs through a series of small, mostly white towns. Groups of white men were drinking beer on their front lawns—a frightening sight for me.

One moment you're a runner, the next you're a nigger. My body took on the weight of the fear, the hypervigilance of what could happen. I thought of white men heckling Ruby Bridges as she tried to exercise her right to an equal education. I thought of how white people see Black people and think *hoodlums,* and how I see white men and register *vigilantes.* The difference is prejudice plus power versus stereotyping and no power. White people could call and report a Black man walking down a street or Black people having a barbecue, and the police would respond, possibly with deadly force. If I called and reported white men drinking, not only would it seem weird, the police would likely not respond.

The miles didn't shake off the hypervigilance—white men drink along the entire course; if not on front lawns, then in pubs. I tried focusing on the crowds, the race energy, but the discomfort never fully lifted. Unlike the Brooklyn Half and the New York City Marathon, where more diversity created greater ease, Boston's whiteness was weight.

As Candice and I came up to the half, the crowds thickened and the volume intensified. Male runners began moving to the right toward a crowd of women. I'd heard about the tradition of kissing the Wellesley co-eds. As I ran past, I watched male runners grab women's faces and plant one on them. It was a horrifying scene, looking to me like a series of sexual assaults, a glorification of the bro culture of dominance. I had to look away.

As I ran, I kept waiting to experience the horrible beauty of Heartbreak Hill, but I never knew I was on it. The whole second half of the race seemed hilly, and, under-trained, I struggled. A brief respite came at mile seventeen when I saw a Black woman from New York who had run with Harlem Run on a few occasions up ahead. "Giiiirl" was all she had to say when I passed, and I already knew. A well-known photographer of color from New York stood at the top of one of the hills. I waved as he snapped a picture of me smiling, though internally I was wincing.

At mile twenty-two, I spotted the group from Harlem Run who'd taken time out of their busy lives to travel from New York to cheer Amir and me. When I passed, I wanted to cry, both with gratitude for their presence—they were the largest group of Black people I saw along the course—but also with fatigue. If I'd had money and known the train system, it's highly possible I would have stopped right then and there.

Up ahead, I spotted the Citgo sign. I couldn't remember what it was meant to signify, but people to my right and left stopped to take a photo. *Should I take a photo?* I wondered, and then laughed at the thought of stopping to take a photograph of a gas sign. I held on and made those famous turns: right on Hereford, left on Boylston. Spectators covered the sidewalk. The finish line loomed large, but it was also far away.

I had pulled ahead of Candice several miles back and ran across the finish with a random woman. We congratulated each other and went our separate ways. I pulled out my phone to text Amir. A woman next to me was crying, seemingly not from pain or relief, but from joy. I wondered what finishing Boston meant to her. Maybe she could fall apart now that 26.2 was over. Maybe she'd hit a time goal. Or maybe, having finally run Boston, she felt part of something she'd been excluded from before.

Around me, I heard a few people say they couldn't believe they'd finished Boston. All I felt walking through the finishing chute was relief at being done. Other marathons ranked higher than this experience for me. Rock 'n' Roll San Diego, because it was my first marathon and represented a turning point in my life. The New York City Marathon, because it lives up to the inclusive spirit it was built on; the race was run as four loops around Central Park until 1976, when the organizers pulled it out of the park and onto all five boroughs so that more people could participate. I felt that energy when I ran it, both in the race's spirit and in the bricks-and-mortar of each beautiful and diverse neighborhood. At Boston, I had no sense of achievement other than another marathon completed. If Boston truly was the pinnacle of running, then I would have experienced its specialness. But you have to buy into the idea of exclusivity to feel it.

What Boston showed me was just how deeply invested runners—and people in general—are in the idea of privilege. Exclusivity makes people feel good. It makes them feel special, better than others, when what it really means is that you've bought into an ideology of exclusion and marginalization. This showed up in a big way later in 2021, when we were deep into the Covid-19 pandemic. Boston held a virtual race alongside the in-person event to recoup revenue, and runners blew up in anger, posting comments like:

"It's not actually Boston if just anyone can run."

"People who run the virtual marathon should not be able to purchase and wear the finisher jacket."

"Why would Boston do this and ruin its reputation for everyone who has ever earned their spot?"

I wished these people had been joking, that their comments were followed by "lol." But they meant it. A Boston Marathon where anyone could participate was not a Boston Marathon they wanted to be part of.

Why? If the race is special, why would that change if it was open to more people?

For me, the issue begs a larger question: Where does your pride come from? Is it in relation to other people, from a position of dominance or being "better"? If you are better, someone else is lesser. If you are above, someone else is below.

Runners talk about the Boston tradition. But a tradition of what? If

Boston is the pinnacle, what does that say about what we value? Exclusivity is antithetical to the belief that running is for everyone. A sport open to all cannot elevate faster runners as more deserving of a race, of being more representative of runners. Can we see all runners as deserving of space and place? It comes down to asking, what is it we truly value: inclusion or exclusion?

THREE

14

Life and Death

first heard about the murder of Ahmaud Arbery while nursing my son, Kouri.

I became aware of Kouri's presence three days after conception. I was recovering from the 2018 New York City Marathon. My body was tired, but I knew something was different in a way I hadn't experienced before. There was a clear shift; it was as if my whole body was weighed down. The pregnancy wouldn't be detectable for weeks, but I already felt heavy.

Very early on, my ob-gyn prescribed progesterone. At thirty-four years old, I was on the verge of what doctors consider to be a geriatric pregnancy, and she wanted to ensure that I would have no trouble carrying the baby to term. The side effect was near-constant nausea, and the vomiting started soon thereafter. Once I got past the major milestone of twelve weeks, another issue arose. Every time I ran, I would bleed, and I landed in the emergency room multiple times, worried I was miscarrying. Each time I was assured that the baby was still fine, but it was as if the universe was telling me to give up the activity I loved. I switched to walking for a bit but was so uncomfortable I stopped exercising altogether and took bed rest.

As the baby grew, I felt my body expanding. Little pulls in the muscles. Fluid buildup. He grew in my uterus head up, in breech position, his head tucked in between my ribs, his bottom pushing on my sciatic nerve. Fibroids, common in Black women, grew outside my uterus, one to the size of an orange, which took up valuable real estate my baby needed to grow. I resigned myself to the pain and discomfort everyday tasks now came with, staying in touch with friends and Harlem Run through social media and home visits.

In July, thirty-six weeks pregnant, I headed to my ob-gyn's office on Fifth Avenue at Eighty-Seventh for a routine checkup. I waddled in (never realizing how accurate that verb could be until eight months pregnant) to the air-conditioned office, relieved at the respite from the sweltering New York heat. The assistant took me in right away and began taking my vitals. My blood pressure was high. "Take a few calming breaths," the assistant advised. She took my vitals again. My blood pressure was still high.

"I feel something pushing on my vagina," I told the doctor when she came in. Sure enough, I was dilated and Kouri's little foot was pressing into the birth canal.

"You're delivering today," the doctor said.

But we haven't even finished setting up his room yet, I thought.

The doctor ordered an emergency C-section and told me to head straight to the hospital.

I left in disbelief. I understood the words but could not make sense of them. My ordinary day had turned into my son's birthday.

Out on the street, I caught a cab, which seemed weird. *What, no ambulance?* Birth was both an emergency and utterly ordinary. I called Amir as we drove across town and asked him to grab the bag I had packed for a day just like this.

At Lenox Hill Hospital, a nurse settled me into a bed. She began a magnesium drip to lower my blood pressure. I tried to relax, but I was anxious. My mind kept returning to a statistic: Black women are three times more likely to die in childbirth than white women. The risk was greater for Black women in New York City, as much as twelve times greater. I was told I was preeclamptic (I had dangerously high blood pressure), which is also more prevalent in Black women; I lay there worried I would die before I even got to meet my baby.

I was at an affluent hospital on the Upper East Side. Presumably the best doctors were here, providing the best care. I had insurance, but none of this would save me. People think economic status is the reason for health disparities, but research points to race as the larger factor. Deaths are linked to institutional racism and the racial bias and stereotyping among medical professionals, who tend to dismiss the concerns of people of color. Black people and other racial minorities receive less accurate diagnoses, less pain management, and fewer treatment options, resulting in higher death rates, notably in heart disease, cancer, and maternal mortality. I worried that if I told the hospital staff I was having pain, they wouldn't believe me.

I thought about what happened to Serena Williams. After delivering a healthy baby girl, she had trouble breathing and told the nurse she was prone to blood clots and requested a lung CT scan and blood thinner. The nurse thought she was confused, so she ordered an ultrasound on her legs instead. The ultrasound was normal. Serena pushed for a CT scan and the hospital eventually complied. The results showed several small blood clots on her lungs, and she was quickly put on a blood thinner. If someone with as much wealth and influence as Williams could almost die during childbirth, what chance did I have?

A nurse gave me a painful steroid shot in my butt, a drug that would help Kouri's underdeveloped lungs mature more quickly. She then took my blood pressure for the fourth or fifth time. "It's not stabilizing," she said. The doctor moved my C-section up by several hours. I was alarmed. I pulled out my phone and began typing an email to Amir. Subject line: "Last will and testament." There was no time for sentimentality. I was straightforward about my wishes: *All my money is to go to you to take care of our baby (sorry about the student loans). Please have my mom help you raise the baby. I prefer that our child be raised without the influence of a religious institution.* I told him that I loved him and that hopefully nothing would happen to me.

Amir arrived just as the nurses finished preparations to take me to the OR. He quickly changed into scrubs and a hairnet. We kissed and took one last picture of us being a family of two. An attendant wheeled me to the operating room where the doctor was waiting. I looked at her. "Please don't let me die," I said, half-joking. She smiled. "I'm the best there is," she assured me. *Yes*, I thought, *okay, but seriously, don't kill me.*

The anesthesiologist administered a numbing agent to my back and told me that she would now give me the epidural. I took a deep breath and exhaled. It was the only time I wished I were a white woman.

Anesthesia hides the pain, but you still feel things. There was a sense of movement, the lifting off of something massive, and then the doctor held up a pale, wiggly, tiny baby above the curtain. "It's a boy!" she said. Amir let out a yelp and I felt myself smiling. I was so high from the anesthesia that I could not wrap my mind around the enormity of the moment. A nurse wrapped the baby in a blanket and handed him to me. We took a few photos—our first as a family of three—but then the nurse took him and whisked him away to the NICU. I remembered my grandmother had feared that the doctors would confuse her babies (she had six), so she never let them out of her sight. "Go!" I said to Amir. "Go! Go!"

No one tells you how painful a C-section is. When the anesthesia wore off, my belly felt like a ring of fire, burning, burning. But there was also the adrenaline of sudden comprehension: I had just birthed a human! My companion for nine months was now his own person in the world. It was hard to sleep, so I stayed up watching Amir sleep in a chair beside me. The nurses told me they would set up a camera for me to have 24/7 access to monitor the baby, but they hadn't done it yet, so the hours passed painfully slow.

Early the next morning, I was moved into what would be my room for the next few days and, good news, the camera was set up. I immediately went to the website on my phone. When I saw Kouri, my hand went to my mouth. *Oh, my tiny baby.* He had breathing tubes taped to his face. It was everything to see him. But I also felt cheated. I didn't get to have that moment of having my child set on my stomach and him climbing up to find warmth in the middle of my breasts.

Hours later the nurses informed me that I could visit Kouri, but I had to be able to walk to the NICU. (Why? Why not bring me in a wheelchair? To this day, I do not understand.) I pushed myself to stand and did a lap down the corridor, making it to the NICU. Amir recorded these first steps for posterity's sake. We entered the room, thoroughly washed our hands, and Amir led me to Kouri's little box. The nurses had created a little sign with his name on it, and my first tears fell since giving birth. I reached in and picked Kouri up. He felt about the same weight as my cell phone. I sat down and placed him on my chest, careful not to nudge the breathing tube. I looked down at him, and one of his hands was covering half his face, just as it had been in the ultrasound images. I felt myself smiling again.

Amir and I took him home three days later. Fear came, too. There was the worry of caring for this tiny human. I had never changed a diaper, never breastfed, never prepared a bottle, never ensured a tiny penis was clean, or that a baby was lain down properly so he wouldn't die in his sleep. I was also still worried I would die. Black women are at higher risk of hemorrhaging or experiencing preeclampsia postpartum. I'd read the stories: Kira Johnson went into hemorrhagic shock and died twelve hours after a scheduled C-section at Cedars-Sinai Medical Center in Los Angeles. Her husband had pleaded with the medical staff to tend to his wife's worsening condition, but they told him she was not a priority. Shalon Irving was an epidemiologist at the Centers for Disease Control and Prevention, where she was working to expose how structural racism and trauma made people ill and exacerbated existing health issues. She wanted to end the victim-blaming leveled at poor Americans and Black Americans for their health problems. Three weeks after giving birth, she died of complications related to high blood pressure.

I nursed the baby, changed the baby, put the baby to bed, and tried to rest myself. Only time released the fear of a postpartum death, but it was replaced by the anxiety that something catastrophic would happen. Objectively, I knew the symptoms and signs of postpartum depression and anxiety from my master's in counseling, but I was so deeply immersed in the fog and darkness, I couldn't make sense of what was happening. I had terrifying visions anytime I closed my eyes or had a moment to myself. I imagined Kouri rolling out of his bassinet and smashing into the floor. I saw myself accidentally slamming his head in the door and his head squishing. I imagined him drowning during bath time. Once, I closed my eyes to rest and saw myself throwing Kouri off a roof. I knew I wouldn't do any of these things or let them happen. Why, then, did I keep having these visions and thoughts? Wasn't this supposed to be the best time of my life, full of bonding and snuggles?

Amir saw my constant crying, he experienced my shouting—*I need you to help with the baby!* (but I wasn't letting him help with the baby)— and he eventually suggested I see someone. A psychiatrist increased my antidepressant dosage and it was only then, when the fear and anxiety subsided, that I could marvel at the tiny human we'd created.

Kouri was so communicative. I understood his different cries (for the most part). I knew his likes and dislikes (loves vegetables, hates fruit). He amazed me daily as he discovered new parts of himself and the world. As the months passed, I learned that Kouri loved music. As he gained control over his body, he began to wiggle and giggle anytime we put R&B on Pandora. During my pregnancy, I had felt the urge to dance more than ever, and I realized now that the urge came from Kouri. He loved to dance, and I had just been the vessel.

Kouri had trouble digesting, some kind of reflux, so anytime he drank milk, it would come out his nose and mouth, causing him to choke. The only way to keep him safe and ensure he wouldn't die in his sleep was to have him sleep on my chest after nursing. The weight of him at nine months felt like comfort, and I would sit for hours in a rocking chair, moving back and forth, flipping through my phone while he slept. One day in late April 2020, I saw that someone had posted a *New York Times* piece about the shooting of a young Black man in their Instagram stories. I swiped up.

The piece described the young man, Ahmaud Arbery, running in a neighborhood near his house when two white men chased him down in their truck with guns and shot him. The white men said they thought he might have been a burglar. They shouted at him to stop, they said, telling him they wanted to talk to him. Two white men with guns wanted a twenty-five-year-old Black man out for a run to stop. What should he have thought, that they'd all chitchat about the weather? There was a struggle over a shotgun and one of the men shot Ahmaud at least twice.

This line in the piece struck me: "a prosecutor who had the case for a few weeks told the police that the pursuers had acted within the scope of Georgia's citizen's arrest statute, and that Travis McMichael, who held the shotgun, had acted out of self-defense." The Black man was presumed violent and guilty. The white men were "protecting" themselves.

Another line: "[The prosecutor] noted that it was possible that Mr. Arbery had caused the gun to go off by pulling on it, and pointed to Mr. Arbery's 'mental health records' and prior convictions, which, he said, 'help explain his apparent aggressive nature and his possible thought pattern to attack an armed man.'" First, I wondered how the prosecutor got access to his mental health records. I also wondered how a man who had been chased and gunned down was now somehow being held responsible for his own murder. Two men go after you with guns. You cannot outrun them. Of course you're going to do everything you can to get the gun. It was Ahmaud who was acting in self-defense.

I was furious. The shooting had taken place sixty-three days earlier but was only now making national news. The men who had shot and killed him had not been arrested. The family was worried the case might disappear and their attempts to protest and draw attention to the murder were hampered by the coronavirus, so they turned to social media to coordinate a campaign with the hashtags #IRunWithMaud and #JusticeForAhmaud.

Not only had this young man been murdered; he had been murdered while out for a *run*. I thought about conversations happening in the running community about the safety of female runners. *Runner's World* had recently published an entire issue on the topic, with sobering data: 84 percent of female runners had been harassed or assaulted, including cases of murder, while running. *People must be talking about this*, I imagined. I flipped through social media, looking at the accounts of multiple running publications.

But there was nothing. I went to the pages of editors and influencers I knew. Nope, nothing. Nobody was talking about it. *Okay, maybe this isn't a big deal*, I thought, questioning myself, gaslighting my own knowing. If nobody was saying anything, maybe it wasn't a story worth writing about.

I called a friend, a Black man who had served in the army but now lived in Baltimore and was a local running crew leader. "This is exactly why I don't run at night," he said. "I run with a group in the early morning when the sun is up." We both heard the fallacy of his safety strategy as he was saying it. Ahmaud was shot in broad daylight. But we clung to his safety-in-numbers approach, which I used, too. We talked about how a Black man had been murdered, shot for running down the street. We talked about how this *was* a big deal. We repeated ourselves. White people had hunted down a Black man and shot him while running. We agreed, these white people were out of control.

Ten days went by. I spoke with a number of my Black and brown friends from Harlem Run. We already knew that doing normal everyday things like running or walking down the street could make us targets of police and vigilante violence. But this one hit too close to home. It had already been a tough year: Covid-19 had hit our communities hard, with a disproportionately high death rate landing on Black and brown communities across the country; the rate was double in New York City. We discussed the ever-present overpolicing in our neighborhoods. Running was essential to our mental health, essential for managing the hypervigilance we live with every day—maybe it was for Ahmaud, too—and yet we had to always consider how we were going to be perceived while doing it.

Then, a video of the shooting was made public. It occurred to me that I should not watch it. I had seen so many of these types of videos—Black people chased, cornered, shot, hands in the air, backs turned, then lifeless bodies on the ground. It had become so commonplace, and I did not need to see another lynching. But my curiosity got the better of me and I hit play.

I saw what I already knew: a Black man had fought for his life to the last moment. He was running toward the white truck that had chased him earlier. Which way to go? Was there a direction that would let him live? The younger white man was on the left. Ahmaud cut right, around the truck, and it was here, in front of the hood, when the first shot was fired, out of camera view. I wondered about the terror Ahmaud must have felt in that moment. I wondered if earlier, when the truck cut him off and he ran the other way, if he thought he might get away. Did he imagine he'd have a story to tell his friends later about the crazy white people going after him? Did he think he had a chance of returning home safely? When did it hit him that he was living the moment we hope will never happen? Was it when the second truck blocked the road? Or was it after, when he'd gotten around the truck, only to have the men and guns appear on the road again?

The scene was different but familiar. Memories that are not mine, but rather ours, our collective memory, surfaced. Emmett Till and the two white men who beat him beyond recognition. The white woman who later confessed to her lie, the lie that led to his murder and his murderers' acquittal. Did she not realize the humanity in Emmett, a fourteen-year-old boy? Memory took me to Freddie Gray, Sandra Bland, Tamir Rice, the Central Park Five. Growing up, grown-ups tell you: don't be caught at the wrong place at the wrong time. But when you get older, you realize that the wrong place and the wrong time could really be any day of the week, any hour of the day. White supremacy dictates the time; it dictates the lessons we all learn and the rules I will teach Kouri. Do not put your hands in your pockets while inside of stores. No, you cannot stay out late. If you're stopped, do what the officer asks. Smile and wave. Do not play with toy guns. Do not wear your hood up.

What good will rules do when a white person sees the color of my child's skin and centuries of anti-Black, white supremacist thinking spin their lies about him? I look at my beautiful, unique baby boy and wonder, at what age will he be discarded and murdered at the hands of white supremacists and police? Will he be twelve years old on the playground like Tamir Rice? Or will he be killed coming back from the store at seventeen like Trayvon Martin? Maybe he will be blessed to make it to young adulthood, only to be gunned down like Ahmaud?

My mind went to Ahmaud's mother, all the love she poured into her child. I wondered how many nights she sat up waiting for him to come home as a teenager. I thought about all of the worries she had for Ahmaud, not just him being a Black man, but worries of whether he'd find a career he liked, a person he loved, if he was happy. I wondered what she was doing right then, if she was in her son's room just to be closer to him. I wondered if she'd always feared this moment. I thought of Ta-Nehisi Coates's lines in *Between the World and Me*: "Black people love their children with a kind of obsession. You are all we have, and you come to us endangered."

Later, I listened to Ahmaud's mom on the news. She talked about how Ahmaud wasn't just a jogger, he was her son. He was loved by many. And they took her baby boy from her. I wondered what my reaction would be. Would I have the poise and composure of Ahmaud's mother, and so many other Black mothers during their prime-time interviews? Or would I fully embrace the burning rage I already felt and take homicidal action myself? A part of me fears that one day I will find out the answer to this question.

15

Confronting Whiteness

People say motherhood changes you. This was certainly true for me. There were the physical changes, of course; I would never have the same body (there would be no bounce back), and the nerve endings in my stomach were still finding and reattaching themselves after my emergency C-section, causing what felt like little electric shocks through my organs. More than that, though, my world had narrowed. The only thing that mattered to me was my son—his health, his safety, his future. What this boiled down to, in the frankest of terms, was giving less fucks about what people thought about me, particularly when it came to the world my son was now living in. I felt empowered to say what I wouldn't have said before on issues of racism and racial justice. My son's life, and the lives of future Black children, depended on it, and so I would speak my mind.

I remembered I had the email of the top editor at the nation's leading running publication. He'd reached out a few months prior to invite me to sit on a panel at the Olympic Marathon Trials, an invitation that told me he knew who I was, and on some level understood the impor-

tance of having a Black woman on a panel about women's running. So
I opened my computer and wrote him an email. I said that I was writing out of fear and anger. I knew the publication had covered the issue
of runner safety for women, most notably in a recent cover story, and
that the brand had launched a new alliance to address the problem. But
a discussion about the dangers of white supremacy for Black runners had
been notably absent from the conversation. I asked the publication to
bring attention to Ahmaud's death with the hashtag #IRunWithMaud,
and to publish an article about the unique and justified fears Black runners, Indigenous runners, and other runners of color have; how our
safety is compromised by white supremacy and the lack of justice we
receive from the legal system.

I took a screenshot of the email and posted it on Instagram. I hoped
people would see it, but didn't anticipate any sort of outcome. I put my
phone down, nursed the baby, took care of some emails. By the time I
looked at my phone again, it was on fire. Former elite runner and national champion Lauren Fleshman had reposted my post and tagged
other running and outdoor publications—*Women's Running*, LetsRun
.com, FloTrack, *Outside*, ESPN, RunnerSpace, *Sports Illustrated*—
calling on them to dedicate front-page space to the issues runners of
color face. Runners tagged other runners and more brands, media out-
lets, podcast hosts, coaches, running clubs, and organizations.

The outcry was loud and vocal, and people were rightly and justly
horrified by Ahmaud's murder. But I felt mostly anger. Why had it
taken my post to get the larger running community fired up about the
murder of a Black man? Where had they been? Don't these same people read the *New York Times*?

Two days later, runners across the country took to the streets to
run 2.23 miles for Ahmaud, the distance a remembrance of the day he
was killed: February 23. In Georgia, the McMichaels had finally been

arrested, almost ten weeks after the murder. It was May 8, on what should have been Ahmaud's twenty-sixth birthday. It wasn't until the evening that Amir and I finally got out to do our 2.23 miles. All day I kept telling myself I would do it, but something in me didn't want to. I was conflicted about honoring his life by running the miles associated with his death. I worried that the complexity of a human being could not be distilled into a day, that running a distance that marked his murder erased the life that he'd lived. Were we honoring Ahmaud? Or was this for us?

Amir and I put the baby in the stroller and headed out. We ran down 132nd to Randall's Island Park, did a small loop, and finished as a family. As always, I gained a sense of clarity that comes after a run. We were running for Ahmaud because that was his place of joy, something we as Black people all deserve to feel while moving through space.

The stories and comments about Ahmaud came, as I knew they would. I received a number of DMs from runners saying Ahmaud's murder had nothing to do with race. Other white runners strung together a narrative about how he had done something bad, that his khaki shorts were evidence that he was not even really out for a run, not really a runner. *What was he doing in that neighborhood?* some white people wondered, as if he had no right to be in that neighborhood. *Why did he not just comply?* others asked.

But the questions should not have been about Ahmaud, what he was doing, or what he was wearing. That's like asking a woman what she had on after being harassed or raped, as if a particular kind of clothing "caused" the crime. Ask about the men who pursued Ahmaud for more than twelve minutes, then cornered him and confronted him with a gun. Ask about the history of the neighborhood he was in, not why he was there. Ask: why did two white men who saw a Black man running down the street feel it was their right and responsibility to hunt him down?

White supremacy, that's why.

The McMichaels had hundreds of years of racial bias, territorial policing, and state and vigilante violence rendered against Black people, with impunity on their side. The history of whiteness and anti-Blackness and its ongoing narrative created the conditions for his murder. It began when the McMichaels saw Ahmaud's Black skin. History had taught them that Black people are criminal and scary. As far back as slavery, ads characterized Black people as physically strong and powerful—i.e., good workers—characteristics whiteness then weaponized by saying that same strength and power, combined with a primitive nature, made Black people dangerous. The stereotype persists. Black people are assumed to be dangerous and criminal, while the reverse is not true. Crimes committed by white people, such as the bombing executed by Timothy McVeigh, the acts of torture carried out by soldiers in Abu Ghraib, the murder of unarmed protesters by Kyle Rittenhouse, the murder of grocery shoppers by Payton Gendron, are assumed to be acts of an individual, not reflective of the white race. But if a Black person commits a crime, it is used as further "proof" that Black people are prone to such behavior. As one researcher put it, a Black or brown person "seems to be always on trial."

Video surveillance of a house being built in Satilla Shores, where Ahmaud was killed, shows that he entered the house, looked around, and continued on his run. It also shows that multiple people had done the same thing: Neighborhood kids, a white couple, a Black man in a white T-shirt who had been caught on camera multiple times. Nothing had ever been taken. No thefts had occurred. "He's been caught on the camera a bunch before," a man told a 911 dispatcher, assuming

Ahmaud was the man in the surveillance video. "It's kind of an ongoing thing out here." A gun, according to the younger McMichael, had recently been stolen from his truck.

That was what the McMichaels would use to justify going after Ahmaud. There was cause for "suspicion." The elder McMichael called 911, and then he and his son grabbed guns and went after him. Why chase him yourself when the police are on the way?

Because they could. White supremacy has allowed white people to police Black bodies for centuries, with little to no consequence. In fact, modern-day policing was born out of slavery. "Slave patrols" were created in the Carolinas in the early 1700s with one mission: to establish a system of terror to control Black people. The patrols' purpose was to squash slave uprisings, and officers were given the power to pursue, apprehend, and return runaway slaves to their owners, using excessive force as necessary to produce the desired behavior. The ability to control Black bodies was extended to all citizens through fugitive slave laws, laws that granted all white people permission to surveil, stop, question, and capture Black people. Even free Black people in slave states were not truly free, as law professor Elise C. Boddie wrote in her seminal paper "Racial Territoriality": They were subject to "being stopped, seized or taken up," a threat born of "the racist presumption that all blacks were subordinate to whites, whether they were enslaved or not." Fugitive slave laws eventually morphed into citizen's arrest laws in the U.S.—the laws the McMichaels would use in their defense. These laws eventually became covers for the lynchings that took place across the South with no arrests. White mobs harassed Black families who moved into white neighborhoods, again, with impunity. The men who killed Emmett Till were acquitted. George Zimmerman, who fatally shot Trayvon Martin, was acquitted. The four officers who beat Rodney King were acquitted. White supremacy lets white people literally get away with killing Black people without consequence. As

Ta-Nehisi Coates so eloquently wrote in *Between the World and Me*, "In America, it is traditional to destroy the Black body."

The history of the neighborhood where Ahmaud was murdered also mattered. Satilla Shores, where Travis McMichael shot Ahmaud, is a historically white suburban area. A couple of miles away is Fancy Bluff, the historically Black area where Ahmaud lived. A four-lane highway separates the neighborhoods, serving for years as the de facto border between the Black and white communities. The color line had blurred over the last decade or so as a few Black families moved to Satilla Shores and white families bought homes in Fancy Bluff. But the racial meaning didn't disappear because a few families crossed the color line. It simply meant that a Black family was living in a white neighborhood or vice versa. A Black person, like Ahmaud, going for a run in Satilla Shores was a Black man running in a white space.

"This country's racial hierarchy has depended to a significant degree on the maintenance of racially distinct spatial territories across neighborhoods and a vast swath of other private and public institutional spaces," Boddie wrote in "Racial Territoriality." "The spatial separation of whites, the exclusion of people of color from white-identified spaces, and the vigilant enforcement of racial boundaries have been integral to this effort. The power of the state has been deployed to 'protect' white space and to 'contain' nonwhite space, while regulating the movement of people of color within and across various racial borders."

The presence of a few Black people can make a space seem diverse to white people. But for Black people, the white space is unchanged, and the rules of engagement are intact. Our survival depends on our ability to make sense of racialized expectations for us in every environment we enter. We know that anything can happen at any time: at a moment's notice, you can go from experiencing a runner's high to being hunted down, and there will be no recourse. So where do you run to avoid the risks? How much do you limit yourself? Do you choose safety, or do you choose exploration? If you choose exploration, what will the consequences be?

No doubt Ahmaud weighed these questions over the years he ran. Had he run at Satilla Shores before? Had those runs given him a sense of safety? We cannot ask him. What we know: the white vigilantes—operating as agents of the state—sought to protect white space from assumed Black criminality and put Ahmaud back in "his place." "Stop right there, dammit just stop," the elder McMichael is heard saying on the video. Another white supremacist action: the expectation of Black people to obey, to do what we are told, to take commands from white people. Would the elder McMichael, if being chased by men with guns, stop? Would he assume the men with guns just wanted to talk?

kept returning to the 911 transcript of a man telling a dispatcher that another man had entered a house under construction.

"Are you saying someone's breaking into it right now?" the dispatcher asked.

"No, it's all open and it's under construction and he's running right now," the man said. "There he goes right now."

"OK. What is he doing?"

"He's running down the street."

"Okay. That's fine. I'll get them out there. I just need to know what he's doing wrong."

Some white runners were able to see that a Black person's agency is very different from a white person's. One runner wrote on Instagram about the freedom a white man knows: "I almost always feel safe while running," he said. "Even when I shouldn't. I've found myself down dark alleys at night. Or on private property, have taken a wrong turn. There are even times I've trespassed knowingly, wanting to get to that beach or down that trail, all the while figuring it'll be all right. Many runners don't have that privilege. To move so freely without fear. Or to make a mistake. To just be human."

Another white man told me in a DM that he was taught that all he needed to do was go out and claim what he wanted. This is what white men do, he said. You want land in the "new" world? Take it. Want to go West? Go West. You get these messages your whole life, he said, that you can take and take and take.

Shortly after I posted on Instagram about the running industry's silence on Ahmaud, I received an email from an editor at *Outside* magazine asking if I was interested in writing an op-ed. There was an inevitability to this moment. I had been surrounded my whole life by white people who did not see whiteness and who did not see me, and the running community was no different. We are divided along racial lines, largely segregated into white running groups and Black ones. We do not talk about this as an industry or community. Running ignores race in the same way the nation does. It pretends that there is no divide, no race problem; it pretends to be color-blind. Running believes it is a sport that welcomes everyone, when it remains a sport that primarily prioritizes and celebrates white experiences while having no clue that there are other experiences.

I imagined this beautiful human being I'd brought into the world, and how hard it was to carry him; for him to then be twenty-six years old and be shot dead? It was my responsibility to care for my son, not just at home, but by ensuring the world is a place in which he can thrive. What kind of world did I want my son to grow up in? It wasn't this one. I also worried that the moment we were in—the one in which

the global running community was fired up about racial justice—
would be a moment in time, rather than a real reckoning. Could I extend that moment by confronting whiteness head-on, by calling out
what the running world did not see? It was worth a try.

So I sat down and wrote, and realized the words had already been
written. They flowed out of me from decades ago, from five minutes
earlier, all coalescing around one identity: motherhood. I wrote everything that I'd been feeling and observing—about the danger my son
was in, the racial climate of the running industry, the fact that we don't
talk about it. I ended by asking people if they were ready to work for
change.

The piece was published on the day we ran for Ahmaud, May 8,
2020, and titled with clarity: "Ahmaud Arbery and Whiteness in the
Running World." I didn't know if anything would come of it, but I
knew nothing would stop me from saying what needed to be said.

16

Running While Black

I didn't leave the house for several days after my op-ed was published. It was unconscious at first. Only after a couple of days of being inside did I realize I hadn't been out. *Maybe I should get some air*, I thought. But I didn't want to. If I never left, I could never be killed.

What is the line between reasonable and paranoid? I didn't know. I didn't judge myself for it. In the local news that week, police officers shot another Black man dead in a high-speed chase. It seemed logical that the safest thing to do was stay inside, and so I did. I ignored news alerts, glanced at social media intermittently, and focused on caring for my son.

I watched him poop and smile and tumble over, and for stretches of time I was lost in the present moment, lost to the singular task of keeping a child fed, clean, happy—and alive. My mind wandered to Ahmaud, to the recent shooting, then Kouri would cry or laugh and pull me back. We paced the house, pausing at the window. I watched people milling on the sidewalk, trucks pulling in and out of the warehouse across the street. Cars honked and the sun hit the Harlem River. The world hummed on and I felt no pull to insert myself in it. It crossed my mind that I might give up running because of white supremacy.

One afternoon I received a request from Amira Rose Davis, host of the *Burn It All Down* podcast, to appear on the show. I was a huge fan of her work. She was a professor of history and African American studies and her scholarship centered the experiences of Black women in sport. The podcast featured guests who were my heroes, like Wyomia Tyus and Gwen Berry. I was honored to be invited to talk about my recent piece in *Outside*.

We started off by talking about Mother's Day and the weight I carried that weekend following Ahmaud's murder and the publication of my op-ed. Then we segued into a wide range of topics, touching on the grand myth of running as the great equalizer and the unique burden white supremacy places on Black youth and us as parents. Amira, a mother of two boys and a girl, said the first paragraph of my piece spoke to her. She, too, worried that her child would be shot or murdered, and discussed how Black children are seen as older than they are. Tamir Rice, for example, was described as a "man" despite being twelve years old. At what age would her sons cross the line from adorable to being seen as a threat?

I told her that when I look at my son, I think about the ways I want to set him up for success and that I want to introduce him to the outdoors and running and give him access to things I didn't have until I was older. But in the back of my mind, I wonder to what extent I am setting him up to feel too comfortable. God forbid he's hiking or running and someone sees him as a threat. Or he's making some ordinary teenage mistake and a cop pulls his gun. How do I prepare him to be self-assured, to own and fill the spaces he is in, while also making sure he understands that shrinking yourself is sometimes necessary for survival?

Amira told me about a debate a colleague of hers has been having.

He wonders if wearing a mask while running will make him look more threatening, but since he's pushing his daughter in a stroller, maybe that'll signal he's not a threat. It's a constant, complex equation.

"High-level math," I said.

"Exactly!" she replied.

I told her about my own debates about a mask—choosing between protecting my health and that of the people around me, or catering to the white gaze for survival. I told her that I think about the relative safety of my neighborhood before heading out, and rationalize that if I am stopped by a cop or have an incident with a white person, I have the ability to stay calm, maybe talk myself out of anything bad happening, even though I know safety isn't guaranteed and the strategy could fail.

I finished the podcast thinking about how living and running as a Black person requires a constant negotiation around what might pose the least harm. What do you do, how do you live, when going outside could get you killed?

After nine days inside, I opened the refrigerator and saw empty shelves. I was confined to roughly seven hundred square feet of apartment space in the Bronx, where we'd moved just before the baby was born. Tiny hands were grabbing at me; the baby's whines came in what seemed like a constant livestream. I wanted air. I wanted to move. Also, with Amir at work all day, if we wanted to eat, I would need to go to the store.

I tucked the baby into the stroller and walked across the Willis Avenue Bridge to the Whole Foods in Harlem and back, 2.5 miles round trip. It felt good to be in motion, to inhale fresh air. I tried not to wonder if walking out in public was a mistake. I tried not to wonder about the people we passed: could this be the person who kills me?

Kouri and I went out every couple of days. I pushed the stroller down 132nd to the bike path over the Bronx Kill to Randall's Island Park. The fields were empty, unused due to pandemic-canceled baseball, soccer, and softball games. What would have been a crowded and buzzing walkway belonged only to us. I could almost feel a sense of peace.

A few days later, I headed out again. This time, just after the Metro-North stop on 125th near Lexington, I stopped short. Twenty cops had descended on two Black men who were fighting. Twenty cops. I pulled out my phone and began recording. I stayed until the men were detained without incident, all the while wondering if this was the moment I would witness a police killing, or if this was the moment I would become a target for recording it all on camera.

A week passed. More news: In Minneapolis, a white police officer held down a Black man by forcing his knee into his neck for nine minutes, taking his life. A Black woman, Darnella Frazier, captured the murder of George Floyd on camera. New York, along with the rest of the United States, took to the streets to protest. Anger turned to rioting and New York City mayor Bill de Blasio instituted an 8:00 p.m. curfew. Amir was coming home from work in those days and I knew the curfew would provide a convenient avenue for police to arrest Black people. Who were going to be more closely scrutinized at 8:05?

When I was a child, I watched Rodney King being beaten on the television. I was in the basement getting my hair braided by my mom when the report came on the screen. My mom wasn't paying attention—she was focused on getting my parts straight as I wiggled around—so the moment went unaddressed. But afterward, I lay in bed at night for weeks waiting for my dad to come home, wondering if that could happen to him. Now, I worried about Amir. I sat on the rocking chair and held the baby and my breath, only exhaling when he walked through the door.

The murders of Ahmaud Arbery and George Floyd resulted in an uptick in reporting on how white supremacy destroys Black people, both in running and outside of it. It was impossible to look at mainstream media and social media without coming across an article or a post.

One was from my friend Mirna Valerio, aka The Mirnavator. She wrote about an experience she had at the end of a long run. She was in Georgia, where she lived at the time, and was decked out in bright clothes—technical attire, gear that indicated she was running. But near the end of a run, a white woman in an SUV passed her and pulled over ahead of her. Mirna ran past and saw the woman on the phone, so she smiled and waved. The woman left. Five minutes later, a cop car rolled by, so she smiled and waved again. A second cop car came from the opposite direction. Mirna was incredulous. "I'm like, what the fuck," she wrote in her post. "This is two miles away from my house. And you know, in my head I'm like, I'm running. I am just running."

Another post, from another friend: Liz Rock, cofounder of the women's running group TrailblazHers in Boston. Liz wrote about running the final miles of the Baystate Marathon with a friend when two white men shouted at them: "FUCKING NIGGERS!!" The men slowed their truck down to make sure the runners could hear them. She and her friend looked at each other. *Did that just happen?* Her friend was riled up, but they took some breaths and finished the race.

I felt every one of the stories I read. I felt the pain and the trauma. I felt the anger and frustration. Their stories tapped into my own fear. You tell yourself it can't happen to you, but it can. You talk yourself into believing such incidents aren't as common as they seem. And yet they are. Every Black person has a story of being policed, surveilled, watched. Of being harassed or othered in one way or another, at work, at a social gathering, at a park, on the street. Every family has their language or ritual around safety—Amir insists I turn on my GPS tracking so he knows where I am when I'm running. I ask him not to go running at night after work if it's dark.

I read an *Outside* Q and A with Olympic marathoner Meb Keflezighi and learned of his family's ritual. When he heads out for a run, his wife says to him, "Safe travels" or "Get home safe," and they both know they're talking about more than traffic. I should not have been surprised to learn that Meb experiences what we all do, but a part of me was surprised because he is so recognizable. I was a little shocked to read that he's been flipped off, been asked what the hell he was doing there, that he takes a white friend to the golf course he likes to run at so he won't get stopped by security. I could relate to him talking about "that *thing*"—the hypervigilance, the wondering, the looking over your shoulder. "Am I really safe?" Meb wonders.

This person was our country's greatest marathoner. If you were to see him running down the street, it'd be clear he was an athlete. I didn't think I was holding on to any shred of belief that any Black person would be exempt from acts of racism, or the possibility of being murdered. I've always said Obama could be shot running down the street in a hoodie. But reading about Meb struck me. If it could happen to Meb, it could happen to anyone, anywhere, at any time. It could happen to me.

Later that summer, I traveled to Seattle to meet with Sally Bergesen, CEO of Oiselle, my new sponsor. I'd first heard of Oiselle when Bergesen confronted Nike and its dominance in track and field by using Photoshop to place the Oiselle logo over a Nike swoosh on the Team USA uniform of Kate Grace and posting the image on Instagram during the 2014 International Amateur Athletic Federation World Relays. Bergesen wanted to show the world who the athlete's sponsor really was. I thought it was a bold move and I started following Bergesen on Twitter. She followed me back. Our relationship built from there. It seemed to me that Oiselle was a company that embraced disruption and was interested in changing the way the industry worked. When my Under Armour contract ended, I signed with the brand.

Since starting to run, I'd made it habit to explore new places on foot. Amir and the baby had come with me, and shortly after settling in to our Airbnb, we put Kouri in the stroller and headed out. It felt good to be outside of New York during what seemed like a safe moment to travel while still in the midst of the pandemic. I didn't know much about Seattle other than it was where Amazon and Microsoft were based, and that it is predominately white, meaning potentially inhospitable and hostile to Black people.

As we ran, I started noticing yard signs, some on lawns, some propped up in front of the front doors or in a window. "In this house, we believe Black Lives Matter, no human is illegal, science is real . . ." Seeing the signs offered a small comfort and I started scanning the neighborhood for them, realizing they could create a safe running route. It was superficial—anything could still happen to me no matter what signs were posted. But the mind adds and subtracts, it multiplies and divides until it lands on some sort of something that might equal safety. *Okay,* I thought, *maybe there are people here who will see our humanity.*

For much of the rest of the year, I collected stories of Black runners harassed while running. I don't know why. But it became sort of an obsession for a while.

A Black man was out for a run in San Antonio, Texas, when two cops stopped and detained him, claiming he fit the description of a suspect.

A woman in Los Angeles verbally assaulted three Black women who were running. "You guys are so violent," she shouted. "You Africans are so (expletive) violent."

A Black man was doing push-ups in lane eight of a public track in Potomac, Maryland, when a white man told him to move out of his way. The Black man pointed out that lanes one through seven were available. The white man replied, "Well, what are you going to do the next time I come around and step on your head?"

Sometimes I shared the stories on social media, or I talked about the reality we face when we run in my posts. Black runners responded knowingly, sometimes chiming in with their own similar situations. White runners typically told me I should stop tainting their running experience because these incidents had nothing to do with running, or they expressed shock that such discrimination and violence was still happening in 2020. Their shock was frustrating; a sign of white privilege, of not paying attention, of racial ignorance.

I did an interview with FloTrack, the running news and race streaming site, and the white reporter wanted to know what running was like for me. He said that in general, runners experience a beautiful feeling of release and joy from being outside moving, and he wondered if being Black meant I didn't feel that. I told him I feel that, but that I also feel a sense of terror. That every time I run, I am subject to forces beyond my control, and I cannot count on the legal system to back me up. I explained that this is our experience and our fear.

I continued searching for stories, and every few weeks I found another. A Black man was handcuffed and detained while jogging in Florida. A white woman threw a bottle and shouted a racial slur at a Black

woman running in Queens. ICE agents in Boston stopped and questioned a Black man who was running by them.

I pasted the links into a Google Doc and titled it "Running While
Black." I see now that creating this list was a reality check, a reminder
to not get too comfortable, to watch my back. It was a reminder that I
am not crazy for worrying. I am not imagining things. The threat is
there all the time. It is real and it is part of our every day.

17

The Unbearable Whiteness of Running

In late June 2020, a graphic of *Runner's World* covers from the last several decades appeared on social media. It featured forty-two covers over multiple decades, lined up side by side. The person featured on nearly every cover was thin and white. It was glaring. The graphic accompanied a post for a podcast episode called "Racing for Representation" on *Keeping Track*, a program hosted by elite runners Alysia Montaño, Molly Huddle, and Roisin McGettigan-Dumas. The women had been talking among themselves about the lack of representation in running media, particularly on magazine covers. They wondered if this was their perception or if the data would bear this out. But they couldn't find any data, so they reached out to fellow runners Francine Darroch and Heather Hillsburg, both sociologists with Ph.D.s, and asked them to conduct a study.

Doctors Darroch and Hillsburg analyzed the covers of three North American publications (*Runner's World*, *Women's Running*, and *Canadian*

Running) over an eleven-year period (2009–2019) and found that yes, the data supported their perception. Of the 284 covers, white people were featured 80 percent of the time. On its own, *Runner's World* featured white people 85 percent of the time, a statistic representative of the publication since it began in the late 1960s. To me, the findings were validating. I'd been running for seven years and had rarely seen Black people featured in the media. I had always known the sport was white. Now there was data that quantified that whiteness. The data and the image proved to me just how white the industry was, how much it valued whiteness, and how it presented whiteness as the standard.

That summer I learned the depth of it.

The August issue of *Runner's World* featured Alysia Montaño on its cover for the first time. Alysia is a hero of mine. She is an amazing runner—a national champion, a world champion, an Olympian—but she is also an activist. Alysia had taken on Nike in an op-ed for the *New York Times* for its hypocritical maternity clause and helped change how the industry approached motherhood in its contracts with athletes. We'd recently gotten to know each other via text and phone calls and had bonded over our love of running and being Black mothers and runners. We discussed the discomfort of being The Only at a race, and the emotional exhaustion that comes from feeling like you have to represent all Black people.

I had mixed feelings when I saw the cover. I was proud and happy for my friend. But I was also annoyed. There were so many moments in her career that had warranted a cover. When she won the national championships in the 800 meters four years in a row, from 2010 through 2013; when she competed in the national championships eight months pregnant in 2014; when she returned the following year to regain her title. But it had taken the murder of a Black runner for the magazine to acknowledge her greatness and the power of her story.

I read the interview, nodding as I went. I recognized myself in the points she made about activism coming naturally, pregnancy not being an illness, and the relief she had after her op-ed was released. She had broken the silence, and other women were now coming forward with their stories. I'd felt similarly when my op-ed was published. By naming the industry's whiteness, I'd spoken about something considered taboo—race—and helped to create space for our stories. I found myself shouting aloud when I read her response to a question about her role as a woman leader in the sport. Her role, she said, has been as the oppressed. Because of that, she's been a fighter and a yeller. Everybody who is not Black, Indigenous, or a person of color (i.e., white people) needs to be asked what their role is, she said. *Yes!*

But as I kept reading, I became alarmed. The reporter asked about the discrimination she'd experienced during her career and Alysia told a story about the U.S. National Championships in 2011. Alysia lined up as the 800-meter defending champion, the woman who'd run the fastest time in the distance the year before, and as the bronze medalist at the World Indoor Championships. But when the announcers introduced the athletes, they did not name her. Instead, they discussed the two blond, blue-eyed women on the starting line. These women were fast, too, and deserved attention. But Alysia was the clear front-runner, and she was not mentioned.

It took me a moment to process this. She was on the starting line of a major race as the defending champion, and she was not introduced? I imagined the mental toll that must have on an athlete in the minutes or seconds before competition. How do you absorb that and not let it disrupt your focus? I couldn't help but think that while all athletes feel the pressure of competition, she had to shoulder the additional weight of racism. That she went out there and pressed the pace from the beginning gave me goose bumps. It was pure brilliance; by taking the lead, she had forced the announcers to name her.

Later that year, at the World Championships in Daegu, South

Korea, Alysia took fourth in the 800-meter final, while one of her white U.S. teammates took sixth. (Positions later changed when Russian women were disqualified for doping.) Alysia said she walked into the media mixed zone knowing FloTrack would want to talk to her. How could they not? She was the highest placing American in the race. But the reporter looked at Alysia, then looked past her to the white teammate behind her. "Maggie," the reporter said to the white woman, "you're the highest [American] finish; you placed sixth."

My jaw dropped. I shouldn't have been shocked, but I was. The racism was so blatant. The reporter literally pretended not to see her.

The incident made it clear that whiteness and white supremacy are embedded in the industry. From the reporters covering the sport, to the announcers at the races, to the editors who decide who appears on covers, who to cast as models, whose experiences are featured—whiteness permeates all of it. While no data exists for running media specifically, a 2021 analysis by the Institute for Diversity and Ethics in Sport found that sports media remains largely white and predominately male. Across multiple newspapers and websites, 79 percent of sports editors were white and 77 percent of reporters were white, with similar numbers across assistant editors, copy editors, columnists, and web specialists.

The same was true of running shoe, apparel, and gear companies. The decision makers across the entire industry were largely white people, specifically white men. This came to light in a story published that summer in the online magazine *The XC*, titled "The Whiteness of the Running Industry." It was written by a brown-skinned man from Toronto who conducted an analysis of the people who sat at the helm of the sport's leading brands—Nike, New Balance, Hoka, Adidas, Brooks, Garmin, Lululemon, and more. He also looked at the people who comprised their executive teams and board of directors.

His findings: In 2020, only one of the eighteen CEOs or COOs at top running brands featured in the story was a person of color. (There might have been two, but how the person identifies was not clear.) Two of the executives were women, both white. Out of the 223 people in executive positions or on the board in those same companies, only five were people of color, or 2 percent.

When all the power is in the hands of white people, Black people are not seen. The reporter didn't see Alysia. Editors didn't see her, nor did the announcers, until they were forced to. A similar erasure happened during the women's Olympic Marathon Trials in Atlanta in 2020. Aliphine Tuliamuk and Sally Kipyego, two Black American athletes, were rarely mentioned by announcers, despite being a constant presence in the lead pack. I remember watching these women compete on TV from a bar on the course—I had been invited by *Runner's World* to be on a panel at the Trials—and then cheering for them on the sidewalk as they ran by. The cognitive dissonance was glaring: all the fans on the sidewalk with me were screaming for Aliphine and Sally; the announcers calling the race hardly said a peep.

Aliphine won, with Sally taking third. The women became the first Black women to represent the United States in the Olympic marathon, a huge milestone. But the media focused on the second-place winner, Molly Seidel, a white woman. Her story was incredible. She'd taken time off from the sport to overcome an eating disorder. Hers was a story of prioritizing one's health, a story of the underdog triumphing, a story we needed. But so was Aliphine's. Her story was the so-called American Dream we are taught to believe in—an immigrant making it to the top. She came to the U.S. from Kenya for college and went on to become one of the best female distance runners in the country. But the press focused on Molly. The *New York Times*, for example, gave her more space in its story and never mentioned the historic nature of the Black women's achievements. Even though America loves a winner, the article treated Aliphine almost as a side story.

In the coverage that followed, the articles that did mention Aliphine often chose details that exoticized her—the large number of siblings she had, for example—rather than humanized her as they did for Molly. In a tweet, Aliphine shared that she broke down watching the Trials coverage. "I cried the 1st time I watched the replay," she said. "I felt uncelebrated, like I wasn't even visible. It hurt, then the 6 more times that I watched it, I got enraged." Sally Kipyego, despite her historic feat, seemed to all but disappear from the coverage.

Before someone told me these two women had become the first Black women to represent the U.S. in the Olympic marathon, I'd had no idea that first was in contention. The historic nature of what could unfold in the race was not a storyline in the buildup to the Trials or as the race played out. The entire running community was not cheering for them to achieve this milestone. The Black women's achievements were not visible or valued.

It is this invisibility that makes running's whiteness unbearable. We are here, but we are not seen. White people's accomplishments are celebrated above our own. We are exoticized. Or we are whitewashed. "Nike," Alysia told *Runner's World*, "was always marketing the lighter, whiter version of anything that was me."

I didn't have to imagine the women's pain and fury. I knew what it felt like to not be seen or valued. But their erasure played out on a national stage and in public, and had financial costs. At one point, Alysia's contract had a clause that offered her a bump in pay if she made the cover of *Runner's World*. She joked about how impossible that was and wondered why the magazine listed in her contract couldn't have been *Ebony*. Media coverage generally shows an athlete's sponsor their value as a marketing voice and influencer, and lack of coverage can reduce an athlete's bargaining power.

The larger social cost is nothing short of deadly. Media shapes perception, biases, and norms. As Dr. Hillsburg said on the *Keeping Track* podcast: "The *lack* of communication communicates to us that racialized people don't belong." It informs who can run freely and who remains a suspect. When everyone sees mostly white runners in the media, Black people are not seen or understood as belonging in that space. A Black person running is not normalized. Instead, the media perpetuates the stereotype that a Black man only runs in public when he is running from trouble; a criminal fleeing a scene—the perception that killed Ahmaud Arbery.

Later, when I looked back at the image of the *Runner's World* covers, I saw an industry that not only valued whiteness, but an industry that failed to acknowledge our presence in the sport. An industry that failed to see us.

18

Doing the Work

Can an industry change? Or rather, will it?

That was the real question my *Outside* story was asking: now that you know, now that I have shown you what you have refused to see for so long, what will you do?

In the weeks following the *Outside* story, it seemed the industry was asking the same question. My DMs and email inbox lit up, and I had countless calls with editors, event organizers, store managers, and podcast hosts. I thought maybe the industry had reached a tipping point, maybe folks were ready to do something about the sport's systemic racism. It was exciting at first—my story had had an impact, and I met each call with a mix of emotions: anger, relief, hope.

But it quickly became clear that even white people wanting to bring about change in the industry were not prepared for conversations on race. They had little to no racial awareness. They had no idea whiteness even existed, let alone that running itself was steeped in it. Honestly, they were clueless. It was as if I'd dropped a truth bomb and the industry was running around trying to make sense of it. *Running is white? Is that bad? What do you mean, "racial divide"? White supremacy? Racism?! Holy crap, what do we do?!* Understanding race seemed mystical, intangible. It was hard not to tell them to get a grip and read a book. It would've been comical if it hadn't been so painful.

This ignorance came alive on a podcast I did with a white store owner who lives and breathes running. He said he believed his store and events were for every runner, and until this moment, that had never been called into question. But after reading my article, he realized the people who made up the vast majority of his customers were white, even though he lived in a city that was nearly half Black. "I go to conferences and it's a bunch of white dudes," he said in the amazed (and what I really want to call asinine) tone of a white person seeing whiteness for the first time. I knew I was Black and what that meant in this world by the first grade, while a white man in his early forties was uncovering his racial identity on this podcast with me. How, Sway?

In the course of conversation, I had to explain the term *white supremacy* to him. He thought it meant extremism, the KKK, white nationalists. "That's not what you're talking about, or is that what you're talking about, or not what you're talking about?" he said, fumbling. So I explained that white supremacy was not simply extremist views or people, but rather the economic, social, and political structure of our nation. It was the idea that white is the norm and everyone else a deviation from it. Talking to him was like doing group work in high school or college when someone doesn't do the reading and expects you to catch them up.

On a call with editors, I was met with ums and sorrys and long pauses as they tried to understand why not having Black people on the cover of their magazine was problematic. They were flummoxed by where to begin. It seemed pretty obvious to me, and I told them as much. Hire editors of color. Use Black sources. Tell the full range of Black stories. Put Black people on the cover of your magazine!

Race directors at trail events were perplexed as to why no Black people showed up at their races. They insisted their races were "welcoming" and "open to everybody," so I had to explain that just because white people think their race (or store or group) is welcoming doesn't mean it actually is to people of color. The wilderness can be a dangerous place for Black people, one that can recall images of strange fruit hanging from poplar trees. This statement drew blank stares from white people. They had no context for my comment, no understanding of the harm done to Black bodies in the woods, no awareness of the collective memory of that harm we carry with us that can make events uncomfortable, if not frightening. Particularly when events are held in historically racist places, or places where white nationalism thrives.

Some white people's reactions were alarmist. They were shocked to learn about racism and insisted we must do something now, resulting in urgent emails—*Can you host a panel this weekend? How do we "fix things?!"*—as if systemic racism could be addressed overnight, with a simple checklist that would make the work easy and digestible for them. White people didn't realize they knew nothing about race and might need to educate themselves. Instead, they were convinced they should be "listening to us," which sounds nice, but it's impossible to have a meaningful conversation on race if the time is spent educating white people on race. It's impossible to feel safe sharing experiences of racial harm when the people you're talking to do not have a historical understanding or awareness to hold space for your experiences.

For a while, I felt it was my duty to answer every call and make myself available. But then I decided I couldn't spend my life answering white people's uninformed questions on race. So I started saying no. It was hard, actually. I felt bad, like I was not doing what I was supposed to be doing. White people were disappointed. I got the feeling that they thought I should be saying yes—*you're Black, aren't you supposed to educate us on race?* Once I accepted that I was not responsible for white people's racial education, I was finally able to let go.

So when a Black woman who did DEI (Diversity, Equity, and Inclusion) work reached out to see if I was interested in hopping on a call with a group of white people who were forming a coalition to address racial diversity in the running industry . . . I wasn't. The idea that white people who knew nothing about race and racial work would be leading a coalition on racial diversity made my eyes roll so far back in my head, I heard my grandmother telling me to be careful or they'd get stuck that way. And really, hadn't I already given enough free labor?

But an Indigenous community leader had already agreed to join the call, and she posted on social media that she wished the running industry had something similar to the outdoor industry's DEI effort. *Okay*, I thought, *I will do this in support of her.* So I said yes.

We met on Zoom. There were two white men and one white woman, all in the running retail business, plus the Indigenous leader, the Black woman who'd brought us on and who was serving as their adviser, and me. The call began with one of the men explaining that they'd all been deeply affected by Ahmaud's murder. Ahmaud was a runner, and he had opened their eyes to racial violence and what it means to run as a Black person. They decided it was time to explore what the industry should do. The man's eyes welled with tears. *Here we go*, I thought. Was I going to have to comfort a white man newly awakened to racial harm? I bit my lip.

The group went around in a circle introducing themselves. When it was my turn, I started by saying that the running industry is part of the problem. It is rooted in whiteness and white supremacy and this was what the industry needed to address.

The white people shifted in their chairs, and their faces went stony save for one man, who blew up.

"Don't call me a white supremacist!" he said, his hands flying up in the air. "White supremacists are skinheads who hate people. KKK. Nazis. I'm not like that."

I'd been on multiple calls with racially ignorant white people, but this was the first time white fragility had exploded in front of me. I took a breath and explained as I had for the podcast host that the definition of white supremacy was broader than the extremist understanding. I also told him that it was his responsibility to understand these terms if he was going to be involved in this work. He couldn't hear me. He was too deep into defending his "good person"—i.e., non-racist—status.

"I am nice to Black people," he said, defiant. "I put a kid in Africa through college. One of my best friends is Black. He, he, he named his son after me." A common tactic, the "I have a Black friend" defense. I believe he actually repeated it. "I mean, my GOD, He. Named. His. Son. After. Me."

I didn't know whether I wanted to laugh or scream. The average Black person without a formal education knows more about racial issues in our country than a formally educated white person. White ignorance is part of what keeps a white supremacist system in place. If we don't acknowledge it exists, then there's nothing to address. White supremacy is the system that allows racism to flourish, and prevents racial diversity from being welcomed and celebrated. I often think of this quote from the hip-hop artist Guante: "White supremacy is not a shark, it is the water."

It was clear to me this group needed to do a lot of reading and personal reckoning with their whiteness before we could move ahead, and so I said as much. After we hung up, I texted the Indigenous runner: *What was that?* She replied, *What a meeting.*

Since college, I had done what I could to avoid white people and white spaces. My friends were Black. The work I did was for Black people. In that moment, there was not a single white person I could've picked up the phone and called to make sense of what had happened.

This was intentional. I had no interest in working closely with white people on issues of white supremacy. I had no interest in building deep relationships with white people that would've made those conversations possible.

But the Black woman, the group's adviser, called me. She talked about the challenge of cross-racial work, how it was hard and uncomfortable. She validated me without trying to calm me down. She let me be angry. She supported my anger. "Anger is important," she said. "But use it." When the white people wanted to meet again, she encouraged me to join, and my respect for her was the only reason I got on another call.

This time, the Black woman opened the conversation. She said I was on point. The problem was white supremacy, and it needed to be named. She acknowledged that this was probably hard for the white people to hear, but necessary. We talked about the idea of meeting each person where they were at, but this did not mean ignorance and denial were okay. I made the analogy that we as runners are always excited to bring new people into running, but we could only do so if the person was willing. We couldn't do the work for them; they had to run the miles themselves.

After the call, one of the white men—the teary one—asked me to cochair the coalition with him and I agreed. I wanted the industry to change. But I didn't do it for the industry or the white people. It felt like it was my responsibility to do the best I could for the Black runners who would come after me.

We brought on two more women of color and began working on defining our mission, vision, and goals. The work, and working with white people, proved much harder than I could ever have imagined.

As our meetings continued, the white people kept resisting the words *systemic racism* and *white supremacy*. The people of color had the same deep understanding of terms like *racism, systemic racism, anti-racism, white supremacy*, and *white supremacy culture*. We knew exactly what these words meant, the history that created them, and the pain they wrought in our daily lives. The white people were lost, so we ended up explaining and re-explaining the terms and the importance of both naming the problem and of white people taking responsibility for the present privileges they'd inherited due to historic wrongs.

"But terms like *white supremacy* and *systemic racism* are not 'joining' language," the white people argued. "They will turn people off and no one will join the coalition."

I spoke up: "Why would we prioritize white people's comfort over Black people's reality?"

White people: "Because we want to bring people in. Once they're here, we can bring them along."

Me: "So you're telling me we're not going to tell white people that our goal is to be anti-racist and to fight white supremacy, so we can coddle them and then later tell them that our goal is to be anti-racist and to fight white supremacy? You're centering white people's feelings. This work is not a bunch of black squares on Instagram. I don't want people to come on board for the sake of appearances. I want to work with people interested in real change."

On the next several calls, we had the same conversation about language over and over again. The white people could not let go of needing to make white people feel good about engaging in issues of race. My cochair would say we should definitely keep the language, then he would backtrack and say no, maybe we should change it. The only way I could get through these meetings was texting one of the other people of color: *Wow, they really don't get it.*

I n between our group calls, the white people were doing their own racial work. They met over Zoom, processing their experiences, with one of them explaining where they were coming from, and another admitting they could not understand the stalemate about language. But they were reading Ibram X. Kendi and Ta-Nehisi Coates. They were sharing articles.

And they were reflecting on their own lives. The white man who blew up on the first call sat back one day and put the pieces together. He grew up in a white city and had the advantages of being white. His bosses were white. *That's white supremacy,* he realized. Now, he's hiring white people at his running retail stores. He's mostly promoting white people and calling his white friends in the industry to tell them to hire this white person or that white person. That's systemic racism. *It's not conscious or intentional,* he realized, *yet I am participating in the system.*

His insight led him to remember a moment in his store eight years earlier. He was on one side and a Black employee was on the other. A Black woman walked in. She looked to be in her sixties and was walking cautiously, looking around. When she saw the Black staff member, her whole demeanor changed. She beamed as he approached her and welcomed her. The white owner has no memory of whether the woman bought shoes. He remembers seeing this exchange, and then going right back to work. Not giving the moment further investigation. Not wondering why the woman looked hesitant in the first place. Not wondering why the presence of a Black staff member was so central to this Black customer. Not wondering what that was *about.*

Often on calls, the people of color shared our experiences with racism. We talked about a lifetime of microaggressions, of feeling dismissed and not being acknowledged. Of our children coming home from a walk with friends and telling us that a white man threatened to call the police if they didn't leave the neighborhood. We expressed how difficult it is for Black people and people of color to feel safe in running groups, in public space, in these meetings. We talked about the stress of being the only person of color at an event. We expressed the reality of racial trauma, the real emotional distress and weight of being a person of color in the United States.

One person at a major running shoe brand disclosed that they were overlooked for a promotion because they didn't have the "right look" for the job. Someone shared that a person they'd recommended was not hired because, as the manager put it, they had dreads. Another person at a different running shoe brand shared that they'd been dismissed in meetings and marginalized by colleagues. Not once, but on many occasions. "No, no, that can't be true," the white woman said. The person of color nodded that it was. The white woman was shocked: *this happens in our industry.*

Over time, the white people came to see how very different our experiences were from theirs. They began to understand that we came to this work weary and exhausted. That we live with the worry and the weight every day while they can step away from race whenever they want to, rest, take a break. We cannot. We are tired of explaining race to white people. We are tired of trying to get them to see beyond whiteness and white comfort to see us. We have little patience for their racial awakening, their processing, their trouble with language. Our lives are at stake. Our children's lives are at stake. *Get up to speed and get on board.*

They did, briefly. We settled on language that included the words *whiteness* and *systemic racism* and acknowledged the industry's complicity in the system and set a date to launch the coalition.

Then the white people backpedaled.

On a final call to discuss what the launch would look like, the white woman said she'd received some feedback from people in the industry that if we used the language they wouldn't join, so she recommended that we acknowledge that racism happened and that we want to change it.

"You have to acknowledge your role," I said.

"It's a legal issue," she said. "I don't know if my company can be a part of this if we use that language. We could be sued on racial grounds."

I texted one of the other people of color: *WTF!*

The other white people began nodding their heads. *This is a valid point*, they were thinking. Someone could bring a lawsuit and say they were fired or not hired due to racism and then point at their involvement with the Running Industry Diversity Coalition: *Look, you admit you're racist, you say it right here in print.*

I was so hurt and angry I had to turn my video off. One of the other women of color did, too. I was done. I was done with white people saying they wanted to address the problem but were actually unwilling to address the problem. They wanted to do what other diversity efforts did. Talk around race. Make sure it was comfortable enough for white people to participate. But initiatives that center white people maintain the status quo. They let the harm continue.

In that moment, our adviser stepped in. "This is a pivotal moment," she said. "If you change course every time someone is uncomfortable with what you're doing, how will you get anywhere? I'm not here to tell you what to do. But how you handle outside influence is going to determine the fate of your group. If you think it's bad now, just wait. There are things that will come up, and you will have to decide how to respond. Are you going to let yourselves be pushed and moved based on what others say, or hold firm to the group's mission? If you want to change the language, I support you. If you don't change the language, I support you. If this coalition does not happen, don't forget that what you've done here is still important."

We postponed the launch and got off the call. There was only one path forward, and honestly, I had little faith the white people would get on board, but they did. I learned later that the person who'd suggested we soften the language worked through her blocks with a biracial friend who'd offered to be a sounding board. The friend explained that white supremacy was not just a phrase or term. It existed physically and historically, as a structure and system, and it thrives on being hidden, she said. The more ingrained white supremacy is in the system, the easier it is to hide and the harder it is to get rid of. So watering down the language actually empowers white supremacy. She added that by suggesting the group soften the language, she was actually muting the voices of the cause she was claiming to support and positioning herself in alliance with people who were not really on board.

The next morning, the white person was the first to speak when we reconvened. "I'm sorry," she said. "It wasn't my intention to offend anyone. Let's keep the language, I'm okay with it, let's keep it, let's do it."

The meeting was a turning point. We talked about honesty, vulnerability, safety, fear, disagreement. At the end of the call, our adviser went around to each person and asked us to verbally state that we agreed to move forward as is, without changing the language, and to stand behind our statements. I can't say that I trusted the white people. And if I'm honest, I wasn't sure I even liked them. But launching the coalition together was doing the work, or at the very least, it was a starting line.

19

Endurance

Over the next year, *DEI* became the buzzword in the running industry. Within four months of launching the coalition, six hundred people had joined. We were fielding so many emails and calls that our small volunteer staff could barely keep up. People were posting our social media graphics that named systems of oppression within our industry and were committing to anti-racist training. The coalition held workshops on how to talk about race, why DEI is important, and other topics. Participation reached 280 people in one Zoom call.

My cochair was blown away that so many people joined. It was exciting to have a positive response. But the numbers were just a start. Signing on to a coalition in the heat of a racial reckoning in our nation and industry was a simple one-off action; it barely scratched the surface. What collective action would people take? How long would the enthusiasm last? How far would they go before settling back into white comfort? White people had "awakened" to racial issues countless times before. They'd been shocked by a beating or a murder and said something must be done, then taken no real action to break down white su-premacist systems. I would wait and see.

Our first educational session introduced the problem: White men held all the power. They were the bulk of the CEOs, store owners, event organizers, editors, i.e., the people at the top with the decision-making power and the purse strings. How could we move a mostly white, mostly male industry toward action? There were four panelists: a Columbia University professor (who studies whiteness) and three white men (two retail store owners and a vice president at a major shoe brand). I was the moderator. The fact that the panel was full of white people proved upsetting for the people of color who joined the Zoom call. In the chat, they said:

Why are white people centered here?

We have to move beyond talk.

When are we going to get to the real issues, the specific issues?

They were also confused about why we were taking the time to define basic concepts like "structural racism" and the "good/bad bi-nary." The runners of color on the call were being confronted by the stark reality of what I'd learned over the last six months: just how far the industry had to go. How little white people know about race. They were, like me, fed up, exhausted, impatient. I responded in the chat with attempts to explain that this was an entry point. The truth is that white people are still on the couch, so we can't tell them to run ten miles, I said. They simply cannot do it.

The phone calls my cochair and I had with industry leaders were characterized by the same white ignorance as all the calls I'd had before; the difference was that these were in service of something larger. These conversations were not meant to be a one-off effort or podcast appear-ances to soothe white people into thinking they'd "done something." The intention was that these calls were first steps toward transparency and accountability. I want to say that this lessened the frustration and pain, but it did not. Before each call, I had to remind myself that I was speaking to a different set of white people who were encountering race and racial work for the first time.

This was true even for people who thought they were already doing DEI work. Many brands, as it turned out, were using the DEI acronym without addressing racism. For example, some brands bragged to us about their DEI work, only for me to realize that their efforts had nothing to do with race, as they completely lacked intersectionality. They shared images and statistics of LGBTIQ+ and disabled athletes, all of whom were white. Black people didn't exist to them. On a call with a major shoe brand, the CEO said the diversity work they'd done had addressed the "easier" issues, like LGBTIQ+ inclusion. In these moments, I let myself turn off my camera, roll my eyes, scream internally—*Black people are also members of the LGBTIQ+ community!*—then come back on.

As the next year unfolded, Black bodies appeared in running publications, on a couple of magazine covers, and in ads and marketing material. More of our stories were told, both the reality of running while Black, but also the joy of finding ourselves through running, the pitfalls of training, our advice as experts.

But as the months passed, the regression I feared came. I watched as brands, stores, and events lost steam. They sprinted instead of pacing themselves. Too often, efforts became examples of what not to do, including:

▶ implementing quick and simple changes that were largely performative: weekly or monthly readings or discussions in staff meetings that fizzled without clear purpose, expectations, or intended outcomes;

▶ stating they were "so committed" to racial justice and posting a statement on their website without allocating funding toward DEI, developing a strategic plan, or dedicating staffing to put their commitment into action;

► attempting multiple actions in rapid succession and burning themselves out, along with the people of color they worked with;

► bringing in DEI consultants and conducting a handful of trainings for staff, and stopping the work when the consultant's contract ended;

► taking advantage of Black staff members eager for change and letting them lead or work on DEI issues for the company without additional compensation;

► recruiting ambassadors of color for the sake of broader representation, but without compensating them for their work; and

► abandoning DEI efforts for more "pressing" matters like supply chain issues.

The small steps the industry took let them feel good about themselves, but they did not change the whiteness of the brand, store, or event; they did not shift the power structure. Their diversity numbers might have been climbing and shifting, but the company's hierarchy ultimately continued to resemble a plantation, with white people retaining senior positions and Black people and people of color in supporting roles, missing the mark.

In some cases, a sense of urgency diluted the possibility of meaningful work. And while the work is urgent, it cannot be done urgently.

It requires strategy, and the mental fortitude to resist white supremacy culture, which prioritizes speed over other factors like including more voices at the table. One simple step—hiring more people of color, for example—is more complex than you initially think. It takes education, planning, thought, and care. It requires an understanding of what certain phrases like "must be professional" signal to Black people and other historically excluded communities: that we won't thrive there because "professionalism" usually translates into a culture that centers white appearance and norms of behavior. It comes with a consideration of whether the company culture will allow a new hire to thrive and feel a sense of belonging. What is good hiring without retention?

One store owner talked about the enthusiasm his staff had for DEI efforts he introduced in the months immediately following the murders of Ahmaud Arbery and George Floyd. But time passed, and while some staff members formed a book club and dove into educating themselves, the majority were indifferent. The store owner struggled with what trainings and work to make mandatory and what should be optional. He hired a DEI consultant to work with him for a year, laying out strategy and outcomes, yet much of the work was at the management level versus staff-wide. In the trainings he did do, some white staff struggled to understand why a Black staff member might not be comfortable at the store. Staff surveys indicated both high appreciation for diversity in running as well as resistance to the boss's efforts, e.g., *why do we need this? It's not why I work here.*

I work with a number of brands both formally and informally, and see both the efforts made and the distance that needs to be traveled. In many cases, brands are confusing diversity with racial justice—increasing diversity is purely a numbers game—leaving efforts largely performative, rather than systemic. Featuring Black people, people of color, different body sizes, and other diverse runners in your marketing material and online is essential. As is diversifying your staff. But diversity is a single step. "Equity" and "inclusion" are essential to the end goal: racial justice.

Racial justice means that every space is a space of belonging. It means feeling free to be your full self without fear and having equal opportunity to thrive. It means everyone present is accepted and celebrated for who they are, and not expected to conform to a white standard or "fit in" to white culture. It is transforming white spaces into what sociologist Elijah Anderson calls canopy spaces, or "diverse islands of civility," what I think of as inclusive spaces. Diversity alone cannot accomplish that goal.

For example, 135 years after the founding of the Boston Athletic Association (BAA), the organization welcomed the first Black woman—and first woman of color—to its board. However, she alone cannot undo the more than a century of systemic racism that is coded into the culture and the fabric of the BAA. Hiring her is but one step of a much longer transformation.

Another example: One brand celebrates the running "tradition," rooting its imagery and references in "Americana." But it fails to see that running's "tradition" is whiteness. The brand romanticizes a time when Black people were fighting for basic human rights and the ability to move through public space with a measure of safety. While the brand includes people of color in its ads and videos, it regularly reverts back to the image of a thin, white male running down a long road, harking back to the "old days." Marketing has the ability to sell product, but also reinforce or change culture. To be truly disruptive—to change the running narrative—the brand would need to do more than put its iconic singlet on Black people. It would have to reject the notion that the early days of the so-called running boom were the "good old days" and look to create a new narrative that centers our stories of running and resistance and joy alongside white people. Then the brand would be intentionally flipping iconic white images on its head with something radical and bold, something that changes the idea of who a runner is and who belongs.

Another common misconception: DEI is a department or bucket. I attended a marketing meeting of all white people. One of the members suggested we create categories for what our social media efforts would focus on. They began listing them: community, product, professional athletes, diversity. I stopped them there. Diversity is not a separate category. It has to be part of every aspect of a brand, woven into the business at large to be effective.

This past year, I watched a CEO with a stated commitment to racial justice hold tight to a hiring belief that made job openings at their brand significantly less accessible to people of color. When I pointed this out to the CEO, they shared that they wouldn't feel comfortable with an alternative approach. This unwillingness to adapt and prioritize people who have been marginalized over white comfort means that any so-called commitments are just words.

When I think about the running industry, I think about an industry in training. It is barely off the couch, just beginning to put in the miles for an ultramarathon. I continue to be in rooms and industry conferences that are disproportionately and overwhelmingly white. Who in those spaces will hold the industry accountable? It cannot be on the backs of us, the few Black people and other people of color who have been given a space. White people must recognize that when they find themselves in a place where everyone is white or mostly white— including at a workout, a race, or a conference—there is a problem, and they are perpetuating it.

At an industry conference in early 2022, a well-meaning race director, a white man from Pittsburgh, pulled me aside to tell me of his efforts to engage the segregated Black community across the bridge. He told me that he understood how history and city planning had isolated, disenfranchised, and disempowered Black people in Pittsburgh and he wanted to do something about it. I felt a warm rush of adrenaline in my body—this guy seemed to get it. My mind began to fill with hope and possibility about the work we could do together. But then he insinuated that the New York City Marathon's new race director—the first Black man to have the job at any of the sport's six major marathons—was only awarded the role because of the recent racial reckoning. I nearly choked. My warmth toward him quickly turned to anger, disappointment, and frustration.

His was one of many in a long line of examples that have shown me how far we have to go. In these moments, I remind myself that we did not get here in a year, and it will take many years—lifetimes?—to break down the system. Our ancestors handed us the torch and we must carry it forward. This thought does not make me hopeful; it makes me tired. It reminds me that endurance requires pacing, it encourages me to take self-care days, shut off social media, cuddle with my son, breathe in the beauty of the Black runners and activists I see doing the work every day. And to pass the baton when I need to; this is not my work alone. I am also aware enough to know that white people have to continually opt into the struggle. This isn't their every day. Even white people with a history of being committed to racial justice often prioritize their own comfort or their own power over marginalized groups. We all want comfort and safety. But for too long racial justice work has been viewed as the work of Black people alone. Our comfort and safety depend on the willingness of white people to resist indifference and ease and take tireless action with us. Will they find the courage—the grit and the endurance—to break the cycle of history?

I don't know. It's a question only the industry can answer.

20

Everything Is Connected

A year into the pandemic, four months after launching the Running Industry Diversity Coalition, I did something I never imagined I'd do: I packed up my seven-hundred-square-foot apartment in the Bronx and moved across the country for a new life in Seattle with my family. New York City, a source of energy and possibility for my entire life, was not a place I wanted to raise my son. Suddenly, I understood why my parents made the same difficult decision to leave Harlem in order to create a better home for my brother and me thirty-plus years earlier.

When I was pregnant with Kouri, we moved to the Bronx into a brand-new luxury apartment because we'd been searching for a new home with laundry in the building and couldn't find anything affordable in Harlem. Our apartment building in the Bronx was a product of the gentrification that has forced many in the community out of their homes and that will likely remake the neighborhood in the next few years. While we were fortunate enough to find a place in the Bronx, the lack of healthy food options surrounding the apartment and the noise and pollution from truck routes and neighboring factories was overwhelming.

The lack of trees in the neighborhood also meant that the temperature was often several degrees higher than in other parts of the city and the air was not as clean. I knew about these correlations because I had read about them in the *New York Times*. Trees absorb pollutants and provide cooling shade. Without them, air quality declines, and surface and air temperatures rise, leading to higher heat levels in the summer in neighborhoods with little tree coverage, like the Bronx.

Going for runs as a family, we often ran on streets without proper sidewalks, avoiding broken glass and garbage to make our way to Randall's Island. Once on Randall's Island, the beauty and expanse of this 480-acre green oasis gave us momentary respite; that is, until the park became home to refrigerated trucks housing hundreds of dead bodies—hundreds of people—lost to the Covid-19 pandemic.

Walking toward the subway meant walking by a poorly maintained public housing project with weeks' worth of garbage that the city had yet to pick up littering the entrance (mattresses, old couches, clothing). Scaffolding covered the sidewalk because of repairs that seemed never-ending and allowed for houseless populations to find much-needed cover. On more than one occasion, I felt nervous walking home from the train at night because the poor lighting and decrepit infrastructure also created the perfect opportunity for crime.

Across the street, a police precinct seemed to do much more in the way of intimidation than in providing actual assistance to community members. Once, during a peaceful protest in June 2020, police aggressively arrested over two hundred people, beating some with batons, and leaving many physically and mentally wounded. Cops were also placed throughout the community, along with SkyWatch towers to keep us "safe," practices you didn't see on Park Avenue. I took special care in these moments to look as much like a runner as I could. With Amir by my side and Kouri in the stroller, I straightened my posture, made sure to look straight ahead of me, whispered to Amir to stop talking so loudly and refrain from joking. *We don't want to give them a reason.*

What I was seeing and experiencing didn't happen overnight. It was set in motion decades ago, the result of federal policies that put the neighborhood on a trajectory of abject neglect. In the late 1930s, much of the Bronx was redlined—graded D (or "red" for "hazardous") or C ("yellow," or "definitely declining") by the Home Owners' Loan Corporation (HOLC), a federal program that appraised neighborhoods in cities and towns across the country. The HOLC used a grade and color-coded system that lenders then used to determine which communities were good investments and which were not; that is, who got loans. The primary factor in determining the grade of a neighborhood was race.

An appraiser in St. Louis, for example, gave a white, middle-class suburb an A and a green label because there was "not a single foreigner or negro." Areas adjacent to Black communities were given C grades and colored yellow, signaling they were declining. "Respectable people, but homes are too near negro area" was the reason an appraiser gave for grading a neighborhood in Richmond, Virginia, with a B. Appraisers gave neighborhoods a D due to the "infiltration of Negroes" and colored them red, thus introducing the term *redlining.* One area of the Bronx, labeled D1 by the HOLC, was redlined because of "Detrimental Influences: Negro infiltration."

Redlining denied loans to Black families, while granting white families access to federally backed mortgages, a practice that was adopted by the entire mortgage industry, and had devastating effects on Black families and communities. Without loans, Black families couldn't buy a house or fix up their home; build intergenerational wealth based on home equity; or move. Ongoing discrimination in housing, education, and jobs pushed many Black families into poverty (or deeper into poverty). City governments zoned white areas as residential and Black areas as commercial and industrial, bringing in warehouses and other business infrastructure, altering the look and nature of the area.

Redlining was part of a larger strategy by the federal government to segregate neighborhoods into Black and white spaces. In the 1920s and '30s, a housing shortage for working- and middle-class families prompted the government to step in and build public housing units and single-family homes—part of President Roosevelt's New Deal plan. Public housing then was a plan to add supply to meet demand for mostly white families. But the federal government, along with city and state governments, used the opportunity to establish white neighborhoods in desirable areas and put Black people elsewhere, deepening segregation where it already existed, and creating segregation where there was none. In Miami, for example, a civic leader said their goal was to "remove the entire colored population" from sections of town they wanted reserved for white people. In Atlanta, government officials razed an integrated, multiracial neighborhood to create a 604-unit, white-only community.

In the suburbs, the government subsidized massive single-home subdivisions, the majority of which had racial exclusion covenants. "The tenant agrees not to permit the premises to be used or occupied by any person other than members of the Caucasian race" read part of the covenant for Levittown, New York, which was among the first white suburbs to be built. Covenants applied to all Black people, including African American veterans returning home from World War II, despite housing promises made in the GI Bill.

By the time racist housing policies were deemed unconstitutional with the passage of the Civil Rights Act of 1968 (also known as the Fair Housing Act), cities had been successfully segregated into under-resourced Black neighborhoods—i.e., the "inner city" or the "ghetto"— and pretty white neighborhoods. While trees were planted and parks were built in white areas, the commercial or industrial zoning of Black areas led to more pavement—parking lots, roads, highways.

With few trees and more pavement to absorb heat, temperatures rose. One study found that previously redlined areas can be five to twenty degrees hotter in the summer than the whiter, wealthier parts of town. More traffic and industry means more pollutants hover over these neighborhoods, leading to declining health. Areas once redlined have higher rates of chronic illnesses like asthma, diabetes, high blood pressure, and obesity—including the Bronx.

The Bronx has one of the highest asthma rates in the United States and ranks the lowest in New York State in both "health factors" (air quality, access to healthcare, tobacco use) and "health outcomes" (quality of life, length of life). Life expectancy for people in the Bronx is seventy-five, a decade less than the eighty-five-year life expectancy for people living on the Upper East Side.

Was this the environment I wanted for my son?

The answer was a resounding no. I could not justify raising my son in a place that was designed to kill him. I could not justify raising my son in an area where his education or opportunities in sports would be compromised, as most schools in low-income areas lack funding for sports and recreation programs. (A 2021 lawsuit in New York City filed against the Department of Education determined that Black and Latino students attended high schools with an average of ten fewer sports teams compared to students of other races.) If I wanted what was best for my son, we'd have to move to a white space.

The decision was difficult but mostly practical. Moving meant leaving our friends and losing our connection to Harlem and the community that is our family. Going to a white space would put a target on our backs. We would forever be outsiders, surveilled and seen as potential criminals, the white gaze always tracking us. But we'd gain a greener space, cleaner air, and maybe even a backyard.

onths later, we landed in Seattle. Amir had applied to various jobs and the one in Seattle came through with a higher salary than he was making in New York. One of my sponsors got wind of the move and designed a position for me that utilized my passion for building community and increasing racial diversity in running. We were lucky enough to be able to afford a house outside the city in a predominately white area. It had a backyard, was surrounded by trees, and area parks were just a short drive or a run away.

It was a relief to finally have space. Rather than hearing police sirens and ambulances, we woke to lake views and the sound of gobbling wild turkeys. I missed my friends, but life was slower, more peaceful. I went out for a run and took in the snow-capped peaks and tranquil water of the lake. I often routed my runs away from houses with American flags and pickup trucks; generalizations, yes, but the worry wasn't worth the risk. I crossed the street if someone looked suspicious. The practices felt both silly and necessary, but every time I made it home to pour coffee and flip through my phone, I put a little more faith in them.

A few months after the move, I came across an article in a running publication listing the best places to live if you're a runner. The article was seemingly just presenting facts and attempting to draw runners to visit these places firsthand. Naturally, the places all had common traits. There were beautiful vistas, trails, tree-lined running paths, and vibrant running communities. Rated fourth out of five was Flagstaff, Arizona. One runner shared, "Flagstaff created my standard for what a town should be like that I want to live in. We have such good trail systems in and around town, the elevation is great for training, and the running community is pretty tight-knit. Even if you don't know every single person, it's just a supportive community."

What the article did not comment on, but was evident in the demographics, is that these places were wealthy and overwhelmingly white. The median house price hovered in the $400,000 range and 70 to 90 percent of residents were white people. My immediate reaction was to think *this didn't happen by accident.* Racism created the "good" parts of town (read: white) and the "bad" parts of town (read: Black). White people didn't just happen to live in the places that were conducive to running, and Black people didn't choose the "other" areas.

But this was one list, so I pulled up other articles on the best places for running and found the results were the same. The cities and towns considered the best for running were predominately white. If cities with large Black populations were included, such as Washington DC and Atlanta, the best places to run were in white areas, the events that were highlighted were historically white events, and the running groups that were featured were largely white.

I saw in these lists the structural racism that underlies running—the gap between overwhelmingly white, wealthy communities where people can easily run, and the under-resourced communities of color where running is less safe and less practical. If you have a good place to run, more people will be running, and the data confirm this. I compared maps of previously redlined areas in Harlem and Brooklyn with activity levels for those areas from Strava heat-map data—maps that register activity levels as "heat" from millions of users around the world. The previously redlined areas of Harlem and Brooklyn were nearly dark, signaling little to no activity, while Manhattan was lit up, showing high levels of activity.

A 2019 article in *Runner's World* dug deeper into the data, using Baltimore as an example. The section with the most runners was along what's known as the city's "white L," an area in the north that travels south along the city's main corridor before turning east to the Inner Harbor and the promenade. The white L, not surprisingly, receives a

big chunk of city resources, and it's where you'll find luxury apartments and upscale dining. In contrast, the areas along the Patapsco River and out toward the county lines have little to no running and biking activity. These areas form what's called the "Black butterfly," neighborhoods characterized by vacant row houses, high poverty rates, and, as the *Runner's World* reporter noted, "generational despair."

The image of the "white L" and the "Black butterfly" is a clear representation of what's necessary to run. A runner is somebody with secure housing, a safe place to train, running infrastructure—parks, paths, trails, well-kept sidewalks—clean air, and the physical, emotional, and psychological safety to run. And the majority of people with those privileges are white, just as it was during the running boom. Said simply: your zip code determines not only your health, longevity, safety, and comfort, it also determines who has the freedom to easily run.

A 2021 survey conducted by TRUE Global Intelligence for Gatorade found that 40 percent of Black respondents cited a safe place to run as a barrier to entering endurance sports like running and cycling.

Nearly half of respondents of color named a safe place to train as a barrier, as well as fear of hate crimes.

This wasn't surprising. Since 2014, the total number of hate crimes in the United States has increased by nearly 42 percent. Black people are the most targeted group by a wide margin, according to the FBI, and white people are the majority of the offenders. In a study conducted by sociologist Rashawn Ray, Ph.D., on why middle-class Black Americans are less active than their white counterparts, Ray found that safety played a primary role. "Black men are criminalized by the

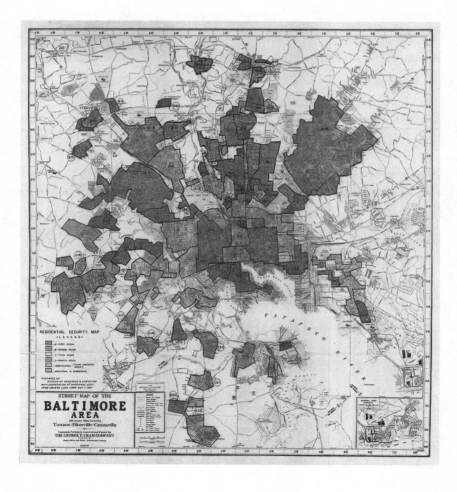

inability of others to separate a Black male from crime," Ray told *Runner's World* in 2013 to explain why Black men tended to avoid running in white neighborhoods. He also found that the cities with the highest concentration of college-educated Black men—Atlanta and Prince George's County, Maryland—had higher activity levels, in part because the men were less likely to be criminalized in these spaces. Black women, on the other hand, were less likely to exercise in Black neighborhoods because these areas are sometimes less safe, or are perceived as being less safe.

The likelihood of a person of color being harmed by police has also risen since 2014; in the year following the killing of Ahmaud Arbery and George Floyd, 229 Black people lost their lives at the hands of a police officer. In 2020, Black people accounted for the highest percentage of police-related deaths, as they had for many years. Also: police shot unarmed Black people at a rate of three times higher than white people between 2015 and 2020.

It's tempting to compartmentalize running into something separate, something somehow detached from the world. But everything is connected: neighborhoods, air quality, bias, violence, safety, running. As basketball legend Kareem Abdul-Jabbar wrote for WebMD's special series on social justice: "The problem with pulling any single thread—Covid-19, health risks, job opportunities—is that each thread is a single strand in a giant quilt that smothers the Black community. One thread leads to another, to another, to another—each forming an interlinking pattern that seems impenetrable and unassailable. A police officer crushing the windpipe of an unarmed Black man is related to not valuing Blacks, which is related to stereotypes about Blacks, which is related to how they are portrayed (or not portrayed) in media, which is related to not having educational opportunities, which is related to . . . and on and on."

When I hear white runners say "keep politics out of running" or that running publications and brands should "stick to running," and that "race" and "social issues" don't belong in running, I hear someone denying structural racism, bias, and white supremacy—denying my reality and the reality of millions of others. These comments demonstrate a lack of racial understanding and a narrow view of our nation's history. And they ignore the fact that running occurs outdoors, in neighborhoods and parks, and on streets and trails. They ignore the fact that politics and racism are embedded in everything—all aspects of American life.

Attempting to silence us isn't the answer. What's needed is in fact the opposite: Every running publication and every brand must feature Black people and other people of color in every issue and online every day, and not just in articles related to racial justice. The more we are seen and heard, the more our voices and bodies are part of the daily running narrative, the faster we'll move toward normalizing Black people running in our society. In the 1960s and early 1970s, white runners were seen as odd; they were ridiculed, even harassed. But as more people started running, as more runners were featured in media and races popped up in communities across the nation, seeing white people running became an ordinary part of American life. We must now make it normal for Black people.

21

***

Reimagining the Run

I n early 2022, Amir and I bundled up Kouri and drove across Seattle to Magnuson Park on Lake Washington to meet with running groups from around the city. In all my time in Seattle—a year at this point—I had never seen so many Black and brown people in one place. We were still the minority, but we were there together, breaking apart the white-centered image of running so typical in Seattle, while also welcoming a number of white running groups. We went for a 5K run along a footpath that offered views of the lake—about one hundred of us in all—and I facilitated a discussion afterward about collaboration and collective action.

It was wild to be doing this kind of organizing in a new place. The setting could not have been more different from our meet-ups in Harlem at Marcus Garvey Park, where we'd run down city streets lined with beautiful brownstones, smiling, giving high fives, and throwing our fists in the air toward our neighbors. Here in Magnuson Park, with its serene views of the lake and well-manicured park lands, I almost couldn't believe I lived in such an un-urban green space. One was not better than the other; I was simply struck that what I once did in Harlem I was now doing here: leading, and making and taking up space. I looked over to see Kouri toddling around and giving high fives to strangers as if nothing much was different. In that moment, I felt the warmth of knowing our move had been the right decision, no matter the compromise it took.

The meet-up was the birth of the Seattle Running Collective, a place for the region's running groups to come together to meet and share ideas and best practices on how to create inclusive and welcoming environments. It's a work in progress, but our goal is clear: fostering a change in running culture to focus on inclusion. What this means to me is rather simple: decenter whiteness and center Black people, Indigenous communities, and other people of color. I don't mean we exclude white people. I mean that by decentering whiteness, we open space for other people, expanding the circle of privilege to include everyone.

When I started running, I bought a new outfit so that I'd have a chance at fitting in. I knew that as a Black woman, I was outside of white culture, and even though I wasn't a runner when I walked into Central Park, I knew (white) running culture prioritizes thinness, speed, and experience. While certainly there are health benefits to weight loss, and getting faster is fun, I learned that defining a runner through a narrow lens, and judging others as "not really a runner" because they are outside of the image, is exclusion.

The running collective is "come as you are," in sweats or sweat-wicking gear. We want to dispel the myth that running is only about getting faster or that it must be about pain and struggle; running can just be about movement, community, and joy. There are so many running groups in Seattle, and we don't know each other because we often don't run outside the convenience of our own segregated neighborhoods. We can change that and increase our power to take collective action by addressing some of the shortcomings and racism we see and experience.

At a meet-up led by Black Girls Run and a group called Club Seattle Runners Division, or CSRD, we encouraged people to run or walk as many laps as possible, pledging a dollar amount per lap. The funds raised went to support Black Coffee Northwest, which has been systematically vandalized over the years for being a Black-owned business. We also plan to organize sneaker and bra collections, two items whose unavailability often make running off-limits to middle school kids. These small contributions might ease the burden for Black and brown youth looking to join a cross-country team—our small contribution to a larger shift in the distance-running talent pipeline, particularly for girls of color, who research shows enter sports later, participate in lower numbers, and drop out earlier than white girls.

The collective cannot undo the historic wrongs in the city, the systemic racism that resides in the Pacific Northwest. But it's the next step I can take in this new community. What we do from here, what we all do—or don't do—will determine the future of our sport. What can you do? How can you help?

Brands and groups are answering this question in meaningful and creative ways. Since 2016, running crews in the Bronx and many other like-minded organizations have been rallying behind the message "Not 62," referring to the Bronx's status of having the lowest health outcomes out of all of New York's sixty-two counties. Their visibility as predominantly groups of color running through a neighborhood that has seen few runners over the decades is a reclamation of the streets and a message to their neighbors that running, and running in the Bronx, is open. These run crews work directly with NYC park authorities to improve lighting, address cracked sidewalks, and create additional recreational and healthy food programming for youth. They also lead park cleanups to make neighborhood parks more inviting and accessible and hold their local community officials accountable for the promises they make for improved facilities and access. They are making change happen.

Strava has realized its data can aid city leaders in improving transportation infrastructure. The brand's Metro program aggregates its heat data and makes it available for free to organizations, companies, and city governments to understand mobility patterns, improve safety, and evaluate projects. By identifying heat islands, as with the Baltimore example, data can make disparities in activity among neighborhoods evident, allowing cities to address infrastructure or other issues preventing people from getting out.

Running events can take an active role in partnering with the neighborhoods they run through by intentionally routing races through neighborhoods of color and engaging with these communities. Races bring excitement and financial opportunities for business, and race directors should seek to partner with Black-owned businesses and center their desires. How can a marathon—or any race distance—ensure collaborative relationships with local officials and community groups? How can the race better communicate to neighborhoods what types of disruption to expect to ease their concerns and plan? How can the race highlight each community and reinvest in their needs? How can an event ensure its demographics match the demographics of its city or town?

The Atlanta Track Club, which puts on the Peachtree Road Race, as well as about thirty other races, has made strides in these areas. It has overhauled its marketing and event management approach to reflect the city's diversity, starting with representation. Marketing photos of the Peachtree race and the club as a whole no longer reflect only the stereotypical runner of a thin, white man. The club's photographers now capture the wide range of participants at its events, and residents now see themselves in the advertising—Black people, white people, people of color, people with all kinds of body types, abilities, and ages. Since efforts began a number of years ago, Black participation in the Peachtree Road Race has risen from 12 percent to 18 percent—not enough, considering that Atlanta is 50 percent Black, but it's moving in the right direction.

The Atlanta Track Club is also an example of a group that diversified the geography of its events. It now hosts races in historically Black communities and other areas to welcome a different audience and build relationships with new communities. It rerouted the Atlanta Marathon to include not only white-majority areas but also historically Black neighborhoods and the campuses of the city's historically Black colleges, Morehouse and Spelman. The Atlanta Track Club is working with these communities to host cheer stations, celebrate heritage, and drive participation.

These should be best practices nationwide. Partner with communities to tell the story of the race. Promote health and wellness in underserved and marginalized neighborhoods. Go beyond shoe giveaways to deeper partnerships with organizations within those communities to support local economies and partners financially. Simply put: consistent and intentional efforts can go a long way toward shifting the image and definition of who is a runner.

W orking to create inclusion is a project that mostly considers the future. But it is incomplete if it doesn't reckon with the past. This came into focus for me a couple of months before the 2021 New York City Marathon when I received an email from Ted Corbitt's son Gary. He was replying to an email I'd sent checking some facts for this book. In his response, Gary mentioned that George Spitz, a white runner, is largely credited with the idea to expand the New York City

Marathon to all five boroughs in 1976, but that in fact it was his father's idea. Spitz was central to the race's expansion—he's the one who took the idea to Percy Sutton, the Manhattan borough president, and who rounded up the funding to get the idea off the ground. But it was Corbitt who gave the idea to Spitz.

Gary passed on supporting documents, correspondence between his father, Spitz, and others. In a letter from Corbitt to Spitz dated May 22, 1976, Corbitt wrote about an article that had gotten the story wrong. The article said that he, Corbitt, credited the idea to Spitz, which was incorrect. It also said that Spitz gave Corbitt the credit, which was correct. In his letter, Corbitt recounted the conversation the two men had shared. Spitz told Corbitt that he wanted to stage a special race, one "worthy of the 'big apple.'" Corbitt replied that "the most unusual race you could set up would be a sweep thru all five boros [sic], providing the distance wasn't too long."

Ted Corbitt sent a letter to the author of the story that misrepresented the situation and later to Fred Lebow after his memoir got the story wrong, too. No one listened. No corrections were issued. Of course, I wanted to set the record straight, so I pitched the *New York Times* an op-ed. After initial interest, I received an email stating there wasn't enough time for the legal department to verify the documents. But then, on November 4, three days before the marathon, a story appeared in the *New York Times* about the growth of the marathon. It credited Spitz with the five-borough idea, and was written by a white man whose version was believed, without documentation.

Why does it matter? Why does a seemingly small detail like whose idea it was to pull the marathon out of the confines of Central Park and do a sweep of the city make a difference? Because it places a Black man in the circle, not the margins. The details of history make up the larger story of our sport. They show who belongs, who was there, and who running is for.

It is not just one piece that matters, but the domino effect of all the pieces lined up. Corbitt as a cofounder of the New York Road Runners, the person who standardized race distances, a champion, and an Olympian. The Pioneer Club. Marilyn Bevans. Ella Willis. Moses Mayfield. The Black men winning marathons in the early 1900s. When we learn the history whiteness has hidden, it expands the story of who running is for. It connects us to our greatness and to our place in the sport.

Over marathon weekend, I met with the person who authored the *Times* piece. He was a white man, age eighty-seven. He knew Corbitt. He knew Spitz. He was there at the 1976 race and was part of the New York Road Runners and the behind-the-scenes creation of the marathon. I told him what I knew about the original documents, and he was humble, willing to accept that he didn't have the full story. But he also wasn't sure what he believed. He wanted to be open, and yet he was hesitant to let go of the story he thought he knew. The stories we think we know bring comfort; they add order and clarity to our experiences. It's hard to let go of that.

Learning and unlearning our history is a necessary part of decentering whiteness and widening the circle of inclusion. History is living and breathing in the present. It does not just explain the past, it sets the future. "What we choose to remember, memorialize, and preserve as a society determines how we understand our present and imagine our future," wrote the curators of an exhibit on the murder of Emmett Till at the National Museum of American History. "When Black history is suppressed or delegitimized, we lose the ability to reckon with systemic racism, from one generation to the next."

The running story being told now is not the full story. Corbitt was correcting history as it was happening, but he was not being heard. We need to hear him now. When we include more Black people and other marginalized groups in the larger story of running, a narrative emerges that opens the sport to more people.

My goal and hope is that we can reimagine running as a sport for everyone, making freedom of movement possible for Black people at all times, in all spaces, where Blackness is seen not as a threat or even a statement, but commonplace and normal. Where Black runners feel welcomed and safe at every race. Where our stories and voices are part of history, part of the universal story of what it means to run. Where we feel like we belong. Only then will the sport live up to what it aspires to be—open to all.

Reclaiming

I n 2022, I hosted a shakeout run the day before the Boston Marathon with two predominately Black running groups, TrailblazHers and Pioneers, named for the group that started it all for us, the New York Pioneer Club. We gathered at the PYNRS pop-up shop, a new streetwear-inspired running clothing line owned by a local Black leader in the running community, on Newbury Street near the finish line. There were about one hundred of us, mostly Black and brown runners, but some white runners, too, as we weaved our way south. The run took us to a place most people in town for the marathon would never see and don't even know exists—Nubian Square, the center of Black culture in Boston, located in the neighborhood of Roxbury, home to a large Black and brown population.

We gathered under a red, black, and green African American flag, and I led us through a short, guided meditation. I asked everyone to close their eyes, breathe deeply, and think about all of the choices and sacrifices they'd made to get to this moment. I asked them to consider all of the choices and sacrifices their parents and grandparents had made to ensure they could be here—some of them leaving everything they knew and the countries of their birth, setting us on a course for us to be exactly where we were meant to be: here, today.

I said that we were still in a place in running where Black people are achieving firsts, yet at the same time we have a long history in the sport. We're not new to this: the first time a Black man ran the Boston Marathon was in 1919. I talked about Marilyn Bevans and Ted Corbitt, and how prolific they were as athletes. Much like those great athletes, what we were doing in this moment would reverberate through history and generations yet to come. I ended by saying that all of us moving together causes the running industry, the community, and the world to take notice. To see that we're here, we've been here, and we're not going anywhere. After a few more deep breaths, I instructed everyone to open their eyes and thank the person next to them for being here. Everyone in the crowd hugged and applauded.

Then we took off, making our way back north to Newbury Street and the pop-up shop. The next day, those of us not running the race gathered at mile twenty-one in Newton to cheer. I felt a lightness in my body as I walked toward the group—a mix of majority-Black running groups from all over the country: District Running Collective from DC, Prolyfyck Run Crew from Charlottesville, TrailblazHers and Pioneers from Boston, Seven on Sundays from Chicago, CSRD from Seattle, and Harlem Run, of course. *This was it*, I thought. We were making a way out of no way. We were dancing and cheering and moving with joy and freedom. We were claiming our space in a place and sport we helped build.

Amir, Kouri, and I stayed only for a few hours—we had a flight to catch. On the way home, back to Seattle, I was flying high, over the moon, filled with the particular joy of belonging.

What I experienced in Boston is happening in communities across the country. Black and brown runners are taking to the streets, rede-

fining what running looks and feels like, building groups with inclusive cultures, reaching back and pulling others along with us. Black and brown people are opening running stores in our neighborhoods—Renegade Running in Oakland and Last Lap Cornerstore on Chicago's South Side—places that not only welcome us, but are built with us in mind. We are hosting events that celebrate our communities. Exhibit A: 26.TRUE Marathon in Boston, a marathon that took place the Saturday before the Boston Marathon and traveled through the city's diverse neighborhoods, including Jamaica Plain, Hyde Park, Roxbury, Allston, and Back Bay. Every event, every store and group, and every Black and brown runner out there moving through space is a call to join us in the sport. Each of us is a tiny revolution that reverberates, expands, and breathes.

We're here. We're doing it for ourselves.

ACKNOWLEDGMENTS

I would like to thank all of the Black writers and activists who came before me and dared to share their truth. People like Zora Neale Hurston, Audre Lorde, Maya Angelou, James Baldwin, Angela Davis, and Edwidge Danticat. Thank you for making space for me.

I would like to thank Alade McKen, who changed my life simply by living his own and sharing his marathon journey. I'm not sure whom I would be—or if I would be—without you.

Thank you to my husband, Amir Figueroa, and son, Kouri Henri Figueroa, for being patient and understanding as I ignored you both and hid behind my laptop screen for months.

Thank you to my parents, Wilfrid and Lucía María Désir, for allowing me to be a pye poudre; for the opportunity to develop so many interests and hobbies that you at times wondered how it would all turn out in the end.

Thank you to my cousin Jennifer Kallicharan, for absorbing so many of my tears over the years and meeting me with nothing but love and encouragement.

Thank you to all the teachers who taught me to be skeptical and challenge the status quo.

Thank you to my very best friends who are always in my corner: Sasha Thompson, Sean Peters, and Amit Pandya.

Thank you to Harlem Run—the leadership team and anyone who has ever shown up. There is no movement without you.

Thank you to the Seattle running community—David Jaewon Oh and Ashley Davies, especially—for welcoming me with open arms.

Thank you to my agent, Daniel Greenberg, and my editor, Trish Daly, for believing in this book.

And finally, thank you to Cleyvis Natera, who saw and nurtured the writer in me, and Michelle Hamilton, for helping me put my story down; without you this book would not exist.

NOTES

INTRODUCTION

4 **"white person would certainly not need to endure":** Elijah Anderson, "The White Space," *Sociology of Race and Ethnicity*, 1, no. 1 (January 2015): 10–21, https://doi.org/10.1177/2332649214561306.

CHAPTER 1 | THE ONLY

10 **build a park for themselves:** "Seneca Village: A Community Lost to Central Park," New-York Historical Society, June 17, 2013, https://www.nyhistory.org/blogs/seneca-village-a-community-lost-to-central-park. See also: "Central Park and the Destruction of Seneca Village," Urban Archive, June 2, 2020, https://www.urbanarchive.org/stories/c4UxttDrUH4.

13 **"project with a deadline, it will get done":** Phillip C. McGraw, *Life Strategies: Doing What Works, Doing What Matters* (New York: Hachette Books, 1999).

CHAPTER 2 | WHITE SPACE

23 **"I am a Black woman in a white supremacist country":** Ijeoma Oluo, *So You Want to Talk About Race* (New York: Seal Press, 2019), 1.

24 **stirring up the crowd at the Apollo:** "Apollo History," Apollo, accessed March 30, 2022, https://www.apollotheater.org/about /history.

CHAPTER 3 | BELONGING

38 **had been criminalized:** Gene Demby, "Sagging Pants and the Long History of 'Dangerous' Street Fashion," *Code Switch*, NPR, September 11, 2014, https://www.npr.org/sections/codeswitch/2014/09/11 /347143588/sagging-pants-and-the-long-history-of-dangerous -street-fashion.

40 **in the Bronx Zoo in 1906:** Pamela Newkirk, "The Man Who Was Caged in a Zoo," *Guardian*, June 3, 2015, https://www.theguardian .com/world/2015/jun/03/the-man-who-was-caged-in-a-zoo.

41 **"degraded and degenerate race":** Newkirk, "The Man Who Was Caged in a Zoo."

41 **"could rival its results by equal efforts":** Newkirk, "The Man Who Was Caged in a Zoo."

41 **in the late 1890s:** "Address by Daniel G. Brinton, the Retiring President of the Association," *Proceedings of the American Association for the Advancement of Science*, American Association for the Advancement of Science (Cambridge, MA: 1896), 12.

41 **"is now far out of date":** Newkirk, "The Man Who Was Caged in a Zoo."

42 **killed myself:** Newkirk, "The Man Who Was Caged in a Zoo."

CHAPTER 4 | LOST

55 **not something the world wanted anybody to think:** Catherine Porter, Constant Méheut, Matt Apuzzo, and Selam Gebrekidan, "The Root of Haiti's Misery: Reparations to Enslavers," *New York Times*, May 20, 2022, https://www.nytimes.com/2022/05/20/world /americas/haiti-history-colonized-france.html.

CHAPTER 6 | OUTSIDE

70 **"animalistic, destructive, and criminal":** David Pilgrim, "The Brute Caricature," Jim Crow Museum, Ferris State University, November 2000, https://www.ferris.edu/HTMLS/news/jimcrow /brute/homepage.htm.

71 **"better adapted for speed and power":** Martin Kane, "An Assessment of 'Black Is Best,'" *Sports Illustrated*, January 18, 1971, https://vault.si.com/vault/1971/01/18/an-assessment-of-black-is-best.

71 **that "explained" their talent in track and field:** Patricia Vertinsky and Gwendolyn Captain, "More Myth Than History: American Culture and Representations of the Black Female's Athletic Ability," *Journal of Sport History*, 25, no. 3 (1998): 532–61, http://www.jstor.org /stable/43609538. See also: David Pilgrim, "The Jezebel Stereotype," Jim Crow Museum, Ferris State University, July 2002, https://www .ferris.edu/jimcrow/jezebel/; and David Pilgrim, "The Sapphire Caricature," Jim Crow Museum, Ferris State University, August 2008, https://www.ferris.edu/HTMLS/news/jimcrow/antiblack/sapphire.htm.

71 **"it was never made available to me":** Jay Jennings, "Why Is Running So White?," *Runner's World*, November 15, 2011, https:// www.runnersworld.com/runners-stories/a20807821/why-is-running -so-white/.

73 **only state with a Black exclusion law:** All history of Oregon's exclusion law found in "Pre-Civil Rights Era: Unwelcome," Museum of Natural and Cultural History, https://mnchexhibits.uoregon.edu /racing-to-change/pre-civil-rights/constitution/.

73 **large white KKK letters on the hill:** Image of KKK sign on Willamette Street, "Racing to Change: Oregon's Civil Rights Years, the Eugene Story," in "Pre-Civil Rights Era: Unwelcome," Museum of Natural and Cultural History, https://mnchexhibits.uoregon.edu /racing-to-change/pre-civil-rights/unwelcome/.

74 **try jogging to come to Hayward Field:** Details of Bowerman and his jogging club from Kenny Moore, *Bowerman and the Men of Oregon* (Emmaus, PA: Rodale Books, 2006), 146–153.

74 **two hundred white people showed up:** Dick Leutzinger, "Bowerman Calls Jogger Turnout at First Meeting 'Very Gratifying,'" *Eugene Register-Guard*, February 4, 1963, 3B, https://news.google.com/news papers?nid=4pF9x-cDGsoC&dat=19630204&printsec=frontpage&hl=en.

75 **Senator Strom Thurmond (R-South Carolina):** Hal Higdon, "Jogging Is an In Sport," *New York Times Magazine*, April 14, 1968, 36–52.

76 **"visas, clothes, tools and blank checks":** Peggy McIntosh, "White Privilege: Unpacking the Invisible Knapsack," *Peace and Freedom*

(July/August 1989), https://psychology.umbc.edu/files/2016/10
/White-Privilege_McIntosh-1989.pdf.

76 **"you are subject to a stop and search":** Natalia Mehlman Petrzela,
"Jogging Has Always Excluded Black People," *New York Times*, May
12, 2020, https://www.nytimes.com/2020/05/12/opinion/running
-jogging-race-ahmaud-arbery.html.

CHAPTER 8 | REFRAMING

94 **"how you navigate the world":** Janel Martinez, "When It Comes to
Latinidad, Who Is Included and Who Isn't?," *Remezcla*, July 30, 2019,
https://remezcla.com/features/culture/when-it-comes-to-latinidad
-who-is-included-and-who-isnt/.

CHAPTER 9 | PURPOSE

107 **higher rates of obesity, heart disease, and hypertension:** "Obesity
and African Americans," U.S. Department of Health and Human
Services, Office of Minority Health, accessed April 21, 2020, https://
minorityhealth.hhs.gov/omh/browse.aspx?lvl=4&lvlid=25; "Heart
Disease and African Americans," U.S. Department of Health and
Human Services, Office of Minority Health, accessed April 21, 2020,
https://minorityhealth.hhs.gov/omh/browse.aspx?lvl=4&lvlid=19.

107 **known in the medical world as weathering:** Tonya Russell, "Let's
Not Forget, Weathering Is Also Killing Black People," *SELF*, July 1,
2020, https://www.self.com/story/weathering.

108 **take advantage of the neighborhood:** Rachel Holliday Smith,
"With a New Clinic on Way, Neighborhoods Decry 'Overburdened'
Harlem," *THE CITY*, September 27, 2019, https://www.thecity.nyc
/health/2019/9/27/21212261/with-a-new-clinic-on-way-neighbors
-decry-overburdened-harlem.

108 **concentrated within 0.4 miles of 125th Street:** "Harlem Tax
Protest," Mount Morris Park Community Improvement Association
via the Harlem Neighborhood Block Association, February 19, 2022,
https://hnba.nyc/tag/5th-avenue/.

108 **nearly 20 percent:** data from analysis of New York City's Office of
Addiction Services and Support (OASAS) by the Greater Harlem
Coalition, "Data and Research," https://greaterharlem.nyc/data
_overview/. Additionally, 75 percent of patients getting treatment in

Harlem do not reside in Harlem, per OASAS 2019 data, as listed on
Greater Harlem Coalition's Data and Research page, point number 2.

108 **commuting from other neighborhoods:** The following notes that
84 percent of patients at East Harlem facilities are from other parts of
the city: NYS OASAS Data Warehouse, CDS extract of December 1,
2018, via Kristin Richardson Jordan, "Addressing the Oversaturation
of Drug Clinics in Harlem," Kristin for Harlem, October 28,
2020, https://kristinforharlem.com/2020/10/28/addressing-the
-oversaturation-of-drug-clinics-in-harlem/; 67.9 percent for Harlem
was found by NYS OASAS Data Warehouse, CDS extract of
December 1, 2018, http://west147block.org/wp-content/uploads/2019
/01/OASAS-FOIL-Based-Charts.pdf.

CHAPTER 11 | MEANING THRU MOVEMENT

123 **March on Washington in 1963:** "March on Washington for Jobs
and Freedom," *King Encyclopedia*, The Martin Luther King, Jr.,
Research and Educational Institute, Stanford University, https://
kinginstitute.stanford.edu/encyclopedia/march-washington-jobs
-and-freedom.

123 **25,000 people walking the final leg to the Alabama State
Capitol:** "Selma to Montgomery: 50 Years Later," The White House
President Barack Obama archives, https://obamawhitehouse.archives
.gov/issues/civil-rights/selma; and "Selma to Montgomery March,"
King Encyclopedia, The Martin Luther King, Jr., Research and
Educational Institute, Stanford University, https://kinginstitute
.stanford.edu/encyclopedia/selma-montgomery-march.

129 **corpses dug up and stolen for science:** Rachel H. Mathis, M.D., et
al., "Grave Robbing in the North and South in Antebellum America,"
American College of Surgeons, 2016, https://www.facs.org/media
/1x0f0byz/03_grave_robbing.pdf. In the late 1700s and late into the
1800s, people dug up graves to supply medical schools with cadavers.
Victims were often poor, criminal, or Black. One analysis in a facility
in Georgia found that 79 percent of the bodies were Black. Black men
were the most common, followed by Black women. Megan Highet,
anthropologist at the University of Alberta, noted: "The theft of
bodies was essentially segregating in death those who had been
marginalized in life," with "death offering no escape from

institutional racism. The white society chose to overlook the practice so long as their graveyards went untouched.

129 **statue in Central Park:** In April 2018, the statue of James Marion Sims that had stood for decades in Central Park, across from the New York Academy of Medicine, was removed after a special commission voted unanimously for its removal. It is, however, expected to be placed in Green-Wood Cemetery in Brooklyn, where Sims is buried. William Neuman, "City Orders Sims Statue Removed from Central Park," *New York Times*, April 16, 2018, https://www.nytimes.com /2018/04/16/nyregion/nyc-sims-statue-central-park-monument.html.

129 **Henrietta Lacks had her cells stolen in 1951:** "Honoring Henrietta," Johns Hopkins Medicine, https://www.hopkinsmedicine .org/henriettalacks/.

130 **that meant Black women and women of color in particular:** "Who's Most Impacted by Attacks on Birth Control," Planned Parenthood, https://www.plannedparenthoodaction.org/fight-for -birth-control/facts/whos-most-impacted-by-attacks-on-birth -control.

CHAPTER 12 | WE WERE THERE

138 **"any previous conditions what[so]ever":** "Black Running History Timeline: William Pegram & Ed Williams," Theodore "Ted" Corbitt, https://tedcorbitt.com/black-running-history-timeline -1880-1979/.

141 **"not yet over Burden winning":** "Black Running History Timeline: Charles Burden," Theodore "Ted" Corbitt, https://tedcorbitt.com /black-running-history-timeline-1880-1979/#Charles-Burden.

142 **"Organize and do something about it":** Pamela Cooper, *The American Marathon* (Syracuse, NY: Syracuse University Press, 1998), 124–25. The history of the creation of the Road Runners Club of America and the New York Road Runners comes from Cooper's book, as well as the RRCA's detailed account. The RRCA puts the founding of the New York chapter as "by April 1958" with twenty-nine members. Cooper's book cites June 1958. NYRR puts its founding in June 1958 with forty members, and Corbitt as president. NYRR offers a look at the history in NYRR Staff, "Six Decades of New York Road Runners History 1958 to 1970," January 31, 2018,

https://www.nyrr.org/run/photos-and-stories/2018/six-decades-of
-new-york-road-runners-history-1958-1970.

CHAPTER 13 | INCLUSION/EXCLUSION

152 **segregation originated there in 1838:** Steve Luxenberg, "The
Forgotten Northern Origins of Jim Crow," *Time*, February 12, 2019,
https://time.com/5527029/jim-crow-plessy-history/.

153 **were still fighting for equal resources for their kids:** Matthew
Delmont, "The Lasting Legacy of the Busing Crisis," *Atlantic*, March
29, 2016, https://www.theatlantic.com/politics/archive/2016
/03/the-boston-busing-crisis-was-never-intended-to-work/474264/.

CHAPTER 14 | LIFE AND DEATH

167 **die in childbirth than white women:** Centers for Disease
Control and Prevention, "Infographic: Racial/Ethnic Disparities
in Pregnancy-Related Deaths—United States, 2007–2016," Division
of Reproductive Health, National Center for Chronic Disease
Prevention and Health Promotion, https://www.cdc.gov
/reproductivehealth/maternal-mortality/disparities-pregnancy
-related-deaths/infographic.html.

167 **twelve times greater:** "Pregnancy-Associated Mortality, New York
City 2006–2010," New York City Department of Health and Mental
Hygiene, Bureau of Maternal, Infant and Reproductive Health,
Executive Summary, 5, https://www1.nyc.gov/assets/doh/downloads
/pdf/ms/pregnancy-associated-mortality-report.pdf.

172 **"had acted out of self-defense":** Richard Fausset, "Two Weapons, a
Chase, a Killing and No Charges," *New York Times*, August 26, 2020,
https://www.nytimes.com/2020/04/26/us/ahmed-arbery-shooting
-georgia.html.

173 **disproportionately high death rate:** Elisabeth Gawthrop, "The
Color of Coronavirus: Covid-19 Deaths by Race and Ethnicity in the
U.S.," APM Research Lab, June 16, 2022, https://www.apmresearchlab
.org/covid/deaths-by-race.

173 **rate was double in New York City:** Jeffery C. Mays and Andy
Newman, "Virus Is Twice as Deadly for Black and Latino People
Than Whites in N.Y.C.," *New York Times*, April 8, 2020, https://www
.nytimes.com/2020/04/08/nyregion/coronavirus-race-deaths.html.

175 **"you come to us endangered":** Ta-Nehisi Coates, *Between the World and Me* (New York: Spiegel & Grau, 2015), 82.

CHAPTER 15 | CONFRONTING WHITENESS

180 **not reflective of the white race:** Pierre W. Orelus, "Being Black and Brown in the 21st Century: Challenges and Pedagogical Possibilities," *SAGE Open*, no. 1–8 (October–December 2012): 5, https://journals.sagepub.com/doi/pdf/10.1177/2158244012464979.

180 **"seems to be always on trial":** Orelus, "Being Black and Brown in the 21st Century," 5, https://journals.sagepub.com/doi/pdf/10.1177/2158244012464979.

181 **"It's kind of an ongoing thing out here":** Rick Rojas, Sarah Mervosh, and Richard Fausset, "Investigators Call Evidence in the Ahmaud Arbery Shooting 'Extremely Upsetting,'" *New York Times*, May 8, 2020, https://www.nytimes.com/2020/05/08/us/ahmaud-arbery-shooting-georgia.html.

181 **establish a system of terror to control Black people:** "History Explained: The Origins of Modern Day Policing," NAACP, https://naacp.org/find-resources/history-explained/origins-modern-day-policing.

181 **"they were enslaved or not":** Elise C. Boddie, "Racial Territoriality, Section II: A Short Spatial History of Race," *UCLA Law Review Rev. 401*, no. 58, December 2010, 10, https://theinclusionproject.rutgers.edu/wp-content/uploads/2020/07/racial-territoriality.pdf.

181 **citizen's arrest laws in the U.S.:** Talib Visram, "The Troubling History of Citizen's Arrests—from Slave Patrols to Ahmaud Arbery to ICE," *Fast Company*, July 20, 2020, https://www.fastcompany.com/90528764/the-troubling-history-of-citizens-arrests-from-slave-patrols-to-ahmaud-arbery-to-ice.

181 **across the South with no arrests:** Emily Jones, "Citizen's Arrest Law Historically a Tool of Lynchings," Georgia Public Broadcasting, June 16, 2020, https://www.gpb.org/news/2020/06/16/citizens-arrest-law-historically-tool-of-lynchings.

182 **"In America, it is traditional to destroy the Black body":** Ta-Nehisi Coates, "Letter to My Son," *Atlantic*, July 4, 2015, https://www.theatlantic.com/politics/archive/2015/07/tanehisi-coates-between-the-world-and-me/397619/.

182 **de facto border between the Black and white communities:**
Mitchell S. Jackson, "Twelve Minutes and a Life," *Runner's World*,
June 18, 2020, https://www.runnersworld.com/runners-stories
/a32883923/ahmaud-arbery-death-running-and-racism/;
Richard Fausset and Rick Rojas, "Where Ahmaud Arbery Ran,
Neighbors Cast Wary Eyes," *New York Times*, May 22, 2020;
https://www.nytimes.com/article/satilla-shores-ahmaud-arbery
-killing.html.

182 **"across various racial borders":** Boddie, "Racial Territoriality,
Section II: A Short Spatial History of Race," 10.

183 **"I just need to know what he's doing wrong":** Jade Abdul-Malik,
"LISTEN: 911 Dispatcher Doesn't Understand What Arbery Is
'Doing Wrong,'" NPR, May 8, 2020, https://www.gpb.org/news
/2020/05/08/listen-911-dispatcher-doesnt-understand-what-arbery
-doing-wrong.

184 **"To just be human":** Peter Bromka (@bromka), "As a white male I
almost always feel safe while running. Even when I shouldn't," Instagram
photo, May 6, 2020, https://www.instagram.com/p/B_3_GWKn0gy/.

185 **"Ahmaud Arbery and Whiteness in the Running World":** Alison
Mariella Désir, "Ahmaud Arbery and Whiteness in the Running
World," *Outside*, May 8, 2020, https://www.outsideonline.com
/health/running/ahmaud-arbery-murder-whiteness-running
-community/.

CHAPTER 16 | RUNNING WHILE BLACK

192 **"Am I really safe?" Meb wonders:** Martin Fritz Huber, "Meb
Keflezighi on Being Black in America," *Outside*, June 10, 2020,
https://www.outsideonline.com/health/running/meb-keflezighi
-racism-running/.

192 **Bergesen confronted Nike:** Elizabeth Weil, "The Woman Who
Took on Nike with Running Shorts," *Outside*, June 7, 2016, https://
www.outsideonline.com/outdoor-gear/run/watch-birdie/.

CHAPTER 17 | THE UNBEARABLE WHITENESS OF RUNNING

197 **thin and white:** Alison Mariella Désir (@alisonmdesir), "The
unbearable whiteness of running," Instagram photo, June 25, 2020,
https://www.instagram.com/p/CB3EYyuAeph/.

198 **85 percent of the time:** Table 1 in Jenna Seyidoglu, Candace
     Roberts, Francine Darroch, et al., "Racing for Representation: A
     Visual Content Analysis of North American Running Magazine
     Covers," *Communication & Sport*, March 24, 2021, https://doi.org
     /10.1177/21674795211000325.

198 **hypocritical maternity clause:** Alysia Montaño, "Nike Told Me to
     Dream Crazy, Until I Wanted a Baby," *New York Times*, May 12, 2019,
     https://www.nytimes.com/2019/05/12/opinion/nike-maternity-leave
     .html.

200 **copy editors, columnists, and web specialists:** Richard E.
     Lapchick, "The 2021 Sports Media Racial and Gender Media Card:
     Associated Press Sports Editors," The Institute for Diversity and
     Ethics in Sport with the DeVos Sport Business Management Program
     in the College of Business Administration of the University of
     Central Florida, 2021, 5, https://www.tidesport.org/_files/ugd
     /138a69_e1e67c118b784f4caba00a4536699300.pdf; Richard Lapchick,
     "Sports Media Remains Overwhelmingly White and Male, Study
     Finds," ESPN, September 22, 2021, https://www.espn.com/espn
     /story/_/id/32254145/sports-media-remains-overwhelmingly-white
     -male-study-finds.

201 **only five were people of color, or 2 percent:** Ravi Singh, "The
     Whiteness of the Running Industry," *The XC*, July 13, 2020, https://
     thexc.org/the-whiteness-of-the-running-industry/.

201 **historic nature of the Black women's achievements:** Matthew
     Futterman and Talya Minsberg, "Rupp and Tuliamuk Win Olympic
     Trials Marathon," *New York Times*, February 29, 2020, https://www
     .nytimes.com/2020/02/29/sports/olympics/olympic-marathon-trials.html.

CHAPTER 20 | EVERYTHING IS CONNECTED

226 **read about them in the *New York Times*:** Nadja Popovich and
     Christopher Flavelle, "Summer in the City Is Hot, but Some
     Neighborhoods Suffer More," August 9, 2019, https://www.nytimes
     .com/interactive/2019/08/09/climate/city-heat-islands.html; Brad
     Plumer and Nadja Popovich, "How Decades of Racist Housing Policy
     Left Neighborhoods Sweltering," August 24, 2020, https://www
     .nytimes.com/interactive/2020/08/24/climate/racism-redlining
     -cities-global-warming.html.

226 **physically and mentally wounded:** Jami Floyd, "24 Minutes in Mott Haven," *Gothamist*, June 4, 2021, https://gothamist.com/news /24-minutes-mott-haven.

227 **C ("yellow," or "definitely declining"):** Bronx map dated 1938 in Robert K. Nelson, LaDale Winling, Richard Marciano, Nathan Connolly, et al., "Mapping Inequality: Redlining in New Deal America," *American Panorama*, ed. Robert K. Nelson and Edward L. Ayers, https://dsl.richmond.edu/panorama/redlining.

227 **"not a single foreigner or negro":** Richard Rothstein, *The Color of Law: A Forgotten History of How Our Government Segregated America* (New York: Liveright, 2017), 64.

227 **"too near negro area":** Camila Domonoske, "Interactive Redlining Map Zooms in on America's History of Discrimination," *The Two-Way*, NPR, October 19, 2016; https://www.npr.org/sections /thetwo-way/2016/10/19/498536077/interactive-redlining-map -zooms-in-on-americas-history-of-discrimination.

227 **"infiltration of Negroes":** Domonoske, "Interactive Redlining Map Zooms in on America's History of Discrimination."

227 **"Detrimental Influences: Negro infiltration":** Bronx, Area Description Images, D1 in Nelson et al., "Mapping Inequality."

227 **entire mortgage industry:** Domonoske, "Interactive Redlining Map Zooms in on America's History of Discrimination."

228 **segregate neighborhoods into Black and white spaces:** Rothstein, *The Color of Law*, 19–24.

228 **reserved for white people:** Rothstein, *The Color of Law*, 21.

228 **white-only community:** Rothstein, *The Color of Law*, 21–22.

228 **"ghetto"—and pretty white neighborhoods:** Rothstein, *The Color of Law*, 17–37.

229 **higher rates of chronic illnesses:** Maria Godoy, "In U.S. Cities, the Health Effects of Past Housing Discrimination Are Plain to See," *Shots*, NPR, November 19, 2020, https://www.npr.org/sections /health-shots/2020/11/19/911909187/in-u-s-cities-the-health-effects -of-past-housing-discrimination-are-plain-to-see.

229 **including the Bronx:** Steve Clark, "Asthma in the Bronx," SBH Health System Bronx, August 30, 2016, http://www.sbhny.org/blog /asthma-in-the-bronx/; "Asthma," Columbia Center for Children's Environmental Health, Columbia Mailman School of Public Health,

https://www.publichealth.columbia.edu/research/columbia-center
-childrens-environmental-health/asthma.

229   **on the Upper East Side:** Sabrina Tavernise and Albert Sun, "Same City, but Very Different Life Spans," *New York Times*, April 28, 2015, https://www.nytimes.com/interactive/2015/04/29/health/life -expectancy-nyc-chi-atl-richmond.html.

229   **compared to students of other races:** Alex Zimmerman, "Settlement to Give Black and Latino Students More Access to NYC High School Sports Teams," *Chalkbeat New York*, November 17, 2021, https://ny.chalkbeat.org/2021/11/17/22788370/psal-lawsuit-sports -inequity-settlement.

230   **best places to live if you're a runner:** Lisa Jhung, "Thinking of Moving? These Are the Best Places in the U.S. for Runners," *Outside* via *Podium Runner*, May 26, 2021, https://www.outsideonline.com /health/running/culture-running/opinion-culture-running/the-best -places-in-the-us-for-runners/.

232   **"generational despair":** Robbe Reddinger, "Baltimore's So Segregated, Even Strava Shows It. These Runners Want to Change That," *Runner's World*, February 19, 2019, https://www.runnersworld .com/runners-stories/a26131774/baltimore-segregated-strava -heatmap/.

232   **barrier to entering endurance sports:** Survey conducted by TRUE Global Intelligence for Gatorade on barriers minority groups face in endurance sports, April 10–23, 2021, https://endurance.gatorade.com /images/virtual/community/slm_survey.pdf.

233   **increased by nearly 42 percent:** David Nakamura, "Hate Crimes Rise to Highest Level in 12 Years Amid Increasing Attacks on Black and Asian People, FBI says," *Washington Post*, August 30, 2021, https://www.washingtonpost.com/national-security/hate-crimes-fbi -2020-asian-black/2021/08/30/28bede00-09a7-11ec-9781-07796ffb56fe _story.html.

233   **the majority of the offenders:** Nakamura, "Hate Crimes Rise to Highest Level in 12 Years Amid Increasing Attacks on Black and Asian People"; "Hate Crime in the United States Incident Analysis," Crime Data Explorer, FBI, United States, 2020, https://crime-data -explorer.fr.cloud.gov/pages/explorer/crime/hate-crime; "2019 FBI Hate Crimes Statistics Report," U.S. Department of Justice,

Community Relations Service, https://www.justice.gov/crs /highlights/FY-2019-Hate-Crimes.

234 **criminalized in these spaces:** Michelle Hamilton, "Black Men Less Likely to Run in White Neighborhoods," *Runner's World*, October 2, 2013, https://www.runnersworld.com/news/a20801993/black-men -less-likely-to-run-in-white-neighborhoods/.

234 **229 Black people lost their lives:** Khaleda Rahman, "Full List of 229 Black People Killed by Police Since George Floyd's Murder," *Newsweek*, May 25, 2021, https://www.newsweek.com/full-list-229-black -people-killed-police-since-george-floyds-murder-1594477.

234 **highest percentage of police-related deaths, as they had for many years:** Julie Tate, Jennifer Jenkins, and Steven Rich, "1,045 Have Been Shot and Killed by Police in the Past Year," *Washington Post*, April 28, 2022, accessed May 19, 2022, https://www .washingtonpost.com/graphics/investigations/police-shootings -database/; GBD 2019 Police Violence U.S. Subnational Collaborators, "Fatal Police Violence by Race and State in the USA, 1980–2019: A Network Meta-Regression," *Lancet*, 398, no. 10307 (October 2, 2021): 1239–1255, https://doi.org/10.1016/S0140-6736(21)01609-3.

234 **rate of three times higher than white people:** "Fatal Police Shootings Among Black Americans Remain High, Unchanged Since 2015," *Penn Medicine News*, October 28, 2020, https://www .pennmedicine.org/news/news-releases/2020/october/fatal-police -shootings-among-black-americans-remain-high-unchanged-since -2015.

234 **"which is related to . . . and on and on":** Kareem Abdul-Jabbar, "Black Lives Matter," WebMD, https://www.webmd.com/story/black -lives-matter.

CHAPTER 21 | REIMAGINING THE RUN

242 **"providing the distance wasn't too long":** Letter from Ted Corbitt to George Spitz, May 22, 1976, PDF of the letter provided by Gary Corbitt.

243 **"systemic racism, from one generation to the next":** "Reckoning with Remembrance: History, Injustice, and the Murder of Emmett Till," National Museum of American History, September 3–November 2, 2021, https://americanhistory.si.edu/reckoning-with-remembrance.